LIVERPOOL'S NOTORIOUS JELLY GANG

CHARLIE SIEGA

First published in Great Britain by True Crime Biography Books in 2018

Second edition published in Great Britain by Gadfly Press in 2023

A catalogue record of this book is available from the British Library.

Typeset by Jane Dixon-Smith

SPELLING DIFFERENCES: UK V US

This book was written in British English, hence US readers may notice some spelling differences from American English: e.g. color = colour, meter = metre and jewelry = jewellery

CONTENTS

Chapter 1:	1958 CHESTER CROWN COURT	7
Chapter 2:	DECEMBER 1956	9
Chapter 3:	PARTY TIME 1956	21
Chapter 4:	GOING OFF BIG TIME JANUARY 1957	29
Chapter 5:	MAKING THE HEADLINES	45
Chapter 6:	HARD ONE TO CRACK	50
Chapter 7:	YOU WIN SOME, YOU LOSE SOME	57
Chapter 8:	AN OLDER WOMAN SHOWS ME THE WAY IT'S DONE 7TH APRIL 1957	64
Chapter 9:	JUST LIKE JESSE JAMES	74
Chapter 10:	THEIR WAY OF LIFE	78
Chapter 11:	A MOTHER'S FURY	86
Chapter 12:	HOW IT'S DONE... BUT FRANCIE WANTS OUT	89
Chapter 13:	A DANGEROUS MISSION	94
Chapter 14:	CARRYING OUT THE TEST	100
Chapter 15:	THE LEMO JOB	104
Chapter 16:	AN EPIDEMIC	117
Chapter 17:	NEARLY ON TOP	120
Chapter 18:	NEAR DEATH AND DISASTER IN THE PARK	128
Chapter 19:	THE SHARE OUT	134
Chapter 20:	A NEW ARRIVAL	139
Chapter 21:	TOSH CALLS IT A DAY AND KEIRON DOES A DISAPPEARING ACT	141
Chapter 22:	THE UPS AND DOWNS OF THE 1950s	147
Chapter 23:	THE SOUNDPROOF JOBS	153

Chapter 24: MY THEORY WAS PROVEN RIGHT 159
Chapter 25: POLICE FIT UP 171
Chapter 26: COPYCAT GANGS 175
Chapter 27: THE DOWNSIDE WHEN FACING THE MUSIC 178
Chapter 28: BAD NEWS 182
Chapter 29: SUSSING THE PLACE OUT 185
Chapter 30: HOME COMFORTS 190
Chapter 31: GETTING IT SORTED 193
Chapter 32: THE LAUNDRY CAPER 195
Chapter 33: BREAKING OUR GOLDEN RULES 208
PHOTOS 216
Chapter 34: VISITORS FROM DIFFERENT PARTS OF THE COUNTRY 219
Chapter 35: MY FIRST TIME IN THE BIG HOUSE 223
Chapter 36: THE TRIAL 225
Chapter 37: THE PROMISE 229
Chapter 38: A GOLDEN OPPORTUNITY 230
Chapter 39: GOING OFF WITH A BANG 245
Chapter 40: BACK ON HOME GROUND – LIVERPOOL 268
Chapter 41: THE END OF AN ERA 271
Chapter 42: WHAT BECAME OF THE JELLY GANG? 273
EPILOGUE 279
About The Author 280
A brief synopsis of Charlie Seiga's other books 288
Reviews of Charlie Seiga's other books 291
Other Books by Gadfly Press 297
Hard Time by Shaun Attwood 309

CHAPTER 1

1958 CHESTER CROWN COURT

My name is Charlie Seiga. I am seventeen years old and I have been accused, along with my brother Fredrick Seiga and his friend Anthony Burns, of one of the highest charges in the land: being found in possession of high explosives, gelignite and detonators and of making use of them to blow open safes.

My brother and his friend had pleaded guilty to this serious charge. They had no other option really, having been caught in the act of safe blowing, 'bang to rights'. As for me, and through good advice from my brother and his friend, as well as my lawyer, I had pleaded not guilty.

Nevertheless, as the crown prosecution put it, we were 'professional safe blowers, using very powerful and dangerous explosives'. The lawyer representing me was trying his upmost with regards to my mitigation. During his powerful speech, he went on to address the court and the right honourable Judge Castle, presiding over the trial:

'My Lord, my client is seventeen years old and I implore you to consider his youth when passing sentence.'

The judge quickly interrupted. 'Yes, yes, I am well aware of his youth as you continue to persistently emphasise.'

Relentless, my lawyer was determined to proceed and he went on to explain to the court that I was not a professional criminal. 'Admittedly,' he finished. 'This youth's two accomplices are. There is no doubt about that'.

I had to hand it to this brief defending me; he did really give it his best shot. However, he and the crown prosecutor along with the judge had no idea what had taken place between my brother, his friend Tony and myself. They were totally unaware that, while being remanded in custody prior to this trial, the three of us had already planned and agreed between ourselves that I was to be portrayed as just a gullible kid, who being easily led and naive, had only gone along to keep a lookout and that I hadn't participated in the using of explosives and the blowing of a safe. This was to be my defence and hopefully, if we could pull this off, and of course, if I got lucky, I could walk altogether. For example, I could just be given a probation order.

Yet all along it was me; the young innocent, ingenuous looking seventeen-year-old kid who had come up with the whole idea of blowing safes open with gelignite and detonators. However, as I stood before the judge I appeared, to all intents and purposes, to be a harmless and inoffensive teenager who showed no evidence of being the instigator of such a high profile and dangerous crime.

Furthermore, as you will see this was by no means the first time we had used this method of safe blowing; there had been many previously. I am not saying that I was the mastermind behind it all but the gelignite and detonator idea was all down to me!

However, it was inevitable that my brother and his friend Tony Burns were both going to prison for a long time. They knew it was the end of the line for the two of them. If this was to happen, and it was more than likely, I would keep the promise that I had made to them both. My brother had not been married for long but he and his wife had a baby boy and although it was a big responsibility for anybody, never mind a kid my age, I vowed that I would provide for them and take care of them as best I could and I also said I would make sure that while he was incarcerated he would get regular visits etc.

The same went for his friend Tony, as he too had a wife and a couple of children. So, I promised that I would look after them whenever possible. That was the pledge I had given to both of them and I had every intention to honour this deal no matter what!

CHAPTER 2

DECEMBER 1956

My story began the week before Christmas on a cold and frosty night. I was just a sixteen year old kid. I had been out with my young friends since earlier that evening, we had all been hanging out together and getting up to all kinds, such as doing a bit of this and a bit of that... if you know what I mean? I had just entered through the back door of our house which led into the kitchen. From there I entered the lounge where the warmth from the dying embers of the coal fire in the grate felt inviting and cosy. My cold face began to sting as it heated up.

In the middle of the room was a large dining table, which had to be big due to the size of the family I came from: seven brothers and one sister along with myself and my parents... so that's ten people all living in one small council house. It makes you wonder how people could exist together in such a small house... but we managed and it was always spotlessly clean, but of course that was all down to our mother. Thankfully though, my two older brothers, Eddie and Ged, as well as my sister Delia were all now married and so lived in their own homes and this helped to alleviate the congestion considerably. Also, my younger brother Billy was now living at my sister's house so that he could concentrate on his school work since winning a scholarship to the Grammar School.

Having said all this, these family members were always calling home to see my mother. At various times one or other of my older brothers would arrive with their tails between their legs carrying their suitcases, staying for a few days or so until the fall out they had had with their wives had blown over and all was forgiven. That is of course until the next time. One of them had two greyhound dogs which he would bring with him and that really did my head in. One of the dogs whose name was Smokey became a right pain in the arse and was also sly. When nobody was around, usually during the night, it would pull the tablecloth off the table and absolutely everything would smash onto the floor. The dog would then eat any food that came off the table, even the sugar from the sugar bowl and the butter out of the butter dish. Then, when anyone entered the room it would be laying there head down and making out it was innocent of all the destruction it had caused. It would look forlorn. You only had to look at it to know it was as guilty as hell. This though spelt the end of the two dogs staying in the house and my brother had to build them a temporary kennel outside.

However, back to my story. On this particular night, sitting at this large dining table was my older brother Freddy, about twenty-seven or eight at the time. Freddy was always well presented and dressed smart in a suit with a shirt and tie, the typical old-school villain. He had dark hair which he wore slicked back and had an olive skin-tone with dark brown eyes, (he got his looks from my mother's side of the family) he was of average slim build and fairly good looking.

Sat next to Freddy at the table was his best friend, a man called Kieron Oates (we called him Kearney). Kieron was another smartly dressed man, same average build as Freddy, again real old school. He had a pale complexion and blue eyes. He was turned out similar to Freddy in a smart shirt and tie.

The other one of the crew called Tosh, he was about forty-ish was the total opposite to Freddy and Kieron; he was smaller in height, a squat, broad shouldered man with a thick neck, sandy hair and thick, black, heavy framed glasses.

I knew who these people were, sitting around the table with my brother that night but there was one man there who I hadn't met before. Now this man presented himself completely different altogether; he had the air of somebody important and respectable.

He wore a dark suit with a shirt and tie. He appeared to be older than the rest of the men; distinguished looking with grey hair. I found out later that he worked in some large affluent shipping company somewhere along the Liverpool Dock Road; he was a card marker (one who gives inside information to villains on the whereabouts of large amounts of stored cash).

The conversation had abruptly ceased the minute I appeared in kitchen; for just those few seconds you could have heard a pin drop.

Then, my brother broke the silence as he rose up from his chair smiling at me, 'It's OK,' he said to the well-dressed stranger. 'This is my kid brother, Charlie.'

'Here you go,' he said pulling up a chair for me. 'Sit down with us, kid; we've finished our little natter (talk).'

I sat myself down with them and as I did so Keiron and Tosh acknowledged me with a smile and a nod.

'How are you doing?' Keiron asked, smiling at me.

'I'm good.'

'I want you to meet a good friend of ours,' said my brother. 'This is Mike.'

He gestured towards the well-dressed stranger who sat opposite me. The man smiled and reached his hand out to me across the table. I leaned across and shook his hand.

It was only a few minutes later that Tosh and Keiron decided it was time to leave; Mike agreed and so consequently, he bid us goodnight and followed them out.

After they had gone, Freddy said he wanted to have a little chat with me. He rose from his seat and in silence he opened the inner kitchen door that led into the hallway. He listened intently for any sound coming from upstairs and then after quietly closing the door again he resumed his seat.

'Everyone is asleep upstairs and I don't want to wake any of them, especially the old lady.' Freddy was referring to our mother, who was vehemently against any of us being involved in any kind of crime. She had been through enough in the past and if she heard Freddy or any of my older brothers discussing it we knew she would put her foot down and maybe even tell Freddy to pack his bags and go!

We all had respect for Mother and so we were discreet with our meetings and plans as we tried to do as we were told.

My mother was a light sleeper, as opposed to my Dad who snored loudly, maybe that's *why* she was a light sleeper; having to put up with all the racket going on from my Dad. Also upstairs were my two younger brothers, Jimmy and Joseph; although we knew they would be sleeping soundly as it was the middle of the night: three o'clock. Therefore, the only one we needed to worry about hearing us was my Ma, so we had to be extra vigilant. Our conversation had to be in whispers.

Freddy looked at me and spoke quietly, 'I know you're 'at it' Charlie, you and your young pals. But do you know what?' He went on, 'You will all eventually come unstuck, the way you are all going about things.'

'What do you mean? I asked him. 'My pals and I are doing OK as far as the graft goes; we're having some half tidy touches here and there.'

'That may be so,' Freddy said, 'but it's mostly petty stuff that you are having away. And another thing kid, can you trust any of them?'

'Aw look,' I said to him, 'they are my best friends and we are all dead loyal to each other.'

'I know, I know,' Freddy replied. 'Unfortunately, I have heard it all before.'

'What do you mean?' I asked.

'Remember what happened to me Charlie? And your other two brothers, Eddie and Ged? We thought we could trust somebody who was a staunch loyal friend, but he turned out to be a rat. All three of us were sent down for a long time because of him. I know you think a lot of your pals and everything, but just think about what I am saying. If the police did happen to get you all on a caper (robbery) there might be a weak link among your little crew, because when they split you up for questioning into different police cells that's when the fireworks start. Never underestimate the police, Charlie, they are clever and ruthless; especially with what goes on in their interviews and their lines of questioning. They will select the weakest one out of your little gang and just keep on at him and on at him until he rolls over. He will then be persuaded to make a statement naming the rest of you. You should know what happens afterwards... he walks and the rest of you go down.'

He stopped talking for a few moments, then with an intensely serious look he said, 'I don't want that to happen to *you* kid.'

I began to realise what my brother Freddy was saying, he made a lot of sense, particularly on how to be aware and avoid making dangerous mistakes.

'Never do anything if the job doesn't look or feel right, Charlie. That way you can stay free to thieve another day. Don't take silly chances.' He told me that he and his friends were into safe robberies. 'When you have one of these jobs away, Charlie, there's a lot more reddies (cash) involved in that sort of graft. Who knows, by the time you are twenty one you can retire,' he said to me laughing.' Suddenly his face went all serious.

'Why don't you come in with *us* kid? That way you won't come unstuck... well not if I can help it that is!'

Some months later he was proved dead right with his predictions; four of my friends got arrested for a robbery they had committed and one of them, called Mikey; who incidentally was my best pal at the time, rolled over (made a statement) blaming it on the rest of the crew. I couldn't believe it... no, not Mikey, he was the one with plenty of bottle. He was the toughest among us all!

It was just two days before Christmas when I started grafting with my brother and his friends, who were right villains, they were all professionals and real old school.

'Come on, Charlie,' said our Freddy, 'I want to show you something that will open your eyes.'

We had just left my mother's house on a crisp, cold Saturday morning. We were walking to Tosh's house which was only a few streets away from home. When we arrived, Tosh was tinkering with an old van outside. He was wearing dirty old overalls with an oily rag hanging out of the pocket. Old tools and van parts were scattered on the floor around him while he worked on the motor. As we approached him Freddy called to him.

'How you doing Tosh?'

Tosh looked up at us, 'Yeah, I'm just trying to get this old banger started. The battery's fucked; it's as flat as a pancake.'

'Never mind, Tosh,' said Freddy. 'You'll be able to buy a new car once we get that peter opened.'

My brother was referring to a safe that they had stolen a couple of nights before. Tosh smiled. 'Yeah, I hope so.' He stood up rubbing his hands, saying, 'I'm freezing, isn't it cold? I see you've got young Charlie with you?'

'Yeah, I'm bringing him in with us. It will keep him out of trouble.'

'Keep him out of trouble?' Tosh replied, laughing.

Tosh and Freddy then looked at me and we all started to laugh. 'Come on inside,' said Tosh. 'We'll have a mug of tea before we get off to the other place.'

'Yeah,' replied Freddy. 'I hope the others have made some progress getting that peter (safe) opened.'

We entered Tosh's house and walked into the front room where there was pandemonium; there were little kids everywhere. They were all hyperactive; running around and playing rowdily. Tosh's wife was sitting in front of a coal fire breast feeding a new baby. As soon as the kids saw Tosh enter they all happily ran over to him, some grabbing and hugging his legs, others tugging his sleeve and in unison they were all excitedly shouting, 'Dad, Dad!'

Tosh gently peeled the kid's hands off his legs. He then said to us, 'Come through to the back kitchen, we will have a bit of peace there.'

Then with a warm smile he told the kids to calm down and behave themselves and immediately they did as they were told.

'He then said to me jokingly and shaking his head, 'Don't have a gang of kids if you ever get married, Charlie, just one or two maybe but not a gang.'

Looking back at that time in Tosh's home I think about how times were so hard in those days for some people, especially if you had a big family to bring up. I admired men like Tosh, at least he had got off his arse and gone out there, he had done something to try to alleviate the poverty they were living in. I mean, men like him had left school at the age of fourteen with no qualifications or prospects. He was older than me; he was of my brother's generation. He went out and had a go, his working tools were a crowbar and a pair of gloves but he did it to feed and clothe his children. He simply wanted to make life a little easier and enjoyable for his family.

After we had finished our hot mugs of tea it was time to go to the place where Freddy had some kind of revelation for me. As we left the house Tosh told us to get into the front of the van. He picked up the starting handle, pushed it into the front of the van underneath the radiator and after a couple of turns the engine sparked to life. Don't forget this was the 1950s and it wasn't unusual for people to use one of these to start an engine, it was primitive but it worked.

I thought to myself, I wouldn't want to be in this situation if we needed a quick get-away. This motor was nothing like the powerful vehicles we have today, which you can start at the press of a button and just put your foot down and speed off.

Tosh got into the driving seat of the van saying, 'I knew all along it was a flat battery.'

The van began to chug away from Tosh's house and we drove to the North end of the city in the Scotland Road area, which was a couple of miles away. We pulled into a yard at the back of an old rundown building. It was a compound that was being used as a scrap yard. Tosh pulled the van into the yard and we all stepped out. We followed Tosh over to an old out-building where before opening the door Freddy turned to me and said, 'This is our slaughter,' (a place where the money or any other stolen gear was chopped-up to share among those involved, hence the name slaughter).

Inside the place were three men all looking exasperated as if they had been working hard and on the floor was a large safe lying on its front with its back exposed. It appeared badly damaged as if part of the back had been ripped open. One of the men had a big steel rail-bar about six foot long like a giant crowbar. He had this bar stuck inside the back of the safe as if he had been trying to lever the back off. The other two men were trying to assist him with this task. The three of them were frustrated. These three men were the Oates brothers: there was Keiron (we called him Kearny); who was our Freddy's best friend; second was Francie who was the youngest and John (we called him Johnny) who was the oldest. They were well known in and around Liverpool as a notorious 'old school' crime family at that time in the 1950s.

They stopped what they were doing when we entered the building and on seeing us walk in, the fella with the steel bar stopped his efforts and stood up straight.

'This is one tough bastard to get open,' he said as he raised his arm up to wipe his brow.

'We have been hours working on this and still can't get some of these fuckin' rivets to snap.'

He was referring to the back of the 'peter' which was always the weakest part on any safe. The back was riveted on with big, strong rivets all the way around the outside of the back panel. The way we opened them was to remove so many of the rivets and then with great effort we would peel the back away and off; it resembled the sardine cans of today, where you peel away the top with a ring pull. Only this was on a much larger scale.

Tosh in his gruff voice said, 'Have you been using the chisel on them?'

'Yeah,' replied Johnny, 'but some of those rivets just won't budge.'

Tosh, who was a strong fella, started to put on a pair of

industrial gloves he had with him. He then picked up a four inch wide steel chisel and a heavy lump hammer and in his gruff voice he said to Johnny, 'Mind out the way,' and with this, he bent over the safe and with these tools he started to chisel away the rivets.

When a few had been snapped away he looked up at us all smiling and said to everyone, 'That's the way it's done.'

After this great demonstration from Tosh my brother Freddy introduced me to the Oates brothers.

'Charlie, say hello to Johnny and Francie, they are Keiron's two brothers.' I already knew Keiron from past visits at our house.

I nodded to them both and said, 'Hiya.'

Johnny smiled warmly at me. 'Hello, Charlie, how are you doing?' He shook my hand.

I would describe Johnny as being fairly well built with blue eyes. His age would be about early thirties. He looked as if he could handle himself and I did learn he used to do a bit of boxing in the past. The younger brother, Francie, was slimmer than Johnny. He had fair hair and blue eyes and he looked to be in his early twenties. He too greeted me warmly.

The Oates brothers, like many professional robbers, had a front; they were real barrow boys in Liverpool. Barrow boys were smart in those days wearing their Crombie overcoats with silk scarves, looking immaculate. Johnny and Francie didn't really stand around selling fresh fruit and veg on their barrows; they had other people to do that for them, obviously they would show their faces now and again but that's about all. No, Johnny and Francie would be sitting in some warm pub negotiating some sort of illegitimate deal or discussing the next move they were going to have off. They, like the rest of us, wanted the good things in life which only money could buy. Tosh had his front too: he had a scrap metal yard, and believe me, he was doing well out of it.

All professional robbers at that time believed in having a 'front'; it was to appear that to all intents and purposes the money they were making was through legitimate means. The Oates brothers and Tosh though were men of decency and had good principals. By that I mean, if one of those men ever came unstuck and were caught on some graft they was doing or had done, it was one hundred percent guaranteed that the rest of his friends would have no fear whatsoever of being informed on. That was the golden rule; loyalties were imperative to the core among these old school gangsters.

'So you're coming in with us hey kid?' Johnny asked.

I just shrugged and nodded yes to him.

'Well, you had better get your sleeves rolled up and give us a hand with this peter,' he said, laughing.

'Yeah, Charlie,' said Keiron. 'It has got our Christmas boxes inside of it.'

Everybody laughed except our Freddy who could be dead serious at times.

'Hey, come on, stop messing about,' he said to us all. 'We don't want to be here all day getting this peter opened. We have been here long enough as it is.'

The jovial banter stopped and was replaced with serious concentration. We were all quiet and within minutes everyone got stuck in. You could hear the grunts coming from Tosh as he and Freddy went to work with a chisel and a hammer on the steel rivets. Johnny, Keiron and Francie were taking it in turns to prise the back off the safe with the metal rail bar. As for me, I could do nothing really except watch and take everything in. It was quite a while before they could get the riveted back off that safe and then there was another obstacle: it had a two inch thick wall of ballast. Ballast resembles a hard concrete that was around the inside of the safe. This ballast material provides the contents of the safe with protection from a serious fire or flood in the building and I remember Tosh saying to me, 'This is the easiest part, Charlie!'

It was a while until the work was completed. Being just a kid at that time I had never seen a safe broken open before; in fact, I had never seen one *opened* before, not in the legitimate *or* the illegitimate way. When I or my young pals – who were 'at it' like me – ever came across a safe when we broke into a place, for example a shop or some other type of property, we would just look at it in awe and then forget about it because in our young minds it would be just impossible to open. That's why most premises were not 'belled up' (alarmed). Most business people even large companies relied solely on the safe, that was their top security. Then of course some firms who *did* take extra precautions, employed night watchmen on their premises and last but not least, as everybody knew – business people and even the thieves themselves – the biggest deterrent in those days was the police who were always on foot patrol at that time. You would see lots and lots of police patrolling the areas in twos; in fact, there were a lot more police than robbers then, unlike today!

However, after me seeing my brother and his friends opening this massive strong safe, which by the way had taken hours of hard manual work, I now knew there would be no more petty crimes for me; this was the way forward and where the real money was to be made.

Talking about money, there was plenty in the safe which they had just opened and I will never forget that Christmas time in 1956!

'Merry Christmas everyone,' Johnny Oates said laughing. He was holding up in one hand a big bundle of twenty pound notes and a big bank money bag in the other which obviously had a lot more inside it.

'This is just for a start,' he exclaimed. Tosh continued passing the safe contents to him.

When the safe had been relieved of its cash it was time for more work to be done. My brother Freddy, being the way he was, meticulous, he always insisted on disposing of any incriminating evidence, for example our work clothes, gloves, tools and most importantly of all... the safe, which was usually dumped in the River Mersey

'We can always buy more gear,' he would say. 'Never leave anything lying around that could get us nicked.'

When all things incriminating had been cleared out of Tosh's scrap yard, Freddy and the rest of them sat down around a big, heavy, old office desk that looked like it had been well used and could tell some tales. They started chopping up the stash from the safe between them while I kept out of the way at the other end of the room. I was making myself scarce while they divided up the money because I didn't want them to think I was being too inquisitive or that I assumed I would get any of the money. After all, I hadn't been with them when they had stolen the safe and brought it in here. It was their graft, not mine.

Eventually, Freddy beckoned me over to the table. 'Here you are kid, it's your Christmas box,' Johnny said smiling as he passed me a roll of notes: ten pounds and five pounds. He also gave me a cloth bank bag consisting of various silver coins like shillings and half-crowns etc. I was absolutely elated and surprised!

I think the amount of cash between them all was just over two grand. When I counted my cut it came to one hundred and fifty pounds. In those days two thousand pounds was a fortune, considering that a working man's average wage was only about eight or ten pounds a week.

Just before we all departed and went our separate ways my brother said to me, 'You know the score, Charlie, don't go splashing that money around, be careful with it.'

Yeah, it was a good touch they had off and it made a happy Christmas for everyone, including myself. I was learning fast and my young life was about to change. I had become deeply involved with these 'peter men'; they were pros, they knew how to make money and how to live!

CHAPTER 3

PARTY TIME 1956

'Johnny and Keiron have invited us both to their Christmas party, Charlie, are you up for it?'

I was with my brother Freddy in the apartment he had just moved into, after falling out with my mother and getting thrown out of the house. I was just giving him a hand with the place. My mother had suspected all along that he had returned to crime, she was no fool, she could see through any cover-ups that Freddy had tried. So inevitably he was thrown out of my mother's house. Let's face it; he hadn't been out of prison long when inexplicably he was dressing in expensive clothes, wearing a nice gold watch and he always had plenty of money; all this and yet he was out of work. How could he hope to get away with all that without being suspected? Especially by my mother! He wasn't flash with it in any way though; he was careful as far as not drawing attention to himself and letting any of the wrong side know his means of support.

'Come on, kid,' he said to me, 'all the other crew will be there.' He was referring to Tosh and the rest of his friends. The lifestyle my brother and his associates lived at that time was something else.

'I don't really know,' I replied. 'I mean, you and them are all a lot older than me and I've already told my own pals that I'm meeting up with them.'

To be honest, I didn't really fancy going to Johnny's party, the reason being, the different music, different age, different conversation. No, it just wasn't for me.

It was 1956, rock and roll had just been born. We danced and dressed different to the older generation. To me, being a teenager, the world seemed dead exciting. When you are aged sixteen, people who are in their twenties and thirties seem ancient and uninteresting. I was really looking forward to the Christmas party, which was being held in our local dance hall, I would be there with my own crowd. All the kids would be jiving to the latest rock-and-roll music. Little Richard belting out 'Tutti Fruitti' on his piano and the beautiful voice of Kay Starr singing her 'Rock'n'Roll Waltz.' A new singer had just been discovered in the States and was having a massive impact on the teenage kids especially the girls, his name was Elvis Presley, his new style of music was just brilliant.

I didn't want to miss out on this rock-and-roll party. I was dressed for it wearing my best clobber (clothes).

I was sporting a black full drape jacket, which was what we called fingertip style, so called because when you were being measured for the jacket of your suit you were asked to stand with your arms down by your side and the tailor would measure down to your finger tips to get the right length for your jacket. I also had sixteen-inch-bottom drainpipe trousers which matched the jacket. Then a crisp shirt and a 'Slim Jim' tie; so called because it was only one half of an inch wide. To complete the outfit, I was wearing black suede shoes with thick crepe soles. This style of dress was created by the English teenager and *only* the English teenager, and if you wore it you were known as a 'Teddy Boy'. The name derived from the English term 'Edwardian'. The nickname for Edward was Ted or Teddy and so hence the name 'Teddy Boy!' If you were dressed like a Teddy Boy and you were out with a lot of your pals, you would be classed as a delinquent by the majority of the older generation. It is true to say that there were a lot of teenage gangs dressed this way in England who often had fights with other gangs and so Teddy Boys, as we were called were regarded as violent by some grown-ups. Of course we didn't mug old men and women or beat up inoffensive people we only fought among ourselves!

The only other difference in our appearance was our hairstyles which were created by the Americans, it was called a crew cut or a 'Tony Curtis'. Tony Curtis was a good looking dark haired famous film star back then, most of the young girls were mad about him. This style had the hair combed with a quiff at the front and a DA at the back and if you did have one of these haircuts you were classed as being dead cool! So, being dressed as I was and attending an older person's party, well it just wouldn't work... or so I thought!

'Well just come for half an hour or so,' Freddy replied. 'Just show your face. It's not asking too much is it? After all, we gave you a nice few quid and we've brought you in on the next graft we will be having off.'

I could see my brother Freddy was getting upset at the way I was behaving. I started to feel guilty over it, I mean, I did appreciate what they had done for me regarding the money and inviting me in with them. Then I thought, Half an hour is not too long really, so I reluctantly agreed to go with him.

Johnny Oates' party was in full swing when my brother and I arrived at his house. It looked packed tight. He was beaming all over when we entered.

'Hiya kid,' he said as he put his arm on my shoulder. 'I want you to meet some good friends of ours.' Then within seconds he was introducing me to some well-dressed fellas.

'This is young Charlie, Freddy's brother,' he said as I shook hands with each one of them. 'He's a good kid.'

Two of the men I had been introduced to were the Cannon brothers, Bert and Harry. These brothers had acquired a notorious reputation among the criminal fraternity *and* the police for their daring safe robberies. Yet to look at them both, you would think butter wouldn't melt in their mouths. They were smartly dressed, small in stature at about five foot five at the most and when they talked to me they spoke softly and politely.

Funnily enough, by this time I was starting to feel great and I was taking everything in. Here I was with these people, who by the way I found out later were the salt of the earth.

'What do you want to drink?' Johnny asked me. To which I shrugged, being just a sixteen year old kid I didn't really drink, in fact, I didn't even know the names of most drinks, so I just said, 'I'll have a beer.'

Johnny smiled at me as he held up a bottle of Champagne. 'Have one of these Charlie, it's Christmas time and we're celebrating.'

There were two or three stunning looking women in his company and one of these ladies, who I think was his wife, handed me a glass from a table which was laden with food and drink. Johnny started to pour the Champagne into my glass. I had never seen a real bottle of Champagne before. By now Freddy, Keiron, his brother Francie and the Cannon brothers had joined us. They too were drinking Champagne. Johnny made me feel a little embarrassed at what happened next; he suggested they all raised their glasses and made a toast to me, the new recruit.

'Here's to young Charlie,' he said loudly.

I just stood there not knowing what else to do. My brother could see the predicament I was in.

'Come on kid, drink up,' he said, encouraging me.

So I did, and I remember Keiron saying to me, 'You're with us now kid.'

Tosh was there and he too patted me on the shoulder. I had never experienced anything like it, being made such a fuss off and I was getting a real buzz out of it.

After all this hype had settled down I suddenly realised the time. I had stayed longer than I had intended to and I had to make it to the Christmas dance to see my friends now. I began to say my goodbyes to Johnny and the others and as I went towards the door Freddy came hurrying over to me. He seemed concerned. 'Will you be alright?'

'Yeah,' I replied.

'OK,' he said, 'but remember Charlie, stay clear of any trouble.' What he was alluding to was not to get into any Teddy Boy fights.

It was approaching ten o'clock and I was now late for the Christmas dance. I should have been there by eight o'clock. My friends and the rest of the crowd would be wondering what had happened to me.

'I will have to step on it,' I said to my brother. 'Otherwise I won't make it to the dance.'

'Don't panic. I'll flag down a taxi for you,' he replied. 'They come along here every two minutes or so.'

Johnny's house was situated on a busy and wide main road. It was the famous Scotland Road or Scottie road as we called it. It was in the North end of Liverpool. If you were to walk down this street on any day of the week the first thing that hit you would be the aroma of real Liverpool Irish food, such as ribs and cabbage, pea soup made from bacon shanks, and not forgetting the pans of good tasty scouse. Every Sunday the menu would change, starting off in the morning with 'salt dolly' (salted cod fish) followed by tasty roast dishes.

This popular street was known for its many ale houses and warm friendly people. Most who lived there were of Irish Catholic descent. It also had an Italian community in the same neighbourhood which was called 'Little Italy' at that time. Both of these communities got on well together even marrying into each other's families at times. My own brothers Ged and Jimmy have sons who married into the Volante and the Ventri Italian families; in fact, our family name Seiga is of Italian decent too.

From most of the pubs along Scottie Road, the sound of pianos and accordions being played could be heard drifting out into the street with the voices of the locals singing along. There was a wonderful joyous atmosphere at that time in the 1950s.

It was starting to get packed with Christmas Eve revellers. Above all the merriment of the jovial festivities, I heard my brother's voice. 'Here you go, kid.' My brother had managed to flag down a taxi, so I started to get into the cab.

'If I don't see you later, I will be at the old lady's tomorrow,' Freddy said. He was referring to my mother's house. As tomorrow would be Christmas Day, I was sure my mother would forgive him in the celestial spirit of Christmas.

'Merry Christmas, kid,' he said to me.

'Merry Christmas,' I replied. We looked at each other slightly tipsy and laughed.

The taxi started to pull away. 'Where to then?' the cab driver asked.

'Huyton.' I told him. Huyton was Liverpool 14; the place where I was born and bred.

I settled down on the back seat of the cab and I could feel my head going into a spin, it was obviously the effects of the champagne I had drunk; yet I had only had two glasses of it.

I did eventually get to our Christmas dance party on that Christmas Eve of 1956, however, I was late. It was just before eleven o'clock when I arrived and I knew it would be finishing before midnight so I would have to get into the swing of things. The dance hall was packed. The kids were jiving to the rock-and-roll music and the atmosphere was electrifying. I remember my friends all gathering around me, Joey Doyle, Yank Myers, Owen Murphy, Frankie Riozzi, Eddie Sabatini and many more who made up our gang. They were all filling me in on what had been going on. These were the kids I grew up with in our neighbourhood and went to school with. Mind you that's when we ever attended school because most of the time we bunked off. Whenever we did bunk off we always headed for the centre of the city or the docks doing a bit of this and a bit that.

Most of us were dressed the same with our Teddy Boy suits on. The girls though were something else, wearing their tight sweaters and skirts with pony tail hairstyles. I tried having a dance with one or two of them but I was really out of it. I even plucked up the courage to ask one of the girls if I could walk her home but she knocked me back. I vaguely remember two of my pals asking me if I was alright and where had I been. I must have looked a right mess to them all!

By the time the end of the party came I was the worst for wear; in fact how I got home that Christmas Eve is a mystery to me, although I do remember waking up late on Christmas Day in the big old double bed that I shared with my two younger brothers.

My two young brothers kept insisting that I get up, pulling at the bed clothes to try to rouse me, which I could do without the way I was feeling. I reached out of the bed with my hand, feeling around for my trousers that I had discarded the night before. I found them and put my hand into one of the pockets which I knew was full of silver. I pulled out what was probably about five pounds in coins.

'Here you are,' I said to my two little brothers holding out my hand full of coins. 'Grab hold of that.'

They both immediately stopped what they were doing and calmed down looking dismayed at the money.

'Here's your Christmas box.' I said. 'Aw, thanks kid,' our Jimmy said.

Little Joe did the same dropping some of the coins on the bedroom floor as he did so.

'Be careful,' I said to them both. 'And don't tell my Ma about this. OK?'

They both nodded together. 'Yeah, OK.'

Although, unbeknown to them, I had already slipped a nice few pounds into my mother's purse. The money was folded tight in a little white envelope with the words 'From Santa, xxx.'

I slowly began to function normally again. I could hear the commotion of my family downstairs with the clattering of crockery and the cheerful sound of my mother's voice rising above it all. My stomach was now telling me I was ready for the Christmas roast dinner!

I entered the room downstairs where the family gathering was taking place. Sat around a festive looking table were all of my close family laughing and chattering to one another as they prepared to tuck into the Christmas dinner. There was such a good atmosphere as everyone was merry. My only sister, who I loved, gave me a big hug as I took my place at the table. She and her husband were both hard working honest people and having two kids to bring up they would often struggled a bit. They too were looked after by me every time I had had a good touch. It was always my mother and my sister who got sorted first. That's the way me and the friends I grafted with did things; we always took care of our own.

CHAPTER 4

GOING OFF BIG TIME JANUARY 1957

In three months' time on the 7th of April, I would be seventeen years old; a youthful and tender age. However, I started to sense within myself that I had suddenly grown up into an adult. Perhaps this was due to me being involved with my older brother Freddy and the rest of his friends. Everything they did was beginning to brush off on me. I was starting to think like them, talk like them and I was even starting to adopt some of their mannerisms. I didn't hang out with my young pals as much as I used to; although we still remained the best of friends. I had moved on and I felt I had outgrown them. They were still doing unplanned petty crimes; crimes that didn't pay; according to my older and more experienced mentors. Safe breaking had become a burning ambition in me. When I first watched my brother and the rest of those Petermen in operation opening a safe, I was fascinated and intrigued. I was impressed at the professional way they went about it all. Little did I realise that in the not too distant future it would be me who became the real expert in the business.

And so it began... a journey that took me on a trail of unbelievable safe robberies, some which were successful and others which were a disaster.

I remember the very first safe robbery I took part in with them, only this time Johnny and Francie were not on the move that we were about to pull off. The reason was because both of them had acquired some brilliant information from a reliable card marker to where the safe was kept, how much money it contained and the best and safest time to have it away. The person who gave the information to Johnny and Francie might become suspects after the robbery had been carried out, so to be on the safe side, as Freddy had said, 'This card marker who gave us the info might seem to be a good fella to us all, but what if he gets a good grilling from the bizzies and under pressure he rolls over on us? We can never take that chance.' He went on to explain. 'We know the only two he can point the finger at are Johnny and Francie so we have to make double sure to protect ourselves.'

So, due to this risk, it was agreed that Johnny and Francie would not be taking part in the actual robbery; instead, they would each get themselves a good airtight alibi at the time the graft was being carried out by the rest of us. It would be Freddy, Tosh (who incidentally could drive), Keiron and me.

It was a Monday when all this was being discussed and planned; the work was to take place on the following Wednesday night. It was a works office on a massive building site, and believe it or not, it was a prefabricated building about the size of a small bungalow. I remember going to have a look at it in the day time with Freddy. We were dressed as builders in working clothes, boots etc. We pretended we were looking for employment as we looked the office over from the outside. It was going to be so easy to penetrate; it had just one lock on the entrance door. Everything the card marker had told us was bang on!

At that time in the 1950s, there was a building boom all over the country, particularly in and around the city centres. Thousands of houses as well as industrial factories were being built on a massive scale around the outskirts of the city centres. Work was plentiful at that time, unemployment was rare. There was no excuse for people not to be working. The working class man had it good then regarding employment. There was so much to go around that the men could practically choose their own jobs.

These gigantic building sites were full of activity and life, they employed thousands of workers and each week they all had to be paid out which amounted to vast sums of money, money which was made up into wage packets by the office staff on Wednesdays when the money had been delivered. Then it was kept in the office safe overnight and paid out to the workers on Thursday the next day.

That's where we came in!

Sometimes though it wasn't all as smooth running as it seemed, a lot of these building firms had security which mainly consisted of an elderly watchman, but really he was there to make sure no petty thieves stole copper piping, timber or other building materials off the site.

Some of these watchmen could doze off at three o'clock in the morning, others though could be more vigilant and stay wide awake. That could be a big problem and it would have to be taken care of. By this I don't mean that the old guy would come to any harm; not if we went about things the right way. None of us would ever stoop to using violence on an old man. You see some of these old-timers who were employed to look after these building premises at night would often pop into the nearest pub for a quick pint or two before they started the night shift and in this instance this was to be the case. Through good information, which Francie had acquired, we knew the location and the name of the pub where our old security guy had his regular drink.

It was decided that Johnny Oates, who had a magnetic personality and could charm anybody, would be the one to make sure that before we pulled the job off, the old watchman had a good nightcap!

Johnny *did* play his part well though. He befriended the old guy while in the pub and he plied him with a few drinks of good old Scotch whisky. Johnny's words to the old guy before they both left the pub were,

'Come on, dad, have another stiff one, it's very cold outside and it will keep you warm throughout the night.'

According to Johnny, as he relayed the story to us later on, the old watchman was more than grateful.

'Thank you, son,' he said to Johnny as he was escorted back to the building premises.

The front of the building compound had eight foot high double steel wired gates which were securely locked with a strong looking padlock. These gates were only opened during the working hours of the day, mostly for the coming and going of the traffic and the people who worked there. To the side of the big gate was a smaller entrance gate, this was the gate where Johnny had walked the old watchman back to. He waited for the old guy to unlock the entrance gate with a key and then watched as he locked it behind him. The time was about half-past nine. The watchman thanked Johnny again and being a gentleman, Johnny said to him, 'You keep yourself warm, dad, the weather is getting colder out here.' He watched as the old guy entered a small hut next to some offices.

Tosh, Freddy, Keiron and I were waiting all geared up in Tosh's house when Johnny, the good Samaritan, got back to us that evening. 'Everything is dead sound,' Johnny told us smiling. 'That old watchman guy will be well out of it. There is no way he is going to wake up, well not until late in the morning at least.' Johnny started to laugh as he went on. 'I'll tell you what, that old fella could drink anybody under the table. He was knocking back glasses of Scotch like there was no tomorrow.'

'Well, seeing as that is taken care of,' our Freddy said. 'Let's get down to business.'

Four of us set off from Tosh's house that evening: Tosh, Freddy, Keiron and me; Francie and Johnny would be taking a back seat while the rest of us went on to carry out the graft and hopefully, if everything went according to plan, we would be returning with a peter (safe) full of readies.

I remember that night so vividly. As I was just a kid, this was my first taste of a big-time robbery and I was extremely excited over it!

Tosh had gone and scrapped the old grafting van and had bought a different one a couple of days beforehand. It had been purchased from the block (car auctions) in a phony name. Obviously using a fictitious name was for our safety, especially if it was to be used in a robbery, and if anything went drastically wrong, like for instance, we got chased or we had to abandon the motor and the bizzies (police) got hold of it, it would be down to nobody.

It must have been about eleven o'clock when we arrived at the scene. I had been sitting in the back of the motor with Keiron while Freddy and Tosh, who was the driver, had sat in the front. It had been quite uncomfortable sitting in the back of the truck, some of Tosh's work tools were scattered on the floor including a sledge hammer and crowbars, and his old faithful two wheeled steel truck was there too. He swore by this truck for wheeling and lifting safes out of places. This truck had been made especially for the purpose of carrying heavy safes. Tosh owned a scrap yard business and this truck had been made at the yard from steel tubes welded together. The steel wheels had heavy duty tyres which made it perfect for this sort of work.

We pulled up a couple of streets away from our target. The place we had parked the van was somewhere where it would not look too conspicuous, where there were plenty of other commercial vehicles parked up for the night. Tosh switched off the engine and Freddy turned around to me.

'Are you ok, kid?' he asked me.

I nodded back to him putting on a brave face. 'Yeah!'

'Now don't forget', he said to me. 'Make double sure that the old guy is fast asleep. And one more thing... don't, whatever happens, get seen coming or going in. Ok, Charl?' Freddy then got out and opened the back door of the van to let me out. It was really dark and quiet. 'Be careful,' Freddy said as I set off towards the building premises.

Walking at a fair pace, I set off up the dark street towards the building premises. At the end of this quiet street, I reached a crossroads and the road that crossed it was big and fairly well lit. I had to be careful here as with it being brighter lit I would be easy to spot by anyone who happened to be around. I looked left and right to make sure there were no bizzies on patrol. It looked all clear, everything appeared to be ok.

Quickly, I crossed this wide road and continued up the street towards my destination. By now my heart was pounding hard in my chest with a cocktail of excitement and fear.

As I progressed further up the street the building premises finally came into sight. This spurred me on until I finally reached the big high double gates of the yard. So far so good, I thought to myself. Everywhere was dead quiet. I had a last good look around and after being sure there was no one about I began to climb the gates. Being young and agile there was no problem with this and I was over them in seconds. I dropped down into the yard on the other side.

I was inside the big building compound and I got between some of the firm's lorries that were parked up in there, just so I could check no one had seen me and that I was alone in there. I quickly began to walk towards the office buildings and the watchman's hut which stood alongside them. I was beginning to get nervous now as I approached the old guy's hut. It looked a fairly strong hut with a slightly misted up window on the side of it. The place was deadly quiet. The silence was ringing in my ears as I could not hear a single sound as I stood there. In my head I was thinking, 'what if he is not in there? What if something has happened?' My inexperienced and young mind had all these thoughts going on. Gingerly, I stretched up and attempted to peer through the window but with it being misted up I couldn't make anything out. So, with my heart pounding, I had to make sure the guy was in there. Freddy had said I should make double sure. I knew the other fellas were banking on me to be absolutely certain it was safe and sound. With my heart still racing I quietly opened the door of the hut. The air from the hut felt warm on my face and there was a strange unrecognisable smell; maybe it was the Scotch Whiskey Johnny had plied him with earlier. I knew that the watchman was in there but I had to be positive and actually see him asleep. Then just at the second I opened the door wider he let out a deep, loud snap of a snore that ended just as quickly and abruptly as it had started. It startled the life out of me. After that one loud snore though, he went straight back to sleeping soundly. For one moment I thought he had woken up but I realised as Johnny had said earlier on, he was well out of the game. Afterall, we wasn't going in there to hurt the old guy or anyone else for that matter, we were just after the wealthy firm's money and nothing else!

After reassuring myself that everything was OK and safe I climbed back over the gates, landing like a cat crouched down on the other side. I cautiously surveyed the area for any signs of life or movement before standing up straight ready to go. Just as Freddy had insisted I was still careful to be sure that no one had seen me. Therefore, with as much vigilance as before I made my way back to the van where the others were waiting.

When I got back to the van I relayed everything back to them.

'Nice going kid,' Freddy said. 'Let's go to work.'

Keiron suddenly and cheerfully piped up. 'Yeah, let's get this graft done.'

Tosh started up the motor and drove it nice and steady, pulling up right in front of the big double gates. Freddy told me and Keiron to stay in the van while he and Tosh got out to make the entrance. Tosh, wearing industrial gloves, opened the back door of the van and picked up a big crowbar and what looked like steel bolt cutters. Then, in a gruff voice and looking at me and Keiron, he said, 'this won't take a minute.'

He closed the van door shut on me and Keiron. I watched them both through the front windscreen of the van. Tosh made for the big padlock on the gates and began to use the bolt cutters, then he prized the lock off with the steel crowbar. This all took less than a minute or so. Freddy quickly took the broken lock off and put it in his jacket pocket. Then both he and Tosh pushed open the gates wide enough for the van to pass through. Tosh got back into the van and at the same time he passed the bolt cutters and the crowbar to me and Keiron. The van was driven and parked right next to the work's vehicles.

Meanwhile, Freddy had pulled the gates shut and replaced

the broken padlock with a new one which was similar. He even locked it behind him. When he returned to the rest of us it was decided that we should all stay put inside the van for half an hour or so. This was important because if anyone had heard or seen us and had gone to inform the police without us realising it then if the police did turn up and catch us while we were trapped in the van the situation wouldn't be as bad because if the worst came to the worst we could only be charged with *attempted* robbery, which would be a lot less serious. After all, an *attempted* could mean we were going to steal some building materials sheets of lead or copper piping etc rather than the safe!

However, that was only if this piece of graft was to go wrong, but *if* is a big word and right now everything was going just fine it was just a matter of having some patience and sitting it out.

Just before we all got settled inside the van Tosh surprised me when he said to Freddy,

'I might just as well put the sign on now.'

On hearing this I was slightly puzzled. Then Freddy said back to Tosh 'Yeah. OK. Just be careful.'

With that, Tosh leaned over the driver's seat and opened a long cloth bag. He pulled out of it a roll of what looked like plastic. He handed Freddy one end of the roll and they both pulled it open between them. Tosh turned around to me with a big grin on his face.

'How does that look Charlie?'

I could not believe what I was seeing. The unrolled sign had the name of the firm we were ready to have off printed on it. It was even done in the same colours, yellow background and red writing so it made our van look just like the other parked up motors next to it.

'I'll slap this on the back of the motor,' Tosh said. And that's exactly what he did.

Incidentally, the back of the van was positioned so that it was pointing towards the big double entrance gates. This was of course so that if any patrolling police just happened to stop and look through the gates our signed van would not arouse suspicion. But then, in those days the bizzies rarely checked premises that were manned by watchmen. It was just a sensible precaution we took, this being down to my brother Freddy who was extremely careful.

After what seemed like hours, Keiron, who didn't seem to have much patience, was beginning to get restless in the back of the van.

'Are we gonna make a move or what? The half hour is up,' he asked Freddy.

'Yeah, yeah, OK,' Freddy replied, turning around and looking at Keiron. 'We will make a start.'

Freddy told me to go and stand by the watchman's hut and to keep out of sight.

'Stay there kid,' he said. 'Don't leave your post unless you have to. OK?'

'OK.' I replied.

He went on. 'We might make a bit of noise going in.'

Just before I got out of the van Tosh looked at me saying, 'Remember kid, eyes and ears at all times.'

'No worries.' I said back to him.

I went and positioned myself right up to the door of the watchman's hut. If I stood there I could also keep an eye on the large gates at the front of the compound. My heart was pumping and the adrenaline was searing through my veins. I decided to have a sneaky peek into the hut. The old guy was still in slumber land.

Looking back towards the van I could see that the other three had got out of it now. I was about ten to twelve yards away from them. Freddy looked over to where I was positioned and gave me the thumbs- up; meaning is everything OK?

I nodded and gave him the thumbs-up back. I watched as all three of them approached the front door of the office building, which ran parallel with the watchman's hut. I noticed that Tosh had only taken a crowbar with them, but then we *had* been told that according to good information the office door only had a brass Yale lock on it.

Looking side on at them from where I was stood I saw Tosh give a sudden single movement and at the same time I heard a slight noise, it wasn't too loud a noise though and after this all three men disappeared inside the place. They were in!

A minute or two later Freddy reappeared and came over to me.

'We're in kid.' He looked cautiously around as he spoke.

'We might make a little noise in there. Are you OK out here?'

'Yeah, I'm good.' I nodded.

'OK, I'm going back. I will keep the office door closed then it will help to keep the noise down inside.'

Freddy then vanished just as quickly as he had appeared. I did hear some slight noise coming from the office building but it was nothing to worry about seeing as I could only just hear it. After a few more minutes, the office door half opened and out came Tosh who spoke to me in his low gruff voice.

'Alright, Charlie? I'm gonna get the truck. We've got everything sorted in there.' He paused and smiled at me as he went on to say, 'It's been a push over. The peter is ready to go.'

I watched as he went to the van and got out the truck. He pushed it back to the doorway of the building where Keiron had appeared holding the door open for him. Tosh wheeled the trolley inside and Keiron left the door to follow him.

A little while later my brother came out and approached me. He sounded a bit out of breath and looked all hot and bothered. He started to bark out his orders as he usually did but in a low voice. 'We are ready to bring the peter out, but before we do I want you to make your way down to the gates.' He paused a minute. 'Now stay put kid; it is very important. Keep your eyes peeled on the streets and if you see anyone, especially the bizzies, give us the wire (warn) straight away. Now get going kid and remember... we are banking on you!'

Quietly and silently I made my way down to the gates. I positioned myself to the side of them where I could get a good view up and down either side of the road and also down the street facing me. I looked back to where Freddy was standing and I gave him a wave and a thumbs-up then I concentrated on the streets looking and listening for anything that moved. It was still and silent. I could feel my heart pumping fast again and I shivered a bit at the thought of anything going wrong, but it was so far so good. I took a quick glance up the compound and saw all three of the fellas with the safe on the truck. Tosh was pushing it towards the van with Freddy and Keiron at either side helping to push the safe and keep it steady. I knew the hardest part would be getting it into the van which could often be really awkward. Tosh though, always seemed to have everything prepared. He had pieces of carpet in the back of the van and that carpet eased the burden. They tipped the safe on its back onto the carpet so that it could be pushed easier into the back of the van. I kept concentrating on the streets looking and listening for any danger. I didn't like being selected for this part of the graft. I thought to myself, Keep lookout! I would rather be handling that peter with them. That's all I am, I thought... a lookout.

Then it dawned on me what my brother had *actually* said, 'Don't forget Charlie, stay put kid, it's very important to keep your eyes peeled on the streets. Remember we are all banking on you!'

I then realised, I was playing an *important* role on this move. It was crucial to have a good reliable lookout. Thinking about that made me feel much better. I had another glance up to the far end of the compound where I could hear a few grunts and puffs. I could vaguely make out my brother and the other two struggling to get the peter into the back of the van. Then to my relief they managed to get it in. Once the safe was in the van my brother Freddy came walking over to me.

'Has everything been OK kid?'

'It's been very quiet and I've seen nothing suspicious,' I replied.

'Good, you can come back up with us now.'

We both quickly walked back to the van where I got into the back with Keiron. Freddy closed the door after me and then he got into the front alongside Tosh who was in the driver's seat.

For a minute or two we all sat in silence. I don't know why but it was just as if we were all lost in our own thoughts. It was Keiron who eventually broke the silence.

'I'll tell you what Freddy. That peter was a heavy bastard.'

Tosh turned around to him chuckling and said jokingly, 'It must be full to the brim with dough, hey, Keiron?'

Freddy being the serious man he was said, 'Look, we have got two choices here. First, we can take a chance and make a move now *or* we can sit it out here and move out with the early morning traffic. What do you think Keiron? And you Tosh?'

'I don't know,' Tosh said. 'What about you, Keiron?'

Keiron shrugged. 'I'm easy whatever we do.'

'Well,' Freddy said. 'I think we should stay put and move out with the flow of traffic first thing in the morning. If we *do* go now with it being only three o'clock in the morning there will be plenty of bizzies hanging about as you all know. We will stand out on the quiet, deserted streets. So it's too risky driving around at this time.'

Keiron nodded and said, 'It's worth sitting it out. After all, it will only be for a couple of hours then that main road will be jam-packed with cars and workers.'

So it was agreed that we would sit it out... not in the van though! The four of us moved into the office where there were more comfortable chairs to sit on and it was a lot warmer.

During the time we were in the office I got tired and every now and again I would drop off. My brother Freddy would give me a shake and insist that I keep having a peek into the old watchman's hut. The last peek I took was getting on to about five o'clock and he was still out for the count.

We all knew that this place came alive with the early shift at eight o'clock in the morning and the office staff would come in at nine. If we stuck to our guns and moved out at six o'clock that would give us a good two hours start before the earliest or workers arrived and by then we would be long gone.

Once again I found myself starting to drop off when suddenly, I was shaken and I heard my brother telling me to stay awake.

I tried my best not to fall asleep. I decided to concentrate on looking around the room just to keep my mind occupied. Tosh and Keiron were sat quietly having a conversation while Freddy, believe it or not, was sitting behind the large office desk looking as if he owned the place, browsing through some paperwork.

On taking a good look around I realised that everything was neat and tidy in here. Filing cabinets untouched, cupboards with all their doors closed, desks with undisturbed drawers and a big wooden table with a big typewriter on it surrounded by the personal bits and bobs of the secretary. Nothing was out of place. If my young pals and I had broken into these premises within minutes it would have been ransacked by us; drawers turned inside out, and cupboards rifled through as we searched for anything of value that we could sell on. Strangely the only thing that wouldn't have been disturbed would have been the safe!

However, being in here with these older guys, nothing in here had been turned over; they hadn't made any sort of a mess even when taking the peter from here.

Still trying my hardest to stay awake, I had a quiet talk with my brother about what I had observed and his words to me left me feeling a little embarrassed.

'We don't stoop to anything as petty as that, Charlie. Pulling open draws and looking for what?' Sarcastically, he said, 'What would we find? Some office staff's lunch money or a little kitty they had been putting into for some charity or maybe for an office night out for somebody's birthday party? Nah, that's not the way we work kid. Besides, these people wouldn't leave any large amounts of cash lying in unlocked draws and cupboards. We have only come here for one thing and that's the prize, which is now safely in the back of that van outside.'

When he finished speaking, I just sat there feeling slightly self-conscious knowing that before I joined up with this crew my friends and I, it's true, were just petty thieves.

My brother could see I was still exhausted; I suppose being a teenager you need more sleep than anyone else. He must have been looking at my sleepy face because he said, 'I'll make you a hot drink, Charlie. What do you want tea or coffee?'

I was startled. I couldn't quite believe what he was asking. A hot drink? How? Where? We were in an office not a cafe. I glanced round the room we were in and for the first time I noticed empty cups on a small table where Tosh and Keiron were sitting. They had only been having cups of tea in here while we had been sitting it out! How cool is that? Still in here, hours later, after robbing a safe and here they were drinking tea! I must have missed this while dozing on and off.

'Have a coffee, kid. It will help you stay awake.'

'Yeah, OK.' I said to my brother.

Tosh who was still in conversation with Keiron piped up, 'Hey Fred, I'll have another cup of rosy-lee if you're putting the kettle on.'

Freddy set about making the drinks in a small kitchenette in the office. I followed him and asked if there were any toilets in here. I needed a pee. He pointed to a door on the right hand side of the kitchenette. Just before I entered the toilet he told me in no uncertain terms that I must not take my gloves off. Obviously, we were all wearing gloves, but mine were thick, old, heavy leather ones that Tosh had given to me.

So, there I was trying to unbutton my flies with these gloves on and finding it awkward to do and really uncomfortable holding my dick with a thick pair of gloves on. At first I was dying for a pee and now because of the feel of the leather glove I couldn't! Then I thought to myself, Sod this for a lark, and took one glove off and commenced relieving myself!

I made sure not to be foolish and leave a fingerprint behind by putting the thick glove right back on rather than washing my hands. I wouldn't like to be the one who incriminated us all by foolishly leaving a finger print behind.

My brother told me some time ago that when a serious crime has been committed, the police, particularly the forensics, turn the place over with a fine toothed comb. They don't leave anything untouched.

At last our time was up, six o'clock had finally come around. We all stretched our legs and yawned after our vigil in the office.

Freddy opened the office door and we all made our exit. Being the last one out Freddy had a quick look around the office before he pulled the door shut behind him.

We all stood outside for a few seconds and listened. We could hear the road traffic as the streets came to life. The plan was that I stay by the old watchman's hut and make sure he was hopefully still sleeping. Freddy was to unlock the gates and Tosh and Keiron would drive quietly down to them in the van.

'Remember Charlie,' our kid said to me. 'Make sure the old guy in there is still asleep.'

I stood at my post by the hut and waited and watched as the rest carried out their roles to perfection. So far so good!

I took a quick peek through the window of the hut and found that the old guy was *still* asleep... after nine hours!

Everything went off smoothly. Freddy had opened the gate and the van had driven out. I made my way down to the gates and got in the back of the van again and that was it really, we all drove away with the bounty. Nice and easy we did it, just mingling in with the early morning traffic!

The plan was that I be dropped off by a bus stop to make my own way home, but that was no problem because in those days the buses were regular and plentiful and at peak hour times, as this was, they carried crowds of early morning workers. It was the other fellas' idea that I split and go home on my own.

Tosh spoke to me before I got out. 'When you *do* get home, get your head down, kid.'

'Yeah,' I nodded, and thought to myself, Yeah that would be the first thing on the agenda... I was dying to get some sleep.

My brother and Keiron were to be dropped off further down the line too while Tosh would drive on alone to park the van up.

I believe he was taking it to the place of somebody they all knew and trusted, as this would be a lot safer.

I remember Tosh saying in that gruff voice of his, 'We will

give it a couple of days before we make a start on that peter as it won't be long before the bizzies are going to be all over that place we have just done.'

Then he turned to me laughing. 'That's why we call them bizzies, Charlie. We keep them fuckin' busy!'

CHAPTER 5

MAKING THE HEADLINES

When I did finally arrive home that morning, it must have been about seven o'clock. My mother, who had always been an early riser, confronted me. She had a concerned look on her face.

'Where have you been? I have been worried sick about you.'

My old fella, who was also up early, was half bending down with a wide steel poker in his hand as he attended to the coal fire, which was blazing away in the fire grate. Without even looking at me I heard him mumble to my mother:

'He's been up to no good!'

During this commotion I tried to explain that I had been out with a girlfriend and had stayed over at her house. My mother looked at me with utter disgust.

'You what?'

She was obviously utterly appalled at this. 'Sleeping with a girl and you are only sixteen?'

Then my old fella had to have his say. 'What's it coming to hey? Where's the decency. That girl's father allowing that to happen in his own house.'

This was 1956 and it was unheard of for kids of sixteen to sleep together; it just was not allowed in those days. So called decent morals were high in the fifties. But worse still, it was God help you if a boy got a girl pregnant.

On reflection, it was hard for a young girl if she fell pregnant, as not only was it frowned upon but in some cases she was completely ostracised by the community. I then tried to soften the blow to my mother as I blurted out, 'I'm nearly seventeen. What's all the fuss about? We never done anything. All we did was kiss.'

'That's enough,' my mother said. 'I don't want to hear about it!'

Just as this miserable exchange of words was going on my two younger brothers entered the room, which helped to alleviate the row. They sat themselves in front of the coal fire and thankfully my mother's attention was quickly turned to them.

'Hey, you lot,' she said to them, 'don't be dilly dallying around. Wash and dressed for school, now.'

She then went into the kitchen to start making breakfast and to my relief it all quietened down. As I was just about to leave the room and go upstairs to bed, I saw my brothers sat grinning at what the row had been about. They had obviously overheard everything.

The oldest one Billy, who was fourteen, said to me, 'Hey kid!'

'What?'

'Was she nice?' They were all giggling now.

'Mind your own business and get to school,' I retorted. 'You might just be late and if you are, with a bit of luck, you will get caned!' Then it was my turn to laugh.

I finally went up to bed and no sooner had I put my head on the pillow, I completely crashed out.

During the course of the following week, the safe robbery had captured the media's attention in a big way. It made headline news:

'Safe Stolen Containing a Large Amount of Cash.'

Another newspaper read:

'The Police are Quoted as Saying 'We Are Determined To Apprehend These Audacious Safe Robbers.'

And another had printed:

'It Is Believed To Be The Same Gang Who Have Orchestrated And Carried Out Similar Raids.'

All of this news had come out before we had even opened the peter!

It wasn't just our crew who was into this sort of graft; the Cannon brothers and Co were just as active as ourselves in this sort of business. So too were others. Old school firms at that time, in 1950s Liverpool, came from and lived in different parts of the city. My brothers and I lived and came from Huyton. The Oates brothers were from the North End of the city and the Cannons from the South End and so on.

The Liverpool bizzies C.I.D. (Criminal Investigation Department) knew who all these firms were and that we were all bang at it. I remember my brother Freddy telling me never to underestimate the bizzies, especially the CID.

'They are clever bastards and if they ever pulled you in they would go to any lengths to make a charge against you stick. More so if they had acquired good information that you may have had anything to do with the crime.'

The newspaper and radio publicity expressing the outrage of this robbery caused a furore from both the bizzies and the public and due to this we just had to wait until everything had calmed down and the papers were full of something else to report.

Therefore, it was decided that the peter, which we had safely stashed away, would not be opened until the heat had blown over. This had all been agreed at a meeting which took place somewhere away from prying eyes and ears. It was just a matter of being extra vigilant and demonstrating patience.

As I was a lot younger than the others and was a new face in the circle they expressed that I had to be extra careful as far as loyalty and trust went. Strictly, I was told not to make any slip-ups whatsoever, meaning keep my mouth shut about the business, especially if I was hanging out with any of my young pals. There was to be no boasting or bragging to anyone at all.

'Our Charlie will be sound,' my brother said.

'I know he will,' Johnny replied. 'After all Freddy, you are the best tutor anyone could have.'

Tosh looked at me and smiled. 'We mean no harm, kid. We've just got to take precautions, that's all.'

I could understand them thinking this way, as I was just a kid. It would be some time in the future when they would eventually see the capabilities that this 'young kid' possessed. However, for the moment I didn't mind them lecturing me with the dos and the don'ts, I didn't mind that at all. I was hungry though, ambitious and eager to learn.

Before we broke from the meeting and temporarily went our separate ways, Johnny put his arm around me and said, 'You're OK, Charlie, don't worry kid.' He went on. 'Everything is gonna be fine. Are you OK for money?'

I told him thanks but I was fine. He then turned to his two brothers, Francie and Keiron, 'Let's get a move on and do some honest work for a change.'

He started to laugh and then winked at me saying, 'It will keep those bizzies off our back.'

'Yeah,' Tosh said. 'I've got a lot of work on in my scrappie.' (scrap yard).

So there it was, everybody was to keep their heads down, mouths shut and not draw attention to themselves from the police CID. It was at times like this when the fronts (businesses) they had come in handy.

I really liked the procedure they had all decided on to take the heat off themselves. The Oates brothers would put themselves about, being seen in the city centre working on their fruit barrows as they peddled their fresh fruit to the white collar office workers and in some cases to the city gents. While Tosh would happily work away at his scrap yard business; wearing his industrial gloves and with tools in his hands he would be completely in his element tinkering with some old car or other.

Freddy though had other ideas; he wasn't into heavy manual work nor any other sort of work if it came to that. Believe it or not, his kind of entertainment was inventing things and he was an ardent reader; he was also intelligent and had a high IQ; he didn't drink at the time, always taking care of himself and was well attired; his only downfall through his life was women.

He had a girlfriend who lived in Glasgow, Scotland, her name was Sadie. I believe he was introduced to her through a friend of his who came from the same city of Glasgow. The guy had served time in the same jail as my brother.

As for myself, I would be going back to hanging out with my pals. To be talking and messing around with my own age group for a change. I could catch up on the things I had missed because the way kids were there was always something going on. We chatted about the latest fashion in clothes, music, girls and then of course who had fought who and who had won a straightener in a fight or what street gang had beaten another. Oh yeah, there were a lot of gang fights going on at that time but only among gangs, naturally. People were still safe as we only fought among ourselves.

It was something else being a youth in 1956, a wonderful era to be part of. Everything was exciting for us kids at that time the world about us was changing; we teenagers were creating our own identity with different music, clothes and lifestyle. This was far removed from the world our parents had inherited. We had fewer inhibitions and we wanted to make our own mark on the world we lived in, and we did!

CHAPTER 6

HARD ONE TO CRACK

It had been almost two weeks since that last piece of graft we had pulled off and now that the heat had died down it was time for us to get to work opening our prize, the peter. I had been waiting for this day to come around and finally it was here. I was dead excited about it all. I felt like a little kid again. It was just like wondering what would be in your Christmas stocking!

I would actually be taking part this time in opening the safe and getting that first look at the contents. We all knew that it contained a large amount of cash, but how much? Well, that remained to be seen.

It was Freddy and Johnny who called to pick me up early that morning.

'Come on,' Freddy had said. 'Tosh and the other two have made a start on that peter.'

Johnny was waiting on the corner of our street in his car. We both got into the motor; Freddy in the front passenger seat and me in the back. Johnny turned around to me with his usual beaming smile. 'How you doing kid?'

'I'm good,' I replied.

The car began to pull away heading for our destination, although where that was I had no idea. I hadn't been told.

After we had been driving a little while I noticed that we had come out of Liverpool and were now on the outskirts of the city and were heading to the sticks (countryside); we drove through a village called Knowsley

'Ever been up this way, Charlie?' asked Johnny.

'Sort of,' I replied.

I had been around these parts a number of times with my pals when we had been bunking off school. We would all be mooching around and messing about. It was like another world to us kids. Knowsley was a beautiful wondrous place back then, in the early 1950s. We passed through the village itself where there were real olde-worlde cottages dotted around. They were surrounded by fresh green, fields and meadows. There were farms and woodland. It was truly picturesque and quaint.

We always knew we would be safe hanging around here when we were playing truant. This was because we were well out of harm's way of the school board and the bizzies; who were always on their push bikes, looking out for kids who were not attending school. They were just like the child catcher! If one of these occasions did arise and we got spotted we would all make for the thick dark woods and hide until the danger had passed.

Suddenly, a voice interrupted my childhood daydream. 'Here you go, Charlie.' It was Johnny. 'We're here!'

The car had turned up a narrow country lane and had entered a big cobbled courtyard lined with old farm buildings. Johnny pulled up the car, switched off the engine and we all got out. I recognised Tosh's van outside one of these buildings. We could hear a loud banging resonating from inside.

A black and white dog came on the scene running around and barking at us as just then a man appeared in the doorway of the old building. He was a tall man wearing breeches, long boots, waistcoat and jacket. He also wore a battered old trilby; he looked about forty years old. He told the dog to calm down. It immediately obeyed him. The man greeted Johnny warmly with a firm handshake. His name was Bob and Johnny turned and gestured towards us to make the introductions then we followed this man into the building.

The banging we could hear was Tosh bashing away at the safe with the tools in his hands. He was there in his old work overalls as usual and was being assisted by Keiron. Francie was just sitting on a chair smoking a cigarette and talking to some other older man. This man who was sat with him was dressed in old work clothes and wore a flat cap. He looked to me like the archetypal farmer with a pipe he was puffing on just about hanging on at the side of his mouth. Later when introduced to him by Francie I found his name was Tom.

Tosh and Keiron stopped what they were doing when they saw us come in. Keiron looking exasperated, pointed to the safe. 'This is a hard one to crack!'

Tosh with his couldn't care less attitude, retorted to Keiron. 'Will you stop complaining? All you have done since you got here is moan. We'll get it sorted in the end.'

I believe they had been trying to open the peter since the crack of dawn and without much success. Because of this I think there had been some squabbling going on between them. Our Freddy interrupted the squabble.

'Now, now, boys, cut it out. Have a blow, take a break. Me, Johnny and our Charlie will have a go at it.'

Keiron looked worn out. 'Thank fuck for that,' he said and sat down.

Bob, the tall man who had greeted us earlier rubbed his hands together and said to us, 'I'll make us all a brew.'

He walked over to a deep, old, white enamel sink, which from where I was standing didn't look clean. It was half filled with dirty dishes too, which was off putting. There was a scruffy, wooden table with a few chairs around it next to the sink where Bob set about making a pot of tea. I thought to myself, I'm glad I don't drink tea. The reason I don't is because I just can't stand tea leaves; they sometimes float on the top of the tea and if those tea leaves get into your mouth... Urgg urgg! There were no such things as tea bags at that time, they hadn't even been invented then.

No... I was into drinks like Coca Cola and Pepsi. These were new drinks that the Americans had only recently introduced to our country. It was all a big new thing then and kids my age liked to be seen drinking Coke and Pepsi from the unique glass bottles; it was considered cool!

Tosh who was standing next me shouted across the room to Bob.

'Make sure you make that tea nice and strong, Bob. The one you made earlier was like a pot of piss.'

Then in a hushed voice he said to me, 'These farmers are tight bastards, Charlie. Too mean to put more tea leaves in the pot. They cut back on everything.'

After the short tea break around the table it was time to tackle the big strong stubborn safe.

The safe was lying on its front on the old stone floor of the building with its back exposed. It was in exactly the same position as the last safe they had opened; the only difference was that this safe here was bigger and stronger. I could see some damage on one of the corners where Tosh and Keiron had been tackling it. Tosh took control once the work commenced. I was looking at it and weighing up the pros and cons of the situation, in particular the size of this big strong-looking monster of a safe, and I thought to myself there and then that it was just impossible to break this massive peter open!

And so it began... Tosh was using a big strong, industrial steel hacksaw with robust looking twelve inch blades. The plan was to literally saw off one of the corners. It sounds easy but this was a tedious, time consuming piece of work. No wonder he and Keiron had been getting irritable with one another. They along with Francie had been at it for hours. When, or should I say 'if' they did succeed in cutting the corner of the safe off, they would then take a thick, steel four foot rail-bar and push it into the open corner of the safe. Then hopefully using all their strength and manpower it would result in the back of the safe being prised open. The back, as I have mentioned before, is the weakest part of a safe.

One must remember though, there was no modern advanced equipment such as a thermos lance, of which the torch can literally burn through steel. That sort of unique invention would come years later. Unfortunately, for now British safes that were made by a reputable firm called Milliners were highly recommended and classed as the best and strongest security by far. This is what not only our crew but other peter men were up against.

I know this was a primitive procedure but we had no other choice with the tools of the time. It was sheer brute force and perseverance that led to our success.

I did hear at that time of some peter men who had actually abandoned the safe they had stolen simply because they found it too difficult to open. However, the way Tosh and our crew were working you could see we had the drive and determination to make it all happen.

It had been over two hours since we had arrived here at these out-buildings of the farm and still not much progress had been made as far as the safe being broken open. It wasn't for the want of trying because everyone was playing their part in this tedious work. I don't know how many hacksaw blades, which were a good foot long and thick, were broken in the process. We were all taking it in turns to use the hacksaw on the thick, steel corner. Keiron started to lose his patience and came over all pessimistic.

'This peter is never gonna open the way things are going!'

It was his turn to have a go at the hacksaw and after only ten minutes or so he threw the hacksaw down in frustration.

Then after what seemed like hours there was a bit of a breakthrough... Johnny was using the saw across the corner about halfway through when Freddy told them to stop.

'Hang on a minute John,' he said. Then turning to Tosh he asked, 'What if we try using the chisel into the part we have sawn? You know, Tosh, maybe it will weaken it?'

'We can try, Fred, but whether it will make any difference who knows.'

Tosh got the wide steel chisel, placed it where the cut marks from the saw were and began to use his lump hammer. Everyone was congregating around the safe hoping and praying (not literally of course) for success. Tosh, who was now kneeling down and using all his strength and stamina, hammered away with the lump hammer and chisel. Eventually, it seemed the cut had widened slightly.

'Go on, Tosh!' Keiron was saying loudly.

But after wielding his lump hammer for so long Tosh put down his tools shaking his head and wiped his brow. The cut had moved slightly, but not enough.

'It does look as if it's a bit wider,' our Freddy said.

But deep down I think we were all becoming disillusioned with it. We stood in silence and contemplated what the next move would be.

While all this had been going on among us, Bob and Tom, the two farmers, had been watching our antics. They approached us standing around the safe and they both took a long look at the damaged corner of the peter. As they examined it, Keiron looked at the rest of us as if to say, 'What are those two up to?' We all shrugged.

After taking a good old look, Bob walked over to the far side of the building and came back holding a massive sledge hammer.

'Stand back for a moment. I'll try this,' he said with authority.

He was a fairly big man with long arms. He began to swing the heavy sledge hammer down onto the edge of the sawn corner. You could hear the thud and almost feel the power every time the sledge hammer connected with the corner of the safe. Then... after a few of these powerful swings the corner started to open. Francie and Keiron shouted in unison:

'Yeah!'

Freddy and Johnny were shouting and encouraging Bob. 'Go on, Bob! Go on, it's going!'

We had renewed vigour!

The corner was opening further and further like a big gaping mouth. It was enough now to get the big four foot steel rail bar inside. Everybody knew by now that we had broken its back!

After all those hours of hard slogging and waiting anxiously to see what the final outcome would be, we did at last finally manage to crack open that peter.

Our spirits were lifted. Was I excited? You bet I was! How much did it contain? Plenty... just under three thousand! This was an absolute fortune back then.

The money was cut up on the big old wooden table inside the farm house building. Besides our crew, other people had to be paid off. This was always a top priority, especially concerning the two guys who had given us all the valuable information about the graft.

Quote from Johnny: "You never stick down on anyone who gives you good info, Charlie. Always give them a decent percentage of the take. A good card marker is worth his weight in gold. You never can tell when you will need them again."

The two farmers Bob and Tom also had to be taken care of regarding the share out. Without them this may never have come off. Tosh told me that he had known them a long time and that they were two good and loyal friends to him. I mean after all, they had been the ones who had actually minded the safe on *their* premises for nearly two weeks and besides that they had also helped us all out on the opening of it. Moreover, another important fact they had agreed on was that they would be responsible for the cleaning up process after we had left the farm. They disposed of the safe and any other evidence that may incriminate us *and* them.

That was my first big-time robbery and it wasn't to be my last!

CHAPTER 7

YOU WIN SOME, YOU LOSE SOME

I was now up to my neck in this business along with my brother and his grafting partners. My life had changed dramatically. Every time we had a good touch there was always a celebration. It was a party time. There were spending sprees etc. Money was coming in fast and it was being spent just as fast!

As time passed, the rollercoaster we were all on started to slow down; things didn't run as smoothly as they had done previously. Taking away and opening safes began to get harder and harder. It didn't take too long for the authorities and the police to make things much more difficult for us. Building firms, which we had been targeting, were now seeking professional and expert advice on security. All of this was due to the sheer magnitude and scale of the recent crime wave regarding safe robberies. After all, it wasn't just us who were targeting these firms. So these companies were given good tuition on how to help combat this. As a result of this, many of the firms had changed their security and used different tactics regarding keeping money in their safes overnight. Their employee's wages were being paid out on the day the cash was delivered to them from the banks. Banks had big strong vaults which were built into the concrete walls. And that to the primitive peter men was virtually impossible to combat. It would be some years later, and through progress, the peter men would be able to combat these vaults with more advanced and sophisticated tools. At the present though we were limited with what we could do. I could see this and so could my brother and his crew.

Another time, we had broken into some business premises.

Through good information we were told that the safe was not built into the wall and could be moved. Of course we were well pleased over this bit of graft. As always we did our homework right. Making sure there was no danger going in and coming out of the place.

Quote from Freddy: "Never go in or do a job, Charlie, if it doesn't look right and you don't feel sure about it, leave it. It's better to be safe than sorry."

These words from my brother have always been etched in my mind. However, what we didn't know and neither did the guy who gave us the information, was that the place had been burgled some time before, and a large amount of cash from in the safe had been stolen. If we had known that at the time we would never had looked at it never mind attempted it. But still being naive about all this we decided to have it away.

The night in question we did the routine as previously and the move went off without any hiccups but somehow it was too easy!

We took the peter away with no problems and we got it to our destination. The only problem we did have was that this was a bigger safe than we had ever done before. I knew just by looking at it myself that this was going to be incredibly hard to open. When Tosh first laid eyes on it inside the premises, he said, 'Aw this is going to be a hard one.'

I remember Freddy having his doubts before we took it. 'Do you think we should take this or should we abandon it? I mean if you think it's going to be too hard to open?'

But Johnny and Keiron wouldn't take *no* for an answer and immediately replied. 'No, let's take it. It looks like there's plenty in it.'

We could hear jingling coming from inside the safe. Francie spoke. 'Did you hear that? There could be gold inside of this.'

We *had* been told that the business owner did a bit of dabbling in gold coins and silver. So we took it! Although, even when we knew it was going to be hard work breaking into this safe, we still got that feeling in our stomachs; that excitement at the thought of opening it and seeing the prize.

Johnny was standing by the safe, which was about four foot high, patting the top of it and looking over at me with a broad smile. 'This could be it, Charlie. We might be able to retire on the contents of this one.'

Francie and Keiron stood there rubbing their gloved hands in glee.

I just thought to myself, The amount of safes you lot have done in the past, you should be retired already. Then again, reflecting back, the Oates brothers favoured the good things life had to offer, they made plenty and spent plenty, living in the fast lane at all times.

Tosh and Freddy were eager to start work on getting this peter open. In fact, we all were, unlike earlier on, when we all stood there looking at the size of it and thinking 'This is going to be tough.' Now, after hearing what sounded like gold coins rattling inside of it, we had a great incentive to really get started.

We were almost sure that, with the information we had been given about the owner's dealings in gold, there would definitely be a good prize in it for us.

We had decided to take it to Tosh's scrap yard. The reason we chose to do it there is because we knew it was going to take a long time working on it but we didn't care, plus the fact that being in Tosh's scrap yard meant we didn't need to hurry. Even Keiron, who often got frustrated and lost it, due to having no patience when opening safes, was keen to get started. I recall him saying, 'I don't care how long it takes or how many fuckin' hacksaw blades get broke getting this one opened. I'll stay here a week if necessary.'

It was typical of Keiron who had some peculiar ways.

I remember Freddy telling me that some other safe they had once worked on was just impossible to open. He was banging on the top of it with his clenched fists in frustration and with tears in his eyes, blaming everybody else apart from himself. I often think back to that time and laugh at what a character he really was.

This time though it was no laughing matter; Keiron's predictions regarding, 'It'll take a week and how many hacksaw blades would be broken was almost proved right!

It did take some long laborious hours to rip the back off that peter. Afterwards, we all stood congratulating ourselves of this great achievement as we stood around the safe. Not only that though, we were buzzing with excitement in anticipation at what this safe was going to contain.

Unfortunately though, those feelings of success and satisfaction we had all experienced were all short lived and were replaced instead, by frustration. An all-consuming cloud of anger descended on us all.

Tosh, as usual, had been passing the contents of the safe to Keiron. The first items he passed to him were two small round tin cans with the words 'Tate and Lyle Syrup Manufacturers' on the side with the familiar face of a stunning golden lion. Keiron stood there holding one tin in each hand. He looked at the rest of us in bewilderment and frowned. On giving both tins a shake we heard the sound of coins rattling around in them. He quickly put the two cans down on the table. Everyone went quiet until Francie looking eager and excited said, 'They're full of gold coins. Open them!'

There was a small knife on the table and immediately Keiron picked it up and began to prise open one of the cans. As he did so the lid fell onto the table and rolled away. He took an expectant look inside the tin and we watched as his face went red with anger.

'The bastards,' he said as he tipped the tin upside down.

They were coins alright... copper coins, pennies and half pennies, which by now were rolling all over the table.

Francie quickly opened the other can and when he saw what was in this one he too became angry. He threw the tin and all its contents across the room hitting the wall on the other side. The pennies and half penny coins scattered everywhere.

'I don't believe it. I don't believe it,' he kept shouting. However, all was not lost... or so we thought...

Tosh went back to rummaging in the safe and recovered a large tin money box. It was black with red and gold lines around the border of the lid. There was a small brass key hole in the middle of the front side. It was locked though. Tosh held the box up in his hands saying to Keiron, 'There you go! You with your whingeing and no patience.'

The atmosphere quickly changed. We were hopeful again.

'This is where the prize is,' Tosh said to Keiron. 'The paper money, not the two cans of loose change what you have been moaning about.' He put the box down on the table.

As all this had been going on our Freddy had been pacing around the room, shaking his head. He came to the table and looked at Johnny.

'Alright,' he said to Johnny. 'Never mind those two bickering, you open up the cash box.'

'It will be my pleasure, Fred,' Johnny replied with his usual big smile.

Tosh leaned over the table and passed an old screwdriver over to Johnny. Looking at his two brothers, Johnny took the screwdriver and attempted to open the box by jamming it underneath the lid and prising it.

The money box began to slide around a bit on the table so Freddy helped Johnny by holding it still. After a few attempts like this at the lid, we all watched as Johnny successfully forced the lid open. Every one of us held our breath in anticipation. What would be inside this money box?

'Fuckin' unbelievable,' Johnny said as he looked inside. He took out a package from the cash box and threw it down on the table.

'Just take a look at what that says, will you?'

Tosh put both hands on the table and leaned down to look at the package. As a puff of air expelled from his disbelieving face he stared down at the package and shook his head.

The package read clearly: **Men's Condoms Durex**

Keiron and Francie had a look of total defeat and they both just sat down on a chair each with their heads down as the demeanour of all six of us became quiet as if in contemplation. Tosh broke the silence.

'Anyone want a cup of tea?'

'It's not fuckin' tea I want,' Keiron said despondently.

Meanwhile Johnny, who was now sitting at the table, had opened the pack of Durex condoms and a look of mischief came across his face. He pulled one of the condoms out and holding each end he started to stretch it expanding it longer and longer. He started laughing as he did this and we all stopped and looked at him. Unbelievably, he then blew into the condom. He looked comical doing this as his face blushed red and almost blue as he gave it his all blowing it up. The condom began to look like a long balloon. Johnny knotted the end of it and held it up by its end giving it a shake as he grinned all over his face and looked over at his sulking brother, Keiron.

'There you go Keiron. Take these down to the market.' (Keiron's girlfriend had a market stall at that time). 'You will sell these easy. Make out to the customers that they are the latest fashion... party balloons!'

Keiron turned to his brother Johnny as if looks could kill.

We all watched these antics of Johnny's, who by now was laughing his head off. Tears were literally coming from his eyes and the comparison of his face to Keiron's gloomy face was an absolute picture. Capturing the differing expressions of the two brothers, one laughing until crying and the other red faced and angry, is all it took for the rest of us to burst out into hysterics too. The spectacle was hilarious and we all pissed ourselves laughing.

Then Keiron picked up the box of condoms and threw them up in the air. They scattered all over the place like lots of little sausage balloons waiting to be blown up. One landed on Tosh's shoulder which caused even more hilarity as he leaned over to pull it off. Even Keiron began to see the funny side now too and joined in. We were laughing uncontrollably.

Freddy who was always a bit more serious than the rest of us tried to play things down a little and in his philosophical way he said, 'Don't worry boys, you win some, you lose some. The owner of that company has had one over on us all.'

Then he continued still being serious. 'He must be laughing his bollocks off by now.'

That was it... again we all went into hysterics of laughter and started picking up the condoms and throwing them at one another...

It was sometime later on that we got the feedback from the guy who had given us the information regarding the details of the safe robbery. He told us what had really gone on at the premises of the robbery.

Apparently, the morning after, when the office staff arrived at work and found that the office had been broken into and the safe had been stolen, the owner of the premises didn't even bother to report it to the police.

'Why should I?' he was heard to say. 'Those robbers did me a great favour by taking that big, old, heavy safe out of here. It was becoming an eyesore in my new office. And, may I add, whoever they may be, I can honestly say they were efficient. While being in here they didn't disturb anything or make any mess. I would like to thank them, whoever they are, and bestow my utmost gratitude.'

The informant guy went on to say that the owner had already had a new style, modern safe installed at the premises even before we had been there taking the old one. Obviously, the information guy didn't know that and so neither did we. It was one of the new floor safes he had had installed. It was buried in thick concrete and steel and was concealed in the floor under a carpet. No wonder we didn't see it... and anyway if we had it would have been impossible for us to open.

CHAPTER 8

AN OLDER WOMAN SHOWS ME THE WAY IT'S DONE 7TH APRIL 1957

On this beautiful spring morning I awoke to the sun shining through my bedroom window and casting sun rays of colour across my room. I had risen from a long blissful sleep. I must have overslept because my two brothers had already got up and left for school.

Today was a special day too... it was my birthday. I was just seventeen years old. What a brilliant age to be, so young and fit, my youthful, supple body full of energy. My young blood coursing through my veins ready to take on all the good things the world had to offer. I was full of vitality and without a care in the world.

I yawned and stretched my young lithe body. Then I relaxed for a moment or two just taking in this early spring morning glad to be alive. Glad to be me.

I could hear the familiar and charming sound of my mother singing downstairs as she got on with taking care of the house. This delightful sound took me back to when my brothers and I were just babies and my mother used to sing lullabies to us in her soft, gentle voice.

Abruptly, I came back to reality as the events of last night came to mind. I had attended a meeting along with our Freddy, Tosh and the Oates brothers. It was held at Johnny's house and it had lasted quite a while. The conversation had become heated at times too. I got the strong impression that Johnny and Francie were toying with the idea of pulling out of the circle altogether. Most of the discussion concerned graft we had been doing and how times were rapidly changing regarding the kind of crime we were into.

I recall at one point in the meeting Johnny said he had had enough of the way we were working. 'There has *got* to be a better way of opening these peters. We are sticking our necks out too much doing what we are doing.'

The other blow to our confidence pertaining to the graft we were doing came from news we had heard about two friends of ours called the Cannon brothers, Bert and Harry. Like us, they were peter men and they had just come badly unstuck on a move they were doing. They were essentially caught bang to rights trying to take a peter away from a place they had broken into. As well as being bad news for us with them being friends this also came as a real wake up call for our crew. Then Francie managed to put us all on a downer when he said, 'There's just no way out for them; you know the way the bizzies work. If we don't watch ourselves, it'll be us next.'

Freddy retorted, 'Hang on, Francie. The way you're talking you have got us all fuckin' terrified here.'

'You know the score, Fred, let's not kid ourselves what they are up against are dead serious charges and any judge they go up in front of will send them down for a long time.'

Doing time in jail in the fifties was hard. Punishments back then were extremely severe; bread and water for days on end was one of them and was dished out quite often. So too was solitary confinement, which was soul destroying for any man. I myself can clarify this from hearing of my brother's experience, as unfortunately, he had tasted those punishments more than once.

My brother suggested that, because of the circumstances regarding the downfall of the Cannon crew and the tenacity of the police right now, we should all disperse for the time being. Also, we should put our minds to thinking of a better way to progress considering future methods.

Even though I was a lot younger and less experienced than the others, I knew in my own heart that it would only be a matter of time before we would be caught in a similar way to the Cannons. That's really how the meeting ended; we all went our separate ways for the time being.

However, today was going to be a good day for me. I had arranged to meet up with some of my friends: Joey, Yank and Owen. We all went down town on a spending spree, buying the usual things that are sought after by kids like clothes, the latest hit records, and catching up on what's what and who's who.

That evening we had met some girls and were all hanging out in our local Milk Bars or Cafes as they are now called; they were something else back then. Juke boxes inside the places would be blaring out the latest music and the atmosphere was electrifying. Everybody was young and carefree. As the night wore on I had pulled one of these girls; her name was Paula. I ended up walking her home, which wasn't too far from where I lived in Huyton, Liverpool 14. While we were walking to Paula's house we were chatting away getting to know one another and she had told me that she was sixteen and asked me how old I was. By this time we had stopped and were stood together not far from her house. I tried to make myself look a bit taller and stuck out my chest attempting to look manly and said to her, with all the confidence in the world, 'I am seventeen!'

I didn't however tell her it was my birthday that very day and that I had *only just* turned seventeen. It's funny, when you are only a teenager you try your best to be grown up; in fact, you can't wait to be an adult. But then, when you do reach that pinnacle *that's* when all your troubles really begin and you then often find yourself wishing you were a kid again!

'Wow, are you really seventeen?' Paula asked looking as if I had made an impression on her. 'When are you eighteen?'

She looked up at me as she spoke and I was thinking, I hope she doesn't ask me my date of birth. That would be embarrassing for me.

'Soon,' I said as I started to put my arm around her getting a bit closer.

'Oh,' she said.

Then we both stood there awkwardly and quiet. I knew I had better make a move, so I bent my head down and clumsily kissed her. This was the worst part for me; I was still a virgin and a little shy.

Sometimes being a teenager was so frustrating at times. It was alright when me and my pals were all hanging out together and there was a crowd of girls in our company; we all put on a big act in front of each other. There was plenty of bravado among us young men together; we were all brimming with confidence and were a bit more forward being in a group. Sometimes talking about it, the boys would brag to each other, usually about a girl they had taken home the night before. They would enthusiastically explain what they had got up to with her but most of it would be lies and certainly exaggerated, as they tried to impress the others, always making out they had done it with the girl.

Right now though, I was at that age and that poignant time in a young man's life when he is on the verge of gaining his manhood regarding relationships and sexual experience.

As far as I was concerned, most of the time, I felt I was more grown up than most; like I was a mature man and yet other times especially like the situation I found myself in right at that moment, I felt totally inadequate and lacking in experience which obviously I was! Yet, there I was with plenty of bottle when it came to committing serious crimes like safe breaking and everything that went with it.

After a few more awkward kisses, this particular moment passed and we went our separate ways probably both feeling the same anticlimax as we walked away.

I remember on one occasion as we had all been hanging out together, one of my pals had been bragging about banging some girl and when he and I were walking home on our own later I stopped him and looked him straight in the eye as I asked him straight out.

'Tell me the truth John, did you really give her one?'

He smirked back at me and said, 'Well, not properly, Charl... but I nearly!'

All he was telling me was that he had only managed what we all had: like standing up against a wall in a cold entry somewhere trying to get it off but it never really happening. There was nowhere private to go. Even if you went into a dark park you always felt someone was watching. If you were at a girls house, of course, that's if you're lucky enough to be invited in, at about half past ten, her parents would say, 'I think it is time you were going now,' and when you stood at the front door saying good bye for too long, one of the parents would come out and tell you to say goodbye! These day's kids have less inhibitions and even parents appear to be more relaxed about the whole thing.

On the way home that night I felt quite down about the uneventful evening. I thought, It's now eleven o'clock... what a *birthday* I'm having, but then again a couple of weeks ago I had confided in my older brother Freddy about the frustrating predicament I felt I was in and what I was experiencing. He had been understanding about it and reassured me.

'We all go through that, Charlie, when we are just kids. Don't worry about it; it will happen in the right place and at the right time and with the right girl. Oh, and by the way,' he added laughing, 'When it does happen, well, then there'll be no stopping you.'

I walked into our house via the back door, which at most times would be unlocked back then. My mother and her friend Christine were both sat chatting in the lounge as I came in.

'Here he is,' my mother said to her friend. 'It's my Charlie's birthday, he is seventeen. Don't the years fly, Christine? One minute they are little babies and the next they have all grown up.'

Christine looked up. 'Happy birthday, Charlie!' Christine smiled at me. 'You are a big boy now.'

I sheepishly nodded and said thanks. I felt a bit foolish, especially with my mother going on about my birthday. I went into the kitchen to make a drink of hot cocoa with milk. I sat by the kitchen table sipping the hot chocolate drink and thinking to myself I wish twelve o'clock would come around and then my birthday would be really over.

Just then my mother called to me from the lounge. Here we go I thought, What next?

I walked back into the lounge. 'Charlie, it's dark outside and getting very late, will you walk Christine to catch her bus home?'

'Yeah, OK,' I said reluctantly.

'I had better hurry,' Christine said. 'The last bus leaves at twelve o'clock midnight and it's ten to now.'

There was no problem really as the bus stop was only ten minutes' walk from our house. I had walked her to this bus stop several times before but this time I thought to myself, I won't get caught out doing this little chore again; next time I'm out at the weekend I will make sure I get home *after* twelve o'clock.

After Christine and my mother had said their goodbye's we both left our house and headed for the bus stop, walking briskly together. After we had walked a few paces Christine put her arm through mine and linked me.

'You don't mind, Charl, do you? I feel safe with you; now you are a big boy.'

I stuck out my chest proudly feeling brave and protective on hearing this. After all, Christine was my mother's best friend and had been for years. I liked the fact that she felt safe with me. We eventually turned onto the main street and could see the bus pulling into the stop and a passenger getting off. It was only about twenty meters away from us.

'Come on,' I said hurrying Christine. 'We will miss that bus if we don't get a move on.'

We both began to run towards the bus stop but we were too late; the bus started to pull away. We just stood there watching the back of the bus as it drove away around the corner and disappeared.

'Oh well. I will just have to get a taxi,' Christine said.

'No worries, Christine, there are plenty that pass around here.' I reassured her.

We had no sooner mentioned it when a taxi came up the main street towards us. I stood at the edge of the kerb and flagged it down. It pulled up right beside us. 'There you go,' I said to Christine, feeling proud of my good deed. I opened the cab door for her.

Before getting into the taxi she asked if I would go with her to make sure she got home safe. She said she would pay the taxi driver to take me back.

'Please, Charlie,' she said.

Her husband Jimmy was away at sea and wouldn't be home for another two weeks.

'I'm a bit scared of going down there on my own, Charlie, but I will be OK once I'm indoors.'

'Yeah, OK,' I said.

I was pleased that I made her feel safe and protected so I got into the cab, and off we went.

The taxi eventually pulled up outside of a block of flats. Christine's was on the third floor. It must have been about half past twelve by now and it was dark and a dimly lit around this quiet little place, so I could appreciate why Christine wanted me to accompany her.

My intention had been to stay in the taxi and head back home, and there was no way I would have let her pay the fare as I had a little roll of money on me. However, everything changed!

She wanted me to take her up to the third floor. I could understand why really because it was a dismal intimidating looking area for any woman being around here alone.

I paid the taxi and he immediately drove away; he didn't appear to want to hang around this area either. Oh well, I thought, I will just get another taxi once I have seen Christine in safe and sound.

We eventually reached the front door of her flat and Christine put her key in the door.

'Come in for a moment, Charl,' she said as she opened the door, 'and have a drink.'

'Yeah, OK,' I said, thinking in my protective way, she must be nervous of going into the dark unlit place on her own.

Christine turned on the lights after we stepped inside and closed the front door behind her. 'Sit down and make yourself comfortable, Charlie,' she said while taking off her coat.

I sat on one of the armchairs and looked around. I noticed how clean and tidy the place was. It was also well decked out with nice furnishings and carpets. She came over to me smiling and asked me what I wanted to drink? I didn't know what to ask for as I wasn't familiar with the names of drinks so I just said to her, 'Whatever,' trying to act confident and casual at the same time. She then went over to a small drinks cabinet and pulled out a bottle of wine and two glasses.

'I like a nice glass of wine,' she said as she opened the bottle and filled the two glasses. Then she came over to pass me a glass and sat herself down in the opposite armchair.

We began to chat about things in general, like her asking whether I was working. She went on to ask about what my likes and dislikes were, just like you do when you are making casual conversation.

As time passed Christine really seemed to be knocking the wine back a bit.

'I bet you have a girlfriend, Charlie,' she said quizzically. She began to giggle.

'No, I haven't, well not really.'

She rose from her armchair and started to leave the room telling me she wouldn't be a moment. I think it was the bathroom she was going to. She called from there saying that I could put on some records if I wanted to. I *had* noticed when I came in that there was a record player on a small coffee table with a selection of records by it. I had a quick look through them before she came back into the room but they weren't my sort of music at all, the likes of Frank Sinatra, Nat King Cole and those types. It was all ancient stuff to me. Kids my age were all into rock and roll.

I sat myself back down in the armchair and had another sip of wine. I don't know if it was the wine I had had so far but, I was beginning to feel good and all warm inside. I had drunk a lot: nearly two glasses and that was considerable for me at that age. Just then Christine came back into the room and surprisingly to me she had changed her clothes. She had a kind of nightdress gown on. She sat in the armchair opposite mine and smiled at me again. I was starting to feel a little embarrassed. It was getting late now and I thought it was time I was going; it was quite obvious she was tired and must have wanted to get off to bed.

Just as I was contemplating leaving and getting myself a taxi Christine stood up and looked directly at me in silence. I expected her to tell me to get myself home now as it was late, but instead she slowly opened up her dressing gown... there she was standing right in front of me completely naked! She also had a sort of sexy smile on her face. I couldn't believe it... I didn't know what to do or where to look. Finally, she spoke to me and her whole demeanour had completely changed as though it wasn't her anymore; Christine my mother's friend!

'What's wrong, Charlie?' she said as her body swayed slowly. 'Don't you like what you see?'

I looked up at the ceiling and then down at the floor and then at her.

'Yeah. Er, no. Er, yeah. Er, er!'

She then half kneeled down in front of me and started to kiss me. I couldn't believe this was happening; and with my mother's friend!

It is a well-known fact that most teenage boys do fantasise a lot about older women and they get themselves excited over it. However, this was real and my young virile body was getting ready to explode... and she knew it.

'Come on,' she said as she straightened herself up and took hold of my hand.

I stood up with her then without another word and still holding my hand she led the way to her bedroom.

I won't go into detail as to what happened between myself and Christine that night; although I will state that not only did my birthday turn out far better than I had ever expected but that night I became a fully-fledged experienced man by the time the morning came around.

The affair went on between Christine and I for the next couple of weeks and I gained more and more experience. Whenever Saturday night came around I would hang out with other teenage kids like me but just before midnight I would make my excuses to my pals and head back to our house to walk Christine to catch the last bus. Although, we always made sure we definitely missed it!

Like everything though, when there's too much of a good thing the novelty soon wears off; especially with me being so young and Christine being in her forties. It seemed like, and she was, a life time older than me and the inevitable happened... it fizzled out. I found myself wanting to be with girls of my own age and eager to share my now matured experience with *them*.

CHAPTER 9

JUST LIKE JESSE JAMES

Almost three months had passed since any moves had been carried out by me and the peter men. My brother Freddy had told me that they had been given advice by a reliable card marker who had approached Johnny and Tosh with information on a good piece of graft. It regarded a safe that was certain to contain plenty of reddies.

However, after carefully weighing up the pros and cons of the work it was decided that any plans to go ahead would have to be aborted. This decision was made after checking out the premises where the peter was situated and discovering that the safe concerned was so large that it would be impossible to move.

A couple of days later, when we were all having a meet at Tosh's scrap yard this piece of graft was talked about and Tosh described the safe as *a big heavy monster* that wouldn't even go on his purpose built truck, apart from which it would have taken hours, if not days, to open. Therefore, they had all agreed it would be too dangerous to even attempt it.

Freddy solemnly said that the way they had always worked, regarding the opening of safes, was now becoming more or less played out.

'It's finished, working the way we have been doing. We have *got* to come up with something better and safer.'

Everyone just sat there looking despondent, especially Keiron.

'Have any of *you* got any ideas? Freddy snapped getting frustrated and irritated. 'And don't be looking at *me* 'cause I haven't!'

No one answered him.

I started to think deeply about what they had just been discussing and to me it sounded as if they were defeated like they had all given up on everything.

I had an idea. I wanted to speak up and suggest something to them but it was out of the ordinary and what was holding me back was the thought of being ridiculed. That would be one thing I just wouldn't be able to handle, to be ridiculed by *anybody.*

The atmosphere among us all was becoming tense and I could tell that they were ready to call it a day.

I sat there and thought to myself, What have I got to lose if I tell them about my idea? The worst they could do was to reject me. So, I spoke up to them and looked at my brother, Freddy, who had posed the question.

'I have an idea!'

'Oh yeah?' Keiron answered back sarcastically. 'And what's that, Charlie?'

This is it, I thought to myself, Fuck it, I'll tell them now.

'What about blowing the safes open?' I said to them as quickly as I could. 'You know? Blowing them open with explosives?'

The room fell into silence and they all just looked at each other for a few seconds.

'And what gave you that idea kid?' Freddy asked.

I looked around at them all. They all appeared to be a bit stunned and puzzled.

'I got the idea from a movie I saw a couple of nights ago.'

'A movie? Oh, what did you see Batman? Hahaha,' Johnny said.

Tosh joined in laughing with Johnny as he obviously thought it was funny too.

I got annoyed with them. 'No, Johnny,' I said, being more serious now. Again, I spoke quickly just in case they took the piss out of me. 'It was a cowboy picture I saw. It was about an outlaw called Jesse James.'

They could see now that I *really* was deadly serious. Then, I couldn't believe it but Keiron came to my rescue. 'Hang on a minute, let the kid speak.' He said, gesturing with his hands to all calm down and listen. 'Go on, Charlie.'

So I began telling them how Jesse James and his outlaw gang had been using explosives to blow open peters on trains.

Francie interrupted: 'Yeah, but that was a hundred years ago, kid.'

'I know it was but have you stopped to think... those old safe robbers were more advanced *then* than we are *now*, in the present day!' As I went on talking I became more and more animated as I got excited. 'They could open a safe in less than two minutes. Yes, minutes, not hours or days. It intrigued me when I saw it and I just know we could do that ourselves, easy.'

Again they all went quiet; they were obviously pondering on this and thinking clearer. I could see Keiron was all for it; I could tell by the look on his face and his mannerisms.

Tosh though shook his head. 'Mmm, I don't know. Explosives? It could be dangerous.'

I immediately, jumped back in. 'Think about it, Tosh. We could open a peter, any peter for that matter, no matter how big or strong, and we could do it is in just a couple of minutes.'

Johnny himself was now getting serious about it all. 'I know what you mean, Charlie, and I know what you are trying to say to us but, let's face it, Tosh is right. Using explosives *is* very dangerous if you don't know what you are doing. And besides, where would we get the gear to blow open these peters?'

I knew in my own heart now that I had them thinking about it, and that was good enough for me. However, what my brother had to say next was the icing on the cake...

'That's the easiest part, Johnny,' he said. Then he looked around at us all. 'There are blasting quarries all over the country. Everything is changing as we all know and those quarries have got plenty of explosives stored there somewhere.'

He went on. 'Our Charlie's right. I have a pal, someone in Scotland, who I did bird with (served time in prison) in 1950, which was a few years ago now. I often meet up with him when

I pay a visit to my girlfriend, Sadie; he is a relative of her family and he's also a dead sound fella, not only that but he is in the same business as us... and in fact he was discussing blowing safes that far back! I think it's the way forward. I'm going up there shortly. I will definitely make it my business to see him and pump him on how to go about blowing peters. I should come back with some good results.'

After this meeting was over we all went our separate ways. Freddy and I carried on talking for a while longer. 'My girlfriend, Sadie and I are getting married there.' He paused for a moment looking concerned.

'She's pregnant. But,' he added quickly, 'that's not the reason I'm marrying her.' He suddenly stopped and looked slightly embarrassed before going on. 'You know the score kid, don't you?'

I nodded yes to him, although I didn't *quite* understand what he meant by it at first and then it dawned on me that he was trying to tell me he had fallen for her in a big way.

'By the way, Charlie, once we are married, don't tell the old lady (our mother) about this because I want it to be a secret and quiet wedding up there, Sadie and I have decided to come back down to Liverpool to live.'

I congratulated him and wished him all the best. Although, before he finally left for Scotland he gave me a stern talking to. 'I will give you a shout when something comes along that's worth having a go at, Charlie, but in the meantime keep yourself out of trouble and don't, under any circumstances, be tempted to jump in with any of those young pals of yours. Just sit tight kid, until I get back.'

So, this was the way it was going to be: waiting for the next move to come along. How long that would take, who knows? Or, could it be that there wouldn't be anymore?

This can't be the end I used to think to myself. I was still a young ambitious kid who had had a taste of the good life and was eager and hungry for more. No, this wouldn't be the end for me this was only the beginning. Safe blowing was definitely the way ahead for us all.

CHAPTER 10

THEIR WAY OF LIFE

The next few weeks I was killing time. I would hang out with my friends and occasionally I would call around to Tosh's place, on my own of course because I still adhered to the golden rule of not mentioning anything about me and the peter men to anyone!

I liked Tosh; he was a great character. He always greeted me with a warm, friendly smile. 'How's it going, Charlie?'

Sometimes, I would sit with him in the big wooden shed that he used as an office in his scrap yard. Inside it had a cast iron stove with a long wide iron pipe going up and out of the roof like a chimney. The fire was always glowing with red hot embers of coke, which was a sort of smokeless fuel back then. On top of the stove there would always be an iron kettle filled with water kept piping hot by a burning fire beneath it. There it was, ready for anyone wanting a hot cup of tea or coffee. So it was a warm and cosy sort of place to be.

Tosh would tell me tales of bygone days when he himself was just a kid the age I was then.

'Times were hard,' he would say. 'But somehow we all seemed to manage.'

I was fascinated by his stories and would sit and listen to him telling me these tales of long ago. He was a man who had had no formal education and yet he was a brilliant philosopher. To sum it up, he was a good man. Underneath all the villainy, he was a genuinely nice fella.

Other times I would call on the Oates brothers, Johnny and Francie... somehow I never called on Keiron; he was a completely different person from his two brothers. He was flamboyant and a vain man; always immaculately dressed and putting himself about with a different bird on his arm. Although, this ostensibly self-centred man showed me a totally different side to himself at times.

I remember on one occasion I was walking with him down some street in the city centre. It was a bitter cold day and we were passing some premises where an old homeless man was huddled inside of the doorway. The shabby clothes he was wearing were in complete tatters. He looked so pathetic, cold and hungry and was visibly shivering in the frosty winter air. There were various other people out that day and from all walks of life: city gentlemen, white collar workers, shoppers, casual people going about their day, but they were all ignoring the poor old guy they saw in this doorway, they side-stepped him as if he wasn't there.

Keiron stopped right in front of him. 'How are you, old timer?'

The guy looked up with his sad weather-beaten face and tried to smile up at us. Keiron then leaned down and pressed a five pound note into the poor man's hand (this was a lot of money in those days). 'Here,' Keiron said to him. 'Get yourself a couple of brandies down you and something to eat.'

The old man looked so grateful. 'Thanks, son,' he said in croaky, shivering voice.

Keiron looked down at him smiling gently. 'You take good care of yourself, dad.'

Then as we walked away Keiron turned to me. 'That's what happens when you get too old, Charlie. Nobody wants to know you.'

After witnessing this and the way he treated that humble old man I realised that this man with his erratic behaviour and bad temper was actually a decent human being underneath it all and had a great deal of empathy.

It's funny but when you are young, time seems to drag. Even more so when you have been promised something and you are waiting in anticipation for it to come around. It's like the feeling you get as a child waiting for Christmas or a birthday to arrive and you are hoping the presents you receive are the ones you have wished for.

This was how I felt while waiting for my brother Freddy to get back from Scotland, hopefully with good news. I had started to miss the danger and excitement that had inspired me. Hanging out with kids of my own age was now becoming a bore. I wasn't getting a buzz out of *anything* we did anymore and even the topics of conversations we had were becoming limited. This was probably due to the fact that I was now socialising with older people. I was even starting to dress differently to the way the kids of my own age were dressing. I was beginning to prefer wearing smart dress suits instead of the Teddy boy look I had previously worn with pride. This Teddy boy look was phasing out of style now anyway, the long draped suit jackets of the Teddy boy were being replaced by shorter jackets. Being dressed the smarter way I was made me feel I had become more accepted when socialising with the older guys, and it not only fitted in with the way they presented themselves but I felt I could converse with them a lot better too.

A couple of days after I had called on Tosh, I paid Johnny and Francie a visit, which was one of Freddy's instructions to me before he left for Scotland: 'Show your face to the others, Charlie; keep in touch with the rest of the crew while I'm away. Keep emphasising to them your idea about safe blowing especially Keiron; he was keen.'

I met up with Johnny and Francie during a lunchtime in a pub in the city centre, which Johnny referred to as his office!

The name of the pub was The Dart. This name was fitting as it was situated on the corner of two streets and one door led onto one street and the other door led out onto the other; hence the name The Dart (one could dart in and out). This was where Johnny had his meetings with various people. If he wasn't hanging out by his fruit barrow then on most days he could be found inside The Dart.

He would always be seated in the back room; which was called the snug or the smoke room. However, as I previously mentioned, Johnny referred to this place as 'the office'.

He had the owner of the place boxed off so that any meeting he conducted there was fairly private and safe. If by any chance some plain clothed C.I.D. came into the pub sniffing around they would be sussed out in no time. The police always managed to give themselves away. Instead of acting normal and like the other drinkers in the place for example, having a drink and a chat in a casual way; they would betray themselves and who they were by their mannerisms alone. They would be constantly watching and surveying anything that moved. This was given away easily just by the fact that their heads were forever looking this way and that... yeah, compared to the average Joe they stuck out like a sore thumb!

One must remember that back then there was no way the majority of people could be contacted by phone as only a small proportion of the population owned a house phone. One had to arrange dates, places and times to meet each other anyway you could and make sure you arrived at the agreed place on the right date and time. Not only were mobile phones unheard of in those days they had never even been thought of never mind invented.

The main way to make contact then was to call on people at home, where they worked or where they socialised. You would organise a time and a day for a meet and each party would be expected to be there. If a person failed to turn up on the meet they would have to give a really valid and good excuse as to why; otherwise, you would be classed as unreliable, and reliability was deemed extremely important among the criminal fraternity...

I arrived at The Dart, which seemed quite dark inside after being outside in the daylight. I made my way to the office.

'How are you doing, kid?' Johnny asked with a big smile as soon as he saw me approaching.

'I'm good,' I said, smiling back at him.

Francie was sat next to him. 'Alright, Charlie,' he said.

'Yeah,' I replied, nodding to acknowledge his greeting.

Just a few short moments after these friendly introductions the three of us had our heads together. We kept our voices down as we talked, but then it was Johnny who did most of the talking anyway.

'Well,' he began. 'We should have a decent bit of news when Freddy gets back. He reckons he has had something of a brainwave!'

Johnny told us that he and Freddy had been keeping in touch and went on to tell us that Freddy had some real good news for us and that if it came off we would all be back in business.

'Well, I hope so,' Francie said. 'By the way, when is Freddy back?'

'I have to pick him up at Lime Street Station in a couple of days. In fact he is ringing me here at The Dart tomorrow bang on two o'clock to confirm it.'

We then changed the topic of our conversation as the pub was beginning to get busier. Some of the people in there were real characters and came from all walks of life.

I noticed a couple of swag-men trying to peddle their wares. One fella had about twenty hula hoops on his arm and was going around the customers to try to sell them. These hoops made of plastic were all different colours and were just big round plastic hoops. The young people at the time, especially girls, used to put them around their waist and twist to keep them going around without dropping them to their feet. This was a new craze which had just come onto the scene. Then there were the flower women who would be in there carrying their big woven flower baskets over one arm and holding a bunch of scented flowers in the other hand, hoping for rich pickings from some of the gents.

You know what? The atmosphere inside this old fashioned pub was unbelievable; what was going on to me it seemed as though no one had a worry in the world.

Some of the other regular customers in there, the old timers, were a different breed altogether. There were women sat wrapped in their thick woollen shawls sipping on glasses of black Guinness and the old fellas sat drinking their pints. They all seemed happy and in good spirits; maybe it was all the snorting they were doing... oh yes, it went on in those days too, except it wasn't cocaine they snorted, no this drug was more addictive than that and it was legal too! It was called snuff.

Every so often you would see them pass around little boxes to each other and all were happily snorting their heads off!

Old nineteen forties music was being played from behind the bar and every now and again somebody, probably a younger bar tender, would put an Elvis song on or Little Richard, singing rock and roll. However, when this happened, the old people, and when I say this I mean people in their forties and fifties, (I considered them old then), would pull their faces. Some of them would shout, 'Get that rubbish off. We don't want to hear all that.'

It was all good fun though.

I couldn't help but notice just how popular the Oates brothers were in this pub: The Dart. Different fellas would come over into our company and say hello and offer to buy us all a drink; to which we would always politely decline... it was day time, and drinking too much so early in the day was out of the question. That was another good quality I admired in these peter men; when it came to conducting a nice piece of graft, it was their top priority to stay as sober as a judge.

'Tongues become loose when certain people drink too much. Always bear that in mind, Charlie,' Johnny had said to me on one such occasion.

Obviously, the conversations we had been engaged in earlier had long since ceased. As I mentioned previously it was busy in the pub now.

A little more time had passed, when three fellas walked in; they looked to be in their late twenties. They walked over to where Johnny, Francie and I were sitting and all acknowledged and shook hands with Johnny and Francie. These three fellas were dressed smart and were wearing expensive watches and rings. I could tell by the way they talked that they were 'at it' (into crime), just like us.

I was introduced to these men by Johnny.

'This is Freddy's young brother, Charlie. He's a good kid.'

The first one to shake my hand was called Johnny McGregor. The other two were called Larry and Brian. They all seemed friendly and little did I realise at the time but, I would meet up with these men later on in my life. I can say that they were 'old school big time' and dead sound people.

One thing that never got mentioned during the conversation that ensued was... crime. Crime would only ever be discussed with our own crew. When I had first been vetted by Tosh and Johnny, I recall them instilling this rule into me.

'Remember, Charlie, never discuss or talk about our business to anybody!'

It was late afternoon when we all decided to split. Francie was the first to make a move. He stood up looking slightly concerned. 'Hey, come on John,' he urged his brother. 'We have got to get back to our barrows. The girls will be wondering where we have got to.'

'Yeah, my wife won't be too happy,' replied Johnny. 'I told her I would only be half an hour or so.' He laughed and turned to me. 'That's what happens, Charlie, when you're in good company and having a nice chat, time flies by.'

Apparently, Francie's girlfriend worked the fruit barrow with him. Her name was Leah, a dark haired, attractive lady who came from the famous Scotland Road in Liverpool. Johnny and his wife worked on the barrow together too. It was a nice little set up they had between them... keep it in the family, as the saying goes.

We all started to make our way out of the pub. Quite a few of the customers acknowledged Francie and Johnny as they passed by them on the way out, smiling at them and saying goodbye.

Once outside, Johnny offered to drive me home but I already knew the predicament he was in by being late getting back to his wife, so I told him I would be alright and that I was going to get a haircut anyway. I wasn't really. I just said that to take the heat off him and I think he was relieved when he heard this too. So after shaking hands with the both of them, I turned and made my way home.

CHAPTER 11

A MOTHER'S FURY

'Charlie, Charlie, wake up! Did you know about your brother and what he has gone and done?'

I had been awakened from a deep sleep. At first I thought I was having a nightmare then I realised it was my mother when I opened my eyes to find her face looking down at me as I lay on my pillow. She looked infuriated and began to pump me for information on my brother Freddy.

It was quite obvious that she had found out about him getting married in Scotland. I think it was my sister who had told her. However, worse was to come... a pregnancy was involved! As my mother was a religious Catholic woman this was considered a great sin, especially in those days.

It was hard for me to lie to my mother but I had been sworn to secrecy by Freddy himself. 'It's the first I've heard, Ma,' I exclaimed as I quickly sat upright in bed.

She just went on woefully, 'He has married a woman who is carrying his child; that's if it *is* his?'

'Aw, Ma, it must be his child,' I replied.

My mother could be vindictive at times.

I know this may sound selfish on my part and I realised all the upset this had caused my mother regarding Freddy but, I wasn't interested in his matrimonial affairs, I was just made up he was back. Hopefully, he had returned with some good news for us peter men and now we could all get back on track concerning the graft.

I was out of bed like a shot on hearing this from my mother. In no time at all I was washed and dressed. All hell had broken loose regarding the news of my brother's surreptitious marriage. In the house now were gathered my sister and her husband and my two older brothers Eddie and Ged.

My mother was frantically going on about Freddy having been married before and how it had all turned out a shambles with a divorce.

As for me, I couldn't get out of there quick enough and leave all this bickering behind. So, discretely, I sneaked out of the back door and headed off to Freddy's place.

'Hello, kid,' Freddy greeted me when I arrived at his flat. 'Let me introduce you to your new sister-in-law.' He smiled.

Oh, here we go, I thought to myself; the new sister-in- law who, through no fault of her own, had caused havoc back at my mother's house.

'Sadie, I want you to meet my kid brother, Charlie. The one I was telling you about.'

Sadie was a rather pleasant looking woman, fairly tall in height and with dark hair. I would say she was about twenty two years of age. She smiled and gave me a hug. 'I have heard quite a lot about you, Charlie,' she said.

We had a chat for half an hour or so. Sadie had never been to Liverpool before and so knew nothing about the city or where she was. I just filled her in on a few things in general. I explained about the famous 'Scotland Road' and of all the warm friendly pubs and bars along it where you could hear the singing and joviality at nighttime. I also told her what I could about the local area where she had come to live. I tried to help her get her bearings on the place. I explained where the nearest bus stops where, which bus would take her into the city, where she would find the little local shops and other public amenities and things like this she may need to know while adjusting to her new surroundings. She seemed to be rather comfortable with everything though and of course to live in a big city like Liverpool was going to be no problem at all for her as she was used to living in the large and tough Scottish city of Glasgow.

'We had better be making a move,' Freddy said. 'Johnny and Tosh are picking us up outside.' He then turned to his new wife. 'Me and Charlie have a business meeting. We won't be too long.'

She seemed to be easy enough with the situation. 'That's OK,' she said. 'I have plenty to sort out here.'

Just then we heard a car beep outside.

'That will be Johnny and Tosh. Let's go kid.'

I said my goodbyes to Sadie and once Freddy and I were outside he asked me, 'What do you think of her kid?'

I told him she was nice and he smiled. As we walked towards the car, he started to grill me about what had gone on at home and what our mother had said about the situation. I briefly told him what had gone on, or at least what *I knew* to have gone on, since my mother had frantically awoken me up that morning. Importantly, I made sure to stipulate that it was not me who told her.

'I know that,' he said, nodding. 'It was our Eddie who spouted his mouth off.' He paused. 'That fella can't even hold his own water. That's one of the reasons I don't have him grafting with me. Anyway, no worries, I will smooth things over with the old lady when I call down to the house.

CHAPTER 12

HOW IT'S DONE... BUT FRANCIE WANTS OUT

Walking to the car, Freddy turned to me and said, 'Listen, kid, I have come up with the perfect solution for knocking those peters off.'

Now he had my attention. I was really listening to him now he was talking about the safe blowing. My stomach fluttered with excitement.

'I know the full score on how to blow them open. I will explain it all fully when we get to Tosh's place and have a sit-down with the rest of the crew.'

At last, I thought to myself. On hearing this and it coming from Freddy, it made me feel on top of the world.

'How are you doin', Fred?' This was the greeting from Tosh as Freddy and I got into the motor.

Johnny was in there too, he was driving and heading straight for the scrap yard. He told us that Francie and Keiron were already there waiting for us.

It was only a short drive to Tosh's place and once we arrived there we wasted no time getting inside that old office shed to start the meeting. I for one couldn't wait to hear what Freddy had to say.

We were all in good spirits and excited. The conversation began about the news of our Freddy getting himself married and not telling anyone about it. What had been the big secret? Why hadn't he told anyone?

Once that had all been discussed and the fellas had teased

him about it, we had another few minutes of jovial banter and catching up before the conversation began to fizzle out.

Tosh stood up and went to open the office shed door. Two fellas, who were employed by Tosh, were tinkering with some old wagon outside about ten yards away. He called out to these men to tell them that we were not to be disturbed. Then he closed the office shed door.

Freddy began to tell us what he had learned in Scotland and we all listened intently. He said his good friend in Scotland had introduced him to a top expert on safe blowing and because Freddy was a man who had a good pedigree (a trustworthy person) he had agreed to show him the ropes on how to blow a safe open. My brother had us all intrigued and eager to learn all about his newfound knowledge. He began to describe to us all in full how it is done.

Firstly, the safe should be placed on its back; that's of course unless it is built into a wall, but even if it was it wouldn't create too much of a problem, because the safe door could still be blown open.

Secondly, the safe door should be sealed all the way around with putty, this is to keep the safe airtight so that the blast caused would be more intense and powerful, therefore being more effective.

Thirdly, and most importantly of all, is to put the gelignite into the keyhole of the safe. This is done by packing it in tight using a narrow pencil or better still a simple lolly-ice stick.

After packing in the gelignite – which by the way is pliable – and after making sure the keyhole is full, the next step, and this too is important, is to place the detonator into the centre of the keyhole and push it in gently. It should be a firm fit within the gelignite, leaving the fuse protruding ready to be lit.

Finally, the safe has to be covered over and packed round with anything soft that might be available in the surrounding area of the place we are grafting. We might be inside an office or a factory building where there could be coats or overalls, rugs or carpet, even if we have to rip the carpeting up to use it, there may be boxes we can stack on top of it. We must smother the door of the safe and all around it with whatever came to hand.

Once this packing covered the entire safe the final thing to do is to light the detonator. All this packing covering the safe ensures that the sound of the explosion will be muffled. It dulls the bang a little and also it can help us out from a safety point of view because, I had been told of times where the safe door has been completely blown off.

We all had to hide away from the safe once the detonator was lit, behind or under desks or even out of the room completely. The second that bang goes off everything has to be done quickly; it's a rush job because there's sure to be someone who will have heard that bang. So we have to grab the contents of the safe and get away fast.

'Well that's about it.' Freddy said finally.

After this speech everybody was quiet. I could tell they were all thinking hard about it. This was new, it was definitely progress. The old way was finished.

To me, the operation that he had described sounded quite easy as long as a few basic rules were followed.

At the time, before I had heard Freddy's explanation of how to blow a safe, I really believed that it would be a more complicated and difficult technique to master. I believed that to be able to perform such an intricate operation one must have to be at the top of one's profession and to know all about explosives and how they worked.

Well, the others might have thought it sounded impressive but to me this wasn't the pinnacle of excellence the way I thought it would be. If this was all we needed to do I knew that I could, and I don't mean to sound arrogant saying this but, I knew I could blow open a safe myself.

I noticed that all the way through the meeting Francie had not uttered one word. He just sat there quietly, unlike his brother Keiron who kept moving around the room looking hyped up and excited; he was even rubbing his hands at times as if he had just been given a nice present.

Tosh got up and went over to open the office shed door. I could feel the fresh air waft through the stuffy room. Tosh yawned and stretched up his arms. 'Anyone want a mug of tea?' He looked around at us all. But no one took him up on his offer. The meeting had come to an end now and it was time for us to split.

Just as we all stood up to leave Francie, who had been sat quietly, broke his silence. 'Listen boys,' he said solemnly. 'I'm gonna deck out of this one, it's not for me.'

We all looked at him not knowing quite what to say; most of us just shrugged and said nothing. I mean, obviously, he was perfectly entitled to change his mind about coming on the graft. None of us had to do it if we didn't want to. It was his brother, Keiron, who for some reason gave him a hard time about it. He had a right go at him over it.

'What's wrong with you? Can't you see this is the best way? You must be mad to pack this in.'

'No, Keiron, *you* must be mad. Think about it... don't you realise what you are letting yourself in for? *Explosives?* No thank you!' Francie turned to the rest of us and said sincerely. 'Look, I don't want any hard feelings between us all. I wish you all the best of luck... but count me out.'

Freddy looked at him said reassuringly. 'That's ok, Fran, if that's the way you feel about it. We're not gonna fall out over this; we're all still family and the best of friends.'

The meeting finally ended with each of us shaking hands with Francie. We all knew Francie was one hundred percent and a good man. We also knew that he had staunch principles right through to the core, so we knew our business would be safe.

We left Tosh's yard in silence. I could see my brother was dismayed by Francie's announcement and so too was I... but we soon snapped out of it.

'Come with us kid,' Freddy said to me as we left Tosh's yard. He wanted me to accompany him to my mother's house while he fronted up to her. 'You know what she's like, Charl, about me getting married again. I know she thinks it won't work after the breakdown with my first wife.'

I told him that I didn't really want to get involved. This had nothing to do with me anyway. However, after a little coaxing he managed to persuade me to go with him and so ten minutes later we arrived at my mother's house.

To cut a long story short, after a few minor arguments the situation ended up with my mother and Freddy hugging each other... thank God!

The thing is, just like every good mother, she was only worried about her son. His first wife was, as my mother put it, 'no good' and she didn't want him to make the same mistake again. Although, if the truth be known, my brother seemed to have no luck with *any* woman.

Anyway, in the end everything was smoothed out with my mother.

CHAPTER 13

A DANGEROUS MISSION

Throughout the rest of that week we looked over various maps and phone books. They had each been carefully studied by us at Freddy's place. The table in the room was covered with maps of different parts of the country where blasting quarries could be located. After a few days of driving around and scouring the countryside we came across a big blasting quarry, it seemed an ideal set up. It was full of activity when we arrived there with plenty of workers milling around and lorries coming and going all the time.

It was Tosh and Freddy who fronted up to the quarry foreman that day. We had driven into the quarry in a moody van (a van not down to anybody therefore hard to trace). I noticed the big sign on the main open steel gates which read: **DANGER KEEP OUT NO TRESPASSING**

I stayed inside the back of the van while the other two set about pretending to look for work. They were both dressed the part too. They looked like proper manual workers, with overalls, work boots and caps on.

I was peering out through the back windows of the van and taking everything in. It was amazing seeing all the big dumping trucks with tons and tons of clay and stone. It was such a huge, noisy and dusty atmosphere with all that was going on.

I kept watch as Freddy and Tosh walked over to a group of workmen, who they began talking to. Obviously, I couldn't hear them speaking but I saw one of them point over to a row of what looked like office buildings. I then watched as Tosh and Freddy walked over and entered one of these offices.

A short time later they emerged from the offices, walked back over to the van and got in. Tosh got into the driver's seat and turned around to me laughing. 'What a shame. They have no vacancies for me, Charlie!'

Freddy was more serious. 'Did you get a good look at that big wooden hut right at the far end of the quarry, Tosh?'

'Yeah, I did,' Tosh replied. 'But I couldn't tell you what it was doing there.'

'Well, I can,' Freddy went on. 'I'll bet you as much as you like that that's where the explosives are stored.'

He then went on to tell us that it was a known fact that the company rules were to keep explosives well out of the way in a remote area just in case there was an accident and they were to explode.

'Phew,' Tosh muttered. 'Imagine that going up, it would cause *some* damage that would.'

'Well, that's the reason it's out of harm's way, Tosh. So that, if it did happen to go up, it wouldn't kill anybody.'

Tosh looked taken aback and more than a little stunned when he heard this. 'No wonder Francie decked out!'

'Come on, Tosh,' Freddy said. 'Don't start thinking like that. Anyway, we have done our homework on the place now so let's get going.'

It *was* a dangerous game we were getting ourselves into... but hey, so what? I was up for it and so too was my brother. I couldn't wait to get active!

A couple of days later it was decided that we would go back to the selected blasting quarry and hopefully would come back with the explosives we needed.

Tosh wasn't too keen on driving a car full of dangerous explosives. Freddy had managed to completely put him off the idea when he told us how dangerous they could be and the damage caused if they were to blow up.

One must remember though, explosives at that time, the early nineteen fifties, had never been used by criminals before, it was unheard of, certainly not in Liverpool or indeed any other major city in England. Indeed, as I look back now I can categorically state that I know we, our team, were the first to carry out safe blowing at that time.

Going to our destination that night was to be myself and Freddy with Johnny driving.

'It doesn't take a gang of us,' our Freddy had said just before we left. 'Three of us will be quite enough to have it off.'

He was of course alluding to the explosives we were going after from inside the selected quarry. At first, it was supposed to be Keiron who was going with Freddy and Johnny but I protested about this as I wanted to go. Reluctantly, Keiron gave in and agreed to it. I remember him rubbing my head and saying, 'Be careful, Charlie, kid.'

We drove out of the city that night at about half past seven in Johnny's car and made our way out into the countryside. The quarry was about thirty miles away.

When we arrived it was fairly dark. Johnny had pulled the car up about twenty or thirty yards before the quarry's main entrance. The plan was for me and Freddy to knock the padlock off the main gates and seek out where the explosives were kept; although Freddy already had a good idea where they would be.

His final words to Johnny were, 'Just stay parked here, John. It's quiet enough here. Me and Charlie will go in. Give us about ten to fifteen minutes and if everything is alright, once we have located the gear we will let you know.'

Freddy and I got out of the car, which was parked in a nice secluded spot obviously with the lights out.

'Come on kid,' Freddy said. 'This shouldn't take too long.'

We both got prepared, putting our gloves on as we made our way down the lane towards the quarry. Freddy had his haversack with him which contained a few light tools, a small crowbar for the lock and some pliers and torches. We were also dressed as workers so as not to draw unnecessary attention if we were spotted.

I was amazed at how lax the security was when we got up to the gates. It just had an ordinary padlock holding them together, which was no problem. Freddy opened this padlock easily with the jemmy (crowbar). We walked in and pulled the gates shut behind us.

'This way kid,' Freddy said and he pointed in the direction of the distant shed.

It was a weird feeling walking through that quarry. It was so deadly quiet. All the huge and powerful wagons and dumpers were parked up silent and motionless. There was just no comparison to the noise and activity of the daylight hours. These same wagons and dumpers that I had witnessed climbing up and down the quarry in the day time looked eerie standing here side by side and unnaturally quiet, like sleeping monsters.

Freddy and I walked at a fair pace, past the office buildings he had entered previously pretending to be look for a job. As we got further round the quarry, the wooden shed came into sight. On seeing this, we made haste and were soon standing right in front of it looking it over.

I couldn't believe my eyes when I saw the big sign on the front of the wooden door: **DANGER KEEP AWAY EXPLOSIVES** Not only these words of warning but also displayed on the door was a big skull and cross bones in white paint which made the whole thing look intimidating and had startled me on first seeing it. However, just like the main gates to the quarry, this shed, filled with such dangerous materials, also only had a measly looking padlock securing it!

Freddy smiled at me and pointed to the skull and cross bones saying, 'It's in here. This is where our prize is... in here!'

He quickly put the jemmy in the lock and snapped it open easily. Then he got out his torch and went inside the shed and I followed him in.

There were cardboard boxes literally floor to ceiling, all different sizes and shapes. Boxes were stacked up everywhere and the labels on the boxes all said the same as we had seen on the door... and with further information like high explosives, gelignite etc.

'Right, Charlie,' Freddy instructed. 'I will sort this lot out and get what we need. You go and get Johnny to bring the car up to the shed then by the time you get back I will have this out ready. I know exactly what to take.'

I was beginning to get excited now. I left Freddy in the hut and trotted back the way we had got there; it seemed further than it did on the way here but I went as fast as I could with adrenaline and enthusiasm spurring me on. When I reached the main gates, I opened both of them wide before jogging the next few yards down the lane to where Johnny was sat in darkness in the car with the headlights out.

'Everything alright, kid?'

I told him everything was sound and that Freddy had it waiting up there for us.

'Ok, jump in,' he said.

We drove quietly and with the light still off. We carried on through the gates and right up the way I had just run. Johnny brought the car to rest right by the side of the hut where Freddy had already placed about three or four cardboard boxes for us to load up. Each one was about the size of a small shoe box.

'Come on,' Freddy urged us. 'Let's get these in as fast as we can and get out of here.'

Johnny opened the boot of the car then Freddy told him to get back in the driver's seat and keep the engine running while we put the boxes in the boot.

Once the boxes were all safely loaded and Freddy had closed the boot he told me to get in the car while he closed up the shed and put the padlock back in position. I don't know if the lock was still in working order but at least it looked as if the shed hadn't been touched.

We drove silently out of the quarry. When we passed out of the main gates, Freddy got out and shut them behind us. Just as he did with the explosives shed, he replaced the broken padlock. When he got back into the car we headed off for home, nice and easy. By now it was about half past eight in the evening. It had taken us literally just minutes to get what we came for and I remember Johnny saying as he drove us away from there: 'Well, at least we have the gear we need now to blow all those peters off!'

We all laughed as we made our way home.

We had to think hard and sensibly regarding the safety of not only ourselves but of other people and also about where the explosives should be stored. It is not as though you could leave these high explosives anywhere!

The boxes that we had taken from the quarry contained gelignite and detonators. Freddy had done a lot of research on this subject; he had read up on and studied these powerful explosives and he went on to explain the danger to us of what could happen if these items were not handled correctly and stored safely in the right place.

For example, if ammonium nitrate gelignite was past its sell by date it could become extremely hygroscopic (absorbing moisture from the air) and for this reason it was packed and sealed in waxed paper to keep out any moisture. So if the seal was broken any water absorbed could expel the nitro-glycerine rendering it unsafe. The aluminium detonators we had were complete with the fuse attached. When this is lit it has a burning speed of just seconds per yard that too can be dangerous if not taken care with.

After careful consideration, the safest place we could think of to store our dangerous goods was Bob and Tom's farm. Therefore, Johnny, Freddy and I paid the two farmers a visit the next day. We explained everything Freddy learned and had told us in full detail to Bob and Tom, so that they knew the full score. We had to be honest with them, let's face it, there are few people who would want to stash high explosive gelignite and detonators on their premises.

Eventually, after they had weighed up the pros and cons of our request to store it all at the farm they agreed. This was ideal because the outbuildings they let us use were situated a good distance away from the farmhouse. It was not as if anything would go wrong but just in case... we were taking the right precautions.

CHAPTER 14

CARRYING OUT THE TEST

The next thing on the agenda and what we all agreed on was to carry out a test. We already had a safe; it was about four feet high with the usual brass keyhole and was manufactured by Milliners the famous safe making firm of the time. We agreed that we should all be there when we carried out this test as we all needed to see what would happen and what each other's reactions would be. The two farmers Bob and Tom agreed to be there too as they were involved with us now regarding this business.

A couple of days later the great test day arrived. This was to be the experiment of a method we hoped would soon make us all rich – or so we thought.

Tosh arrived in his van with the safe on his now infamous safe carrying truck. We were all present minus Francie (who had now left our crew) and we were all eager to see what the outcome of our testing would be.

Freddy had all the right equipment with him in his trusty haversack and was more than prepared for the job. Freddy was about to follow the instructions he had received in Scotland to the tee. The safe was laid down on its back and we all stood around it attentively watching as Freddy set to work, looking like an experienced surgeon about to operate!

He began the operation by sealing all around the safe door while we all nodded our approval at his technique. Then, from his bag he pulled out a stick of gelignite sealed in wax paper. He began to push some of the gelignite into the keyhole and pack it in tightly using a small lolly stick. Once he was satisfied that it was all packed in tightly enough and could fit no more in he took the detonator with a fuse attached from his bag. It felt like we all held our breath as we observed him intently as he placed the detonator carefully into gelignite in the centre of the keyhole leaving several inches of the fuse wire protruding so it could be lit. Then he stood up and looked down at his handiwork.

Keiron was the first to speak. 'Is that it?' he sounded excited and eager.

'Don't be silly,' Freddy retorted. 'It's got to be packed all over yet.'

'Oh, OK,' Keiron said less eagerly.

All of a sudden the local church bells began to ring out in the background.

'Listen to them bells,' said Johnny. 'They're a bit loud aren't they?'

'Not as loud as the bang this will let out when it explodes in a minute,' said Freddy laughing.

The two farmers were standing well back out of the way and looking slightly concerned by now.

Freddy shouted over to them. 'Hey, have you got any old bags or rugs to pack over this?'

Bob went into one of the old barns and came back with a load of potato sacks all held together like in bails. 'Will these do?'

'They'll do fine,' replied Freddy.

So, we all started to pack them tightly around the safe, concentrating particularly over the door. All we left exposed was the fuse.

'Have you got anything heavy, Bob? Just to hold everything down 'cause we don't want these bags just flying off all going over the place before the blast even happens.'

Bob disappeared again and returned this time with a heavy looking bag.

'What's in that?' Tosh asked.

'Old potatoes!' replied Bob.

'Oh, right,' Freddy said looking a little bemused.

Just then my mind began to wander. I remember looking at the potatoes on top of the safe and thinking to myself, This is Sunday, a day when everybody sits down to a traditional Sunday dinner with roast potatoes. A funny thing to think of at a moment like this but it must have been seeing the bag of potatoes plonked on top of the safe. It made me think, Oh yeah, it's Sunday. Then I smiled to myself, Well, I bet there is no one else in the whole country doing exactly what we are doing right now on this Sunday lunch time!

I was shaken from my thoughts by the sound of Freddy's voice. He picked up his bag of tools and proclaimed loudly. 'Get ready everybody. I'm gonna light this now.'

He had taken Bob's big old brass lighter that he used for his pipe. 'Hurry up everybody. Take cover.'

He lit the fuse and we all disbursed. Most of us ran over and into one of the farm buildings which looked like a stable and we watched anxiously over the stable door at the spark and smoke that came from the safe. I recall looking at Tosh with his hands over his ears and his eyes tightly closed. I could hear my heart pounding loudly in my chest. Then it happened...

BANG!

It was a dull, thud-like bang rather that a loud crack of a bang and for a few hesitant moments we all just stood there and stared at the safe.

'Come on,' Freddy said as he opened the stable door and stepped out.

We all ran over and pulled the sacking away. Freddy took hold of the handle of the safe. It opened. The first time we had tried it and it worked!

'Well, I gauged that right didn't I?' Freddy said with great pride.

Keiron started to clap with applause. Tosh just stood there and muttered bewilderedly. 'I can't fuckin' believe it!' I don't know where they emerged from, but the two farmers came walking over to us as calmly as anything.

Freddy looked pleased with himself; we could all see he felt dead chuffed about it all. 'There you go,' he said. 'What do you think of that? We're ready to do some graft now!'

'That's brilliant!' Keiron said grinning all over his face.

CHAPTER 15

THE LEMO JOB

Now that we had the ability to open safes more efficiently and with less effort and time, every one of us was eager to proceed further and to start grafting as soon as possible. Within a matter of days we were 'at it'. We had been put on to a well-established factory which manufactured lemonade and other soft drinks.

Lemonade back then was in great demand along with other soft drinks such as Tizer, cream soda and dandelion and burdock. These drinks were favoured by the majority of the public. Therefore, as you will realise it was *big* business. There were no supermarkets around at the time either so every day lorries would be seen making their deliveries to almost everywhere including shops, pubs and other businesses selling drinks and they would even deliver to the front door of the general public. Everyone bought from the 'pop man'. Obviously, a massive business had to have a massive workforce!

The information that had been put our way regarding this place appeared to be reliable. There was also a good piece of information in relation to the cash takings. Apparently, these takings were placed inside the safe each night and delivered to the bank at ten o'clock every Monday morning by the manager of the factory, accompanied by one of the office staff. Therefore, this would mean that on a Sunday night the safe would contain a hell of a lot of cash. Armed with this knowledge we decided we would have this away on a Sunday evening.

When I heard about this Sunday graft I thought to myself what a coincidence, it was only last Sunday that we tested the safe blowing for the first time and it will be on this Sunday just one week later that we would hopefully blow this safe.

Subsequently, the next couple of days were crucial. We had to do our homework thoroughly to make sure everything was primed. The office that contained the safe was situated within a big old Victorian building which was adjacent to the factory itself. This building was set back, off a wide main road. It was a thriving business and it looked impressive from the outside; there were gigantic signs up around the place advertising the soft drinks they manufactured and one could see just from the outer appearance of the place that this was a successful and highly profitable business.

We went over everything like a fine toothed comb before we went on that move, making sure there could be no slip ups whatsoever. After all, we were about to commit what would be regarded as a highly serious crime and if we came unstuck we could all be facing a long time in prison. So we really *did* have to be extra vigilant on this one.

The first thing on the agenda was our safety and by that I don't mean the danger of using explosives. It was our liberty that was our top priority. This was our lives we were gambling with. As I have previously mentioned, back then in those years there were more police patrolling on the beat than there were criminals. They were even more evident at nighttime. The police that patrolled the streets would check properties more than anything else; they were active in crime prevention and they seemed to be everywhere at that time... and *they* were our danger!

Once we were all satisfied that our preparation was complete and that we had planned our move perfectly, without flaws, we were ready to go. It was decided that on the Sunday night we went into action we would only need three of us to enter the building and this would be myself with Freddy and Keiron. Tosh and Johnny were to remain outside one of them in the street at the back of the premises and the other in the street out front. They would both be sitting off in their motors. It was a necessary precaution we had to take to ensure ourselves of an escape route just in case something went drastically wrong. Apart from which, we were well aware that once the safe had been blown inside the building we would have to get out of there as fast as possible!

We went over everything meticulously and for the last time on that Sunday afternoon. We had arranged for our last meeting to be at Bob and Tom's farm. This was ideal because we could also pick up the jelly and dets (gelignite and detonators) while we were there, so it made sense really.

Although Freddy insisted that we should make this our last visit to the farm as it could be dangerous for Bob and Tom if we were seen by any inquisitive neighbours or worse still nosey bizzies. All these comings and goings could bring it on top and we just could not afford for that to happen; not just because of the jelly and dets being stored there, but Bob and Tom had to be considered. They were, as I was beginning to learn, loyal and trustworthy men.

We had been at the farm for a while and by now the afternoon had turned into evening. It was starting to get dark. Tosh happened to mention the time was almost seven o'clock. Then he turned to Freddy. 'Fred, when are we moving out?'

'Give it another half hour or so and we will start making tracks then,' Freddy replied.

Before we *did* leave the farm, Freddy gave us his final instructions.

'Remember Tosh, and you, John... when us three make the entrance don't under any circumstances leave your cars. Stay put at all times. If by any chance it does happen to come on top while we are in there, you still stay put, we will get to you both somehow. But if it gets too drastic and we get a chase by the bizzies we will just ignore the motors you are in and run straight past. Obviously, I hope it doesn't come to that but it's no good you two getting roped in with us. OK, John? Tosh?'

They both nodded back to him.

Every one of us was tense at hearing the way Freddy was talking but it had to be said and we all accepted that. This was the way these peter men worked. I recall Johnny once saying something similar to me: 'If you are ever caught bang to rights, Charlie, and you have a chance to save your friends from going down with you, do it. It's much better for them to go free than the lot of you being banged up.'

This made a lot of sense to me because then those who were free on the outside could help those who were locked up on the inside. I respected what Johnny was saying and I carried that old school principal with me throughout my career, except of course towards the lowlife scum.

'OK, boys, times up. Let's go to work!' Freddy was ready.

We left the farm at around half past seven that evening and headed for our, as Freddy put it, place of work. That sounded so funny to me: here we are, all going off to work but instead of carrying our lunch boxes and clocking on at a factory like good honest people do, we are carrying our tools consisting of high explosives to break in and cause havoc. This is crazy, I thought, but being just a kid I loved it all.

Tosh drove me and Freddy, and Johnny took Keiron in his car. The target was only about twenty minutes away. We eventually arrived there and just as we were getting out of the car Tosh uttered some words of warning to Freddy: 'Play it safe, Fred.'

'That goes without saying!' my brother replied.

We set off walking towards the factory. Keiron, who had travelled in the car with Johnny, was to join us from where he had been dropped off on the road at the back of the factory as arranged. As I walked along with my brother that evening, I couldn't help but think how unbelievable this all was, We are about to commit the serious crime of safe breaking and what are we armed with? A pair of gloves each, two crowbars one of which had been shortened to go up my coat jacket sleeve, and a stick of jelly and a couple of detonators which Freddy had in his coat pocket... that was about it. Talk about travelling light! There was definitely no comparison to what we used to have to take with us on past graft. We would have the likes of a steel truck, sledge hammers, big heavy steel rail bars and a large holdall bag filled with other various tools. Thankfully, we no longer had to lump that lot around!

As the front of the factory was set back from the main road it was well lit on the outside. This was so that the building could still be seen by passers-by along the road in spite of its distance away. This was obviously to highlight to people that it was there and so served to promote and advertise the company and its products.

There were other factories on either side of the one we were interested in as this was a large industrial site. Our targeted factory had a wall of about eight feet high surrounding its perimeter. Along the streets up either side of the building the lighting was far dimmer as there was no advertising along these walls and our plan was for me to climb over the wall to the left of the building to make sure everything was quiet and safe for us to continue.

There was a long loading bay the length of the back wall where the lorries would be filled with their cargo to distribute throughout the day. At the left end of the loading bay, just where I would jump over the wall, was where we wanted to get in to, as this was where the office was situated that held the safe. We had arranged to meet Keiron along this left hand side street and just as we got there we could see him strolling down to meet us.

As he approached us, Freddy spoke to him quietly. 'Alright, Kearn?'

'Yeah, everything seems sound enough around here, up to now that is.'

The dark side street of the factory was quiet and after a quick look around the area I prepared to go over the high brick wall, just to make sure nothing was out of place and to check out the main offices where the safe was kept. Just before Freddy and Keiron hoisted me up, Freddy said, 'Give us your stick (crowbar), Charlie.'

I pulled the stick out from my jacket sleeve, gave it to Freddy and then they both helped me over the wall by cupping their hands for me to put my feet in and then they hoisted me up enabling me to climb cleanly over and drop down on the other side, which I did easily enough.

I knew exactly where I was going as Freddy and I had wandered in here a couple of days ago on a lunch time. We had been sussing the place out and nobody had taken any notice of us while we had been there. It had been easy to mingle in with the workers during the busy lunchtime.

The first thing you look for in this sort of game is the best way to break in and out without looking too suspicious. Freddy and I had cased the place thoroughly. We both had spotted a small side gate. We had no idea what the purpose of the gate was but we could tell by looking at it that it had not been used for quite some time. On the inside it had a bolt at the top and one at the bottom and while we were stood there pretending to be two workers talking, I had my back against the gate and I discreetly tried the bolts. They were both stiff due to lack of use but I did think to myself at the time that they wouldn't be too much of a problem.

So after jumping over the wall that night I went straight back to the old side door as it was going to be our way in. Freddy and Keiron, still on the outside, were on opposite sides of the street strolling up and down casually so as not to look suspicious. Obviously, if they were stood together waiting around they would look conspicuous.

The plan was for me to give them a wave when I was ready but I was having some difficulty opening these old unused bolts. I was trying to wriggle them up and down to get them loose but it was taking a while and the other two must have been wondering what was wrong. I was also unintentionally making some noise as I struggled with the bolts and I was wishing I had a tool with me to help prise them open. Just then, coming from the other side of the door, I heard my brother's voice: 'Are you OK in there, kid?'

'I can hardly move these bolts they are really stiff.'

'Hang on.' He suddenly appeared looking over the wall holding the crowbar. 'Here, try to use this on them.' He dropped the crowbar down to me. Then he disappeared back over the wall and back down onto the side street. The small crowbar worked a treat and started to loosen the bolts. Eventually, I managed to get the two of them open. Cautiously, I opened the door slightly and peeked out onto the side street to look for my brother. I saw him across the other side of the street. He had been keeping an eye on the door and on seeing me pop my head out he made his way over. Keiron was on the opposite side of the street to him and when he saw Freddy make his way to the door he came over too, keeping a lookout as he did so.

They both quickly came in through the door. Freddy came in first and then stood back holding the door to let Keiron come in past him. He took a final look up and down the street to check it was still all clear and that no one had seen them come in. After this he closed the door quietly behind him and re-locked the bolts.

Now that we were inside the yard we made our way to the main office building where we knew the safe was held. This office building was older than the factory and loading bay building. The factory side had been added more recently.

This was an old Victorian building and it had a couple of wide stone steps leading up to large imposing double doors with wood panelling, typical of the period and polished to a high gloss shine. There was a brass plate on the wall next to them which proudly displayed the name of the firm and there were two big brass door knobs, one in the centre of each door. The left hand door had the letter box in it and the one on the right had the lock. It was a solid old brass mortice lock and it also had a Yale lock just above it. These doors were solid and impressive and would work to our advantage as the thickness of them would help to deaden the noise from the blast when we blew the safe. On either side of the double door were two long windows.

We knew by looking at the locks on the door that this was going to be fairly difficult to open with the crowbars but we knew we could do it; it would just take a little time and could be noisy. At one point we contemplated breaking in through a window but that could be messy, take just as much time and probably be noisier. So we began to jemmy the door with the crowbars using one as to prise and the other one to insert into the prised gap and use as leverage. It was a struggle but we managed it and we burst in through the door and entered a large reception area.

From the information gathered we knew which office held the safe. It was the one off to the left of the reception so we went straight to it and entered. It contained all the usual office furniture: a desk with a large important looking chair behind it; other chairs set around the room obviously for guests and co-workers to use in meetings. However, it was just the safe we were interested in and we spotted it immediately over in the far corner of the room. It was built into the wall like the typical safes of the day and had the big brass keyhole in the centre. More and more offices were building their safes into the walls for extra security, to prevent the safe being taken away or tipped over and worked on to break into.

We all stood and looked at each other as we anticipated our first attempt *for real* at this safe blowing game. I'm sure Freddy and Keiron could also feel their hearts pounding hard and fast in their chests the way mine was at that moment. I felt nervous but also quite excited at the prospect of blowing this completely open.

Freddy took the gelignite and detonators out of his pocket and this time it was Keiron who kept lookout at the window while I helped Freddy with the work, passing him whatever he needed. Firstly, I passed him the putty and he proceeded to put it around the safe door as he had done on our rehearsal safe in the farm yard the other day. He then pressed the pliable gelignite into the key hole and made sure it was tightly packed in there with space for no more. Then I passed him the detonator and watched as he carefully inserted it into the centre of the jelly leaving a small amount protruding for him to light.

When this preparation was done we stood back and observed. Freddy turned to me: 'Before we blow this we have to look round to see what we can pack it with.'

Scanning the office we could see nothing that we could use so we went back out into the reception area and looked into the other rooms. In one of them we found stacks and stacks of boxes containing orange cordial in cartons and other soft drinks, so, thinking they would do the job we hand-balled them out of there and back into the room of the strong looking safe.

We stacked them in front of the safe against the wall several boxes high and about five boxes deep and then we pushed the office table right up against them and butted them up tightly thinking this would also help with the packing. We only left enough of a gap for Freddy to reach through to light the detonator. The big thick office door would also make a good buffer of the sound so once Freddy had lit the detonator the plan was to run out of the room and shut the door tight to use it as a good barricade from the blow.

Before Freddy leaned over to the gap where he could light the det I went out into the reception area where Keiron was still lookout at one of the windows. I went to be the lookout at another window and we waited to hear instructions from Freddy.

'Everything OK out there?' Freddy called out.

We both shouted back that all was OK. We could see traffic right over where the main road was but that was a good thing too as it would help to disguise any noise that may be heard on the outside. Incidentally, all this work was done in the dark. The only light we had was what was being cast naturally through the windows from the lights outside. Therefore, as it wasn't pitch black inside we didn't need to put any light on, which again was in our favour as even less likely to arouse suspicion.

Once we knew everything was packed up tightly and we were ready to blow it, Freddy shouted a reminder of a warning to us: 'Remember, the minute that blast goes off we have to be on our toes in case anybody hears it. We have to empty this peter as soon as and get the fuck out of here fast.' Then after a slight pause for thought he shouted again: 'I'm lighting this right now. Are you ready?' We shouted back that everything was OK and we were ready. He lit the fuse!

I was just thinking to myself that I hoped nothing would go wrong. This was our first attempt at this and I hoped to God it all went well. I'm sure too that the others were thinking exactly the same. Suddenly, there was an almighty **bang!**

I don't know if it was just my imagination but, it seemed to me as if even the room shuddered. All three of us knew we had to be gone from here within seconds of the bang. As arranged, Keiron stayed lookout at the window while Freddy and I ran into the room to grab the contents of the safe. The place was in a right mess. The orange juice had splattered all over the place. Boxes and cartons had burst open with the force of the blast. My heart was in my mouth as I watched Freddy grab the handle of the safe to see if it would open and I held my breath as he attempted to turn it. There was no problem at all though... it turned and opened. We had done it!

We had brought with us two leatherette bags which were rolled up and secured with an elastic band around them. As fast as we could we opened them up and filled them with the contents of the safe. Then we ran out of the room and back into the reception area where Keiron was still at the window looking at us anxiously.

'Is that it? Are we ready?'

'Yeah, come on lets go,' said Freddy.

We immediately ran outside to the side door. Just before Freddy opened it he paused and we listened for any noise outside. There wasn't a sound.

'I wonder if Tosh and Johnny heard that blast? Freddy said. 'We did tell them to keep the car windows open and listen.'

Keiron and I just looked at him and shrugged. We just wanted to get out of there and away. Freddy unbolted the gate quietly and looked out onto the street. Everything was still quiet and still so the three of us walked quickly out. Keiron with one of the bags went in one direction towards where Johnny was waiting with the car and Freddy and I walked briskly the other way to where Tosh was waiting for us in his car. I was carrying the few tools we had taken and Freddy was carrying the bag of stuff we had just taken from that first safe blowing job. We got back to Tosh who was sat in the car with the engine ticking over and we got in.

As soon as we got into the car, Tosh began to drive away, and when I say drive away, I don't mean screeched away, the way they always portray it on television and in the movies. Of course the right thing to do was to distance ourselves from the scene of the crime as soon as possible but why go at a high powered speed and draw attention to ourselves when there is no need? Particularly on this piece of graft we had just pulled off, because to me so far, everything was perfect.

'Did you hear that explosion from where you were parked, Tosh?' Freddy asked.

'I did hear a slight bit of a boom. That's when I switched the engine on just in case, Fred.'

'It must have been heard.' Freddy said. 'It sounded loud inside the office.' Then he turned to me. 'Didn't it, kid?' I nodded to him. 'I don't think it will be too long before the bizzies are on the scene.' He went on to say, as the car drove further away.

'How did it go, Fred?' Tosh asked. 'Have we made out OK?'

Freddy lifted up the bag of cash. 'Well, up to now we have.'

We had arranged that if everything went according to plan we would all meet up at Johnny's house, which wasn't too far away from the scene of the crime and fortunately, we all eventually arrived there without any hiccups.

The others had arrived there just before us and had been discussing how things had gone. I will never forget the atmosphere in Johnny's house that night – we were all buzzing.

Keiron being his usual excitable self was pacing up and down and around the room. 'I was telling our John how it went in there.' He said referring to the safe we had just successfully blown. 'You should have seen it, kid,' he said to Johnny. 'It was incredible.' He laughed. 'And it only took a couple of minutes. Tell you what? If we carry on the way we are going like this, we will all be on Easy Street.'

'Now, now, Keiron, don't start counting your chickens yet.' Johnny laughed. 'OK, let's chop this up,' he went on.

We all sat down around Johnny's table and he emptied the

bag of money onto it. It was left up to Freddy and Johnny to divide up the readies, the total of which came to just under three grand, an absolutely brilliant amount of money in those days. The two farmers were well taken care of and the man who gave us the information about the graft, he too was well looked after. We all decided to chip in for Francie, to give him a nice little touch as a good will gesture. Just think about it though, I was only a seventeen year old kid and I had just received all these, if I can put it this way: *ill-gotten gains.*

My brother and the rest of the crew sat and had a talk about me having such a large amount of cash on me all at once and that maybe it was not such a good idea. Johnny turned to me. 'We don't mean to underestimate you or anything like that kid, but one of us will mind a majority of the money for you. That way it will be safe and whenever you *do* need any out of it, it will always be there for you, anytime.'

Tosh was to be the one who would take care of my cut as he had a good little front with the scrapyard business. This all made good common sense to me really. And after all, they were only taking care of my welfare. The move that we had just pulled off made headlines in the papers. The media had a field day with it all:

GELIGNITE GANG BLOW OPEN SAFE AT FACTORY

Police reported gelignite was used to blow open a safe.

Gang escape with thousands of pounds.

Police at first thought it could be a Scottish gang of criminals who had carried out this audacious crime but then after further investigations they had discovered a blasting quarry had been broken into and thieves had gained access to dangerous explosives that had been stored in the compound of the quarry according to some reports.

As far as we were aware this safe blowing was the first of its kind in England. From then on there was no turning back for our crew.

CHAPTER 16

AN EPIDEMIC

Safe-blowing was the way forward and it became a new modern type of crime. We had become true underworld pioneers and yet it was so simple.

Due to all the attention this was creating in so far as the media etc, it was inevitable that gangs who were still using the old method would put two and two together and turn their hands to safe blowing which was fast and efficient. This is what happens when progress is made in crime by criminals: there are copycats. This was all down to the police and the media, who only had themselves to blame as it was these who subsequently exposed how a blasting quarry had been broken into and gelignite and detonators (which incidentally were the trade tools of the safe blower) had been stolen. Therefore, the old fashioned safe breakers now knew they also could get hold of this valuable equipment from these unmanned and unsecured blasting quarries.

In the forthcoming months this began to escalate, there wasn't a week that went by without the police and the public being informed of another safe blowing happening. The place was in the grip of an epidemic, particularly in and around Liverpool and as a matter of course it eventually spread to other major cities.

Initially, the police didn't have the ability to control this sort of crime. Referring back to those days in the early fifties, the police force was comparatively primitive. They patrolled on foot and some may have used a bicycle as there were few in cars. They had to get to a telephone box to call the station for assistance or to report anything untoward as they had no walkie-talkies or mobile phones then either. The only thing the police could do was to have more police patrolling areas in which businesses may be regarded as vulnerable, and if they heard a bang they would instantly know that it was a safe being blown. Perceptibly, this situation meant that almost everything worked in favour of the offenders.

Primarily, there was no longer a need for a gang of several men to go on a safe job. Just one or two men would now be sufficient: one peter man to blow the safe and another to assist with breaking and entering the premises and then to keep lookout while the peter man went to work on the safe. Obviously, there could still be another couple of men involved and as well as lookouts they could help with the packing of the safe prior to blowing it but there was no longer the *necessity* to have a gang of men.

Also, the old way would involve the gang being weighed down with tools, a truck and heavy equipment including the five foot long, weighty steel rail bars, sledge hammer and other cumbersome equipment previously needed or having to drag out a big heavy safe, to take in a van to be opened elsewhere. With this new method of safe breaking the modern peter man would travel light to carry out the graft and sometimes would be on foot. They could even be dressed in smart suits and look extremely well-heeled and yet he could have gelignite and a couple of detonators in his suit pocket. No one would know this by looking at him!

Secondly, the police couldn't catch them because the minute that peter was blown the men would exit the premises immediately and with no tools to carry and only paper money taken from the robbery, again they would be carrying no weight. Providing they were lucky enough to get out of the premises unseen by police they would get out onto the street and just look like any other passer-by. The peter men would always split up and walk separately on opposite sides of the road and maybe even in different directions so they would rouse no suspicion in either their appearance or carrying content. Consequently, looking just like an ordinary man walking down the road they could leave the area confidently and above suspicion.

Another tactic the peter men deployed was to change the time they would carry out the graft. Whereas before they would be working in the dead of night and would obviously look suspect had they been spotted, they were now hitting the premises not long after they had closed for business and while there was still traffic around on the roads. This was a much less conspicuous time of day.

The police C.I.D. (Criminal Investigation Department) did however find an alternative way to charge a safe blower called fitting up! As soon as they had a good idea who was doing the graft they would go all out and use devious ways to get them arrested and charged. They would even go as far as planting and fabricating evidence.

CHAPTER 17

NEARLY ON TOP

However, having said all of this about the new way there was one occasion when we had to revert back to the old. So although it was a bit like three steps forward and two steps back we had to take the safe far away from the premises due to there being a police station in the vicinity.

We always insisted that whichever one of us gained the information from the card marker, he stayed away from the graft and got himself a good alibi. This was just in case the card marker got found out and taken in to be questioned where there was always a danger that he would confess under strong police interrogation. Therefore, Johnny didn't come on this move with us as he was the only one connected to the card marker. So, it was my brother Freddy and I along with Tosh and Keiron who went down by the Liverpool dockside on this cold night in 1958.

The long and wide dock road was lined with huge adjoining warehouses several stories high. These austere buildings with their weather-beaten, industrial brick fronts seemed to stare down ominously at the uninhabited dockside. It was a cold winter's night at about three o'clock in the morning. A mist hung over the river giving an ethereal feel to the darkness. Everywhere appeared bleak and foreboding, particularly the dark and murky River Mersey, which seemed to stretch endlessly along the dock.

Inside one of these warehouses in an office on the ground level, Freddy, Tosh, Keiron and I were all standing around staring down at the floor. There had just been a heated discussion and we were all a little agitated.

'It's too risky, we can't blow it in here,' Freddy said sternly.

Keiron had been pacing around the office. 'Why can't we do it in here? We have the jelly with us and it will save us all a lot of time.'

Freddy looked at Keiron and raised his voice. 'No! We all agreed to take it away with us, didn't we? Isn't that right, Tosh?'

Tosh cut in. 'All right, all right, take it easy will you.' He looked sternly at Keiron. 'Freddy's right: it would be suicidal to open it in here, especially when we all know there's a police station just a couple of streets away. The minute it went off, this place would be crawling with bizzies. Keiron, you're out of order the way you are behaving.'

Keiron shrugged his shoulders and conceded, 'OK, whatever!'

I was glad that the heated conversation between us had ceased. For a brief moment the three of us stood in silence looking down at the big strong heavy Milner's safe, positioned right up against the office wall; it had the usual dark green colour with a large brass handle and a separate brass keyhole on a thick steel door. It was possibly made in the late forties or early fifties.

'OK, let's make a move,' Freddy said breaking the silence. 'We have been hanging about here a bit too long now.'

He looked over at me. 'You alright, kid?'

'Yeah, I'm alright.'

'Do us a favour,' he asked. 'Shoot up those stairs and have a look out of the window while we get this peter out of here.' As I left the office, Freddy called, 'Don't forget, kid, keep your eyes peeled for any plod hanging about.'

'Yeah, OK. You don't have to keep telling me what to do, Freddy. I know the score!' I instantly regretted saying this to my brother but I was getting a bit fed up with all the arguments and atmosphere that was being created by Keiron. And another thing anything like running upstairs or climbing it was always me that they asked. Then again maybe it's because I was young and fit. I quickly climbed the stairs two at a time. I entered the room above the office and positioned myself at a window which overlooked the dimly lit, cobbled main street below. I knew this street like the back of my hand and my young mind wandered back to when I was just twelve.

I was constantly bunking off school with my young pals. And we always gravitated towards these docks, jumping on and off the open back of the haulage lorries as they drove slowly along the bustling dock road. We would rob the sacks of goods, throwing them off the lorries and being just young kids at the time, we preferred to steal the sacks of brown sugar and peanuts.

I looked through the dusty warehouse window to the left and right and down the empty dock road. There was none of the usual hustle and bustle of the busy docks; no cargo ships being unburdened, no goods being loaded onto waiting trucks and carts. There was none of the heavy, noisy dock traffic now, that's because it was three o'clock in the morning. Here in the still of night all that I could hear was the distant sound of a ship's foghorn out on the dark and cold River Mersey.

I wished they would hurry up down below in the office. I hated doing this part of the graft, being the lookout. It always seemed to be me Freddy picked. Then again he knew that I was meticulous like him and he could trust my judgement. I had only been in the room a few minutes but it seemed like an eternity.

My mind was brought back to the present and the task at hand and I concentrated on the job and my observations of the street below. I intently looked and listened for any signs of the dreaded enemy... 'the plod' who were always patrolling the streets on foot and they usually came in twos.

Suddenly, a noise from the office below broke my concentration. I heard my name being called. It was my brother Freddy. 'Charlie, is everything alright out there kid?'

'Yeah, everything seems OK.'

'Good. We're almost ready. I'll tell you when we're going out and then you can come down, alright kid?'

Freddy, Keiron and Tosh had somehow managed to manhandle the big heavy safe onto a two wheeled truck and out of the office.

I heard the gruff voice of Tosh talking to Keiron: 'I can't do this by my fuckin' self, Keiron. Give us a hand will you?'

I thought to myself, Here they go again. Arguing. I heard him say to Freddy, 'Open that door for us while me and Keiron get it through that door. It looks like it's going to be a tight squeeze here.' I could hear the bickering going on with Tosh and Keiron.

'Come on,' Freddy shouted. 'It's going through. Come on. I've got my eye on it.' There was a pause. 'Hang on, stop a minute. I will jam this chair against the door and I'll give you a hand to pull it through from the other side.'

Somehow they managed to get it through. 'Thank fuck for that,' Tosh said.

Outside the office was a large wide reception area, with a great high ornate ceiling. The walls were adorned with dark oak panelling which gave you a feeling of insignificance as these heavily panelled austere walls towered above you and upwards to the grandiose ceiling. There were several dark oak chairs around the reception area where visitors could sit and await their business appointments with the company. The illustrious reception area had a polished floor of marble tiles; this was obviously an affluent and successful company and you could almost smell the money. Opposite the large elaborate entrance doors there was a marble counter along the wall; this was the reception desk to where any visitors would report on entering the building.

Freddy walked across the reception area followed by Tosh pushing the truck with the safe on and Keiron holding onto the side of the safe to keep it steady and prevent it from falling off. They made their way to another door which leads out into a side street. Freddy began to unbolt the side entrance door by which we had all entered earlier. I had climbed through a side window and unbolted the door from the inside, letting in the rest of the crew. The information Johnny had received from an employee on the inside was accurate. He had been employed by this big wealthy dock merchant's establishment for some time.

Freddy opened the door cautiously. He peered up and down

the quiet old cobbled side street which was lined on both sides with adjoining warehouses. He saw that the street was deserted. He stepped back inside the building, slowly closing the door, while keeping watch all the time. Then he spoke to Tosh and Keiron: 'Everything seems OK out there. You go and get the van Tosh; try to drive it up to the door here... but quietly.'

Tosh and Keiron lowered the truck and safe down onto the floor. Before Tosh could go out of the door Freddy reminded him about what to do. 'You know the score Tosh, if you see any bizzies hanging around here when you're on your way back, drive straight past... just keep going; we'll know something's wrong.'

'Yeah, alright,' Tosh replied.

Freddy opened the door and took a final look around then motioned to Tosh to get going. 'Be careful,' he said as Tosh left.

Tosh began to walk quickly and quietly in his soft rubber soled footwear, which we all wore on moves like this. Freddy watched as Tosh disappeared down the dark, dimly lit side street. He pulled the side door shut again. Freddy came to the bottom of the stairs and shouted up to me. 'Is everything OK there, kid?'

I was still standing on lookout at the window. 'Yeah, dead sound,' I replied.

'Tosh has gone for the motor, he shouldn't take too long. I'll give you a shout when he comes back. Alright?'

'Yeah,' I shouted back.

Freddy went back to the side door entrance, where he waited with Keiron as they listened for the sound of the van. I remember the van getting parked up along with several other commercial vehicles. It was Freddy's idea to park the van among them as he said it wouldn't arouse suspicion.

Tosh was the only one of us who could drive at that time; being the 1950s few working class people could drive a car. The transport in those days was mostly buses, tramcars and bicycles. There was maybe one in every hundred men who could drive in those days and certainly no one owned their own cars; in fact, you never saw a car parked outside any of the working class people's houses. Unlike today, where there are rows and rows of streets that are congested with cars.

I was with them when the van was stolen from outside of town a few days ago, Johnny had driven us up there in his motor. I remember Freddy saying, 'Get a good reliable motor, Tosh. We don't want an old banger; the peter we're going to have away is a big, heavy, strong one and has plenty of reddies inside it.' And that's exactly the van that we stole, good and reliable. It looked the part. It must have only been a few months old. It was a 1957 commercial truck, just right for the job.

Freddy had told him to only rev the engine as lightly as possible and to always keep his eyes peeled and make sure no bizzies were patrolling around. And that if he did see any bizzies patrolling around by the warehouse, just keep driving past until they were gone. That way nothing would be fucked up.

Freddy and Keiron were waiting patiently behind the side door listening for any sound of Tosh in the motor. Then they heard it! Freddy opened the door and peered out; he could see the van coming towards the warehouse. 'Here he is, Keiron, go and tell our Charlie to make sure the main road is clear and to come down right away.'

Keiron quickly ran through the reception area and shouted up to me. 'Is everything clear, Charlie?'

'Yeah,' I shouted back.

'You had better come down now, we're moving out.'

I took one final look through the window; I could clearly see there was nothing and nobody on the main street. I quickly left the upstairs room and ran down the stairs two and three at a time making my way to Freddy and Keiron.

By this time, Tosh had reversed the vehicle right up to the side door and pulled on the hand-break. He left the engine ticking over and got out of the van. Then with Freddy and Keiron they tried to manhandle the safe into the back of the motor. With instructions from Freddy, I ran up to the top of the side street about fifty yards away and discreetly positioned myself on the corner but backed into a small doorway out of sight. I kept a watchful eye for danger.

The three others were having a bit of a struggle getting the big heavy safe into the back of the van. One must remember that in those days it was mainly man-power and horse-power that were available. There were no electric tailgates or sliding doors like there are on today's modern vehicles. Eventually, Tosh took most of the weight of the safe by holding the bottom while Freddy and Keiron held onto each side and, with their collective man-power, they managed to heave it into the van.

Meanwhile, I had spotted movement on the main street. My young heart started to pound and my adrenaline rushed as I saw the enemy... the bizzies! Two policemen were walking down the road on the same side as the warehouse along the side street where Freddy and the others were and they were not too far away. I took one final look to make sure they were definitely the 'plod.' When I was sure, I turned and ran down to where my brother and the other two were. Freddy, Tosh and Keiron were startled to see me running towards them. When I was almost on top of them and breathless, I hurriedly informed them: 'It's the bizzies; they are only around that corner.'

Keiron got all wound up. 'Come on, let's get the fuck away from here.'

'How far away are they kid and did they see you?'

'I don't know for sure but they'll be around that corner any minute now.'

On hearing this, Tosh jumped into the driving seat and Keiron got in the passenger seat beside him. Freddy told me to get in the back and at the same time he threw a black holdall into the van which contained their working tools and equipment. Before Freddy got in, he attempted to close the door of the warehouse but he had some difficulty. Tosh had got the window wound down and spotted the two policemen at the top of the street. As he tried to keep his voice down, he hissed to Freddie: 'For fuck's sake, let's do one, it's on top!'

The policemen looked down the side street and saw the van and the commotion that was going on. Freddy quickly got into the back of the van and pulled the door shut. Tosh revved up the engine and put his foot down. The two policemen were now running towards us and shouting for us to stop. One of them took his helmet off and threw it aside while running down the street at speed. The other had his whistle in his mouth manically blowing it loud and shrill but to no avail, as the van was now disappearing out of sight. Tosh quite rightly didn't turn the van's lights on until we got out of the way of the two bizzies.

After a few blocks, he took a left turn and then just before he hit the main dock road, he put the vehicle's lights back on. Freddy told Keiron, who was sitting in the passenger seat, to try to crouch down low out of sight, so that it looked like only one person was in the motor. By doing this it would help us avoid getting a pull from the police. Tosh looked the part with his flat cap on, so he could easily be taken for a worker on an early shift, as plenty of time had passed by now and it was the early hours of the morning. On the getaway we started having all kinds of ideas about what would happen next.

This wasn't really supposed to happen, but like all best made plans there are often little hazards that come along, especially in our chosen game. Everything had been going perfectly and exactly the way the robbery had been organised. The plan was obviously to get inside the premises, which was the easy part, as according to good information there were no security alarms to bypass. The next step was to bring out the safe and leave it inside the truck which would be parked up. The most important thing was to make sure the side door of the premises, that we came out of, was shut tight again as we left, that way the robbery would not be discovered until the work employees arrived the next morning, which was usually between eight and nine o'clock. So we just needed to sit off until the early morning traffic started and then we could just mingle in with it and drive away. One thing was for sure though: the break-in at the warehouse was well and truly discovered now!

CHAPTER 18

NEAR DEATH AND DISASTER IN THE PARK

This is when the police would really get a move on. Road blocks would probably be in progress and any suspicious looking vehicles would get pulled over. Tosh, though, was concentrating on his driving; not going too fast and keeping his eyes on the mirrors. He turned the motor off the main drag (road). We were well away from the docks by now and heading for the outskirts of the city, driving towards one of Liverpool's large main parks.

Freddy made a suggestion: 'Let's get into that park, Tosh, at least we will be off the beaten track.'

Tosh drove the van through the park entrance which had a huge pair of austere looking Victorian gateposts flanked either side. They were made from sandstone and were elaborately decorated. As we entered the park, Tosh turned off the van lights again and as we were now safely away from the road, Keiron no longer had to crouch down. He was sitting-up in the passenger seat with both windows of the van wound down.

The engine was switched off and all was silent except for the cold winter wind blowing and whistling through the bare branches of the tall trees. This park was a pleasant place to be during the daytime but at this hour of the night it felt foreboding. There was something unnerving and sinister about it. For a brief moment we all stopped, deep in thought as we sat in total silence contemplating what to do next.

Tosh broke the silence: 'What's the score now then, Freddy? Are we going to dump this peter or what?'

Keiron instantly turned around annoyed and gave Tosh a stern look. 'You must be joking... dump it? Dump it, after us getting it this far without a pull? I say we should stash it in the woods until the dust has settled and then pick it up in a couple of days' time.'

'I don't know about that,' retorted Freddy. 'I don't fancy coming back here for it. What if someone finds it, like kids maybe? The bizzies are not stupid; they would 'sit off' and wait to ambush us all. No we can't take that chance.'

Tosh was getting agitated and more than a little annoyed. 'Well, we can't sit here all night can we?'

We all went silent again. Then I startled them. 'Why don't we blow it here?' They all look at me, amazed but amused; a young kid my age and not long since left school coming out with a suggestion like that.

Freddy laughed. 'Will you listen to my kid brother. What do you think, Keiron? And you Tosh, what do you reckon?'

They all look at one another bemused then Freddy said, 'Well, why *not* do it here?' They all looked at each other and then nodded in agreement.

'OK,' Keiron said. 'Let's get a move on. Let's do it and get the fuck away from here. What about you, Tosh?'

'Yeah, I'm up for it.'

Freddy agreed too. 'Alright then, let's make a move. Drive the van onto that big field over there, Tosh,' he said pointing out the field.

Tosh drove the van off the road side and onto the field going further into the park. He eventually pulled up in a secluded spot and turned off the engine. Everybody got out.

After looking around, Freddy said, 'This'll do.'

Tosh, Freddy and Keiron started manhandling the safe out of the back of the van while I was closely surveying the road into the park, making sure that there were no police cars or anyone around. By now, they had the safe out of the van and on its back. Freddy opened his tool bag and told Tosh to go and park the van further away and out of sight. He then started quickly preparing to blow the safe by using the highly explosive gelignite and a detonator.

Keiron and I were standing over Freddy as he was bent over the safe carrying out the work. As he had successfully done before, first he rolled a ball of putty around between the palms of his hands to warm and soften the texture, making it pliable and easier to use. When this was done and it was soft enough, he began to push the pliable putty into and around the entire door of the safe, thereby sealing the gap around the edges and making it as airtight as possible. When this was properly carried out and he was happy that it was sealed, he took a packet of gelignite from the tool bag. The gelignite came rolled up in thick greaseproof paper and was about six inches long. When it was opened, it resembled beige coloured plasticine. The gelignite was pushed into the keyhole of the safe and packed in as tightly as possible using a wooden pencil he took from his pocket. Then finally and most importantly he pushed a fused detonator into the centre of the gelignite until it was flush with the end of the keyhole. The detonator fuses were usually about six to eight inches in length and it hung out to enable the detonator to be lit and give time for the user to get well back before the gelignite went off.

We all knew by now that time was of the essence; if we had had a lot more time on our hands, blowing the safe would have been done much more professionally. We would usually look around the environment wherever we were going to blow it; like we had done previously in the office on the 'lemo job', for anything we could find that could be packed on top of the safe to muffle the loud bang that would inevitably be made as it exploded. However, there was nothing here to pack it with so we knew there would be an extremely loud bang.

'I'm about to light this,' Freddy shouted to us all. 'Everybody spread out and get down on the grass.' He lit the fuse quickly and moved away from the immediate area. We were all spread out lying on the grass waiting for the explosion, but it never came... not even a flicker. We waited for another minute or so... still nothing happened. Due to this delay we were all becoming anxious, knowing the police could enter the park at any given moment.

'What's gone wrong?' Keiron asked.

'Give it one more minute,' Freddy said. 'It might just be a slow burn.'

Again we waited. With every second we became more nervous as we awaited the big explosion. However, it still didn't happen and time was running out for us.

Freddy got up from the grass. 'I'll go and check it out.'

Keiron also got up and chose to go and investigate too, eager to see what had gone wrong.

As I watched Freddy and Keiron walk slowly and cautiously towards the safe my heart was in my mouth. I was worried about what could happen to my brother if anything went wrong. While I stood there, it brought back to me one bonfire night a couple of years ago when a banger firework had failed to go off. I had gone to investigate, thinking it was probably a dud, but it did go off, just as I got up to it. It didn't half give me the fright of my life and I was lucky not to be injured. However, this is not a little firework with a small bang but a big metal safe packed with highly explosive gelignite and a lit detonator. I couldn't look anymore, so I turned to watch the park road again, hoping that no police cars would enter while all this turmoil was going on.

Freddy and Keiron finally got to the safe and discovered that the detonator fuse had gone out. Both men were sweating and nervous but they remained determined to proceed. 'I'll cut the fuse shorter,' Freddy said to Keiron. 'And when I light it we will run further back on the field and get our heads down.' As he was about to light the fuse, he muttered. 'Get ready!' He lit it and then both he and Keiron ran away as fast as they could shouting to me to do the same. All three of us spread out and lay down quickly, and watched the safe. We were spread-eagled on the cold hard grass, peering over our arms, which were folded out in front of us, as if trying to shield any blast.

Meanwhile, Tosh appeared from between some big Rhododendron bushes and was heading towards the safe totally unaware of the drama that had just ensued. Freddy, Keiron and

I all shouted to him to get down and keep away from the safe, warning him that it was about to blow, but it was too late; he walked right up to it just as the detonator and explosion blasted. It was the dead of the night and the blast was so loud it must have been heard for miles. Unfortunately for Tosh, the safe door was catapulted into the air and by sheer luck alone, it just about missed his head! The minute this happened all three of us ran up to him. He was just stood frozen to the spot with shock and he just kept repeating in his gruff voice over and over: 'Fucking hell! Fucking hell!' Then he said, 'I felt it touch my hair... I could have been killed!' Tosh had just cheated death and was in total shock and disarray... he had narrowly missed being decapitated! The whole incident was frightening for all of us

'Come on, Tosh, snap out of it. You'll be alright.' Freddy reassured him.

Keiron went over to the now wide open safe. There was plenty inside and amazingly it was all still intact. The door had been blown away but nothing else. 'Let's step on it now 'cause that noise will definitely have alerted the bizzies. They'll be swarming around here in no time.'

I was staring ahead across the park shocked at what I had just witnessed. I watched as lights went on here and there in some of the surrounding houses around the outskirts of the park. I shouted with urgency to Freddy and Keiron. 'Hey, look at those houses! Look at that! That bang has woken people up.'

Freddy and Keiron grabbed the contents of the safe. Keiron opened up two cloth bags full of paper money. The rest of the contents were abandoned there. They consisted of things like bank books, ledgers, stamps etc. There were also two large tin boxes full of coin money. 'We won't take those boxes with us, they're a bit heavy and awkward,' Freddy said. 'We might come unstuck now that that noise has brought it on top, especially if we all have to make a run for it.'

Keiron hated to leave them behind, not because he was greedy but he would rather give those coins away than let the bizzies get them. He then did something extraordinary: he opened up the two boxes of coins and started to grab them and throw them in different directions as far as he could.

Freddy was agitated by now and shouted to him: 'Come on, Keiron, we have no time for this.'

'OK,' Keiron said. 'I just hope some poor kids find them and not the bizzies.

Tosh was still looking terribly shocked at almost losing his head. Freddy asked him again if he was alright. We were all now really concerned about him and whether he would ever snap out of this.

Our luck had held that night and we took away a large amount of money. We were cautious and kept a lookout for police and road blocks and after abandoning the van, which was down to nobody anyway so there would be no come backs over it, we all set off going our separate ways. Obviously, Freddy and I went off together. It had been a fruitful night for us and certainly one that Tosh would never forget!

We planned to meet at Johnny's house the next day so that the money could be chopped up fair and square.

CHAPTER 19

THE SHARE OUT

The next morning, after waking up bright and early, I set off round to my brother's place. We had arranged for Tosh to pick us up from there and to drive us all to Johnny's house but we weren't sure whether he would show up after the terrifying ordeal he had gone through the night before. Keiron was to meet us there too.

I arrived at Freddy's and knocked on the door. It was opened by a nervous looking Freddy. He greeted me saying that his new wife Sadie was ready to give birth at any moment. 'You and Tosh will have to go to Johnny's without me, kid. I can't leave Sadie here by herself. At least not until the nurse arrives. She should be here by now, but there's no sign of her yet. So I have no other choice but to wait here. The baby is due anytime now!' My brother was full of contradicting emotions; he seemed really nervous and yet also excited and happy at the same time.

'No worries, kid,' I said to him. 'Me and Tosh will explain it all to Johnny and Keiron. Hey, by the way, Freddy,' I said cheerfully. 'We will have to have a little celebration when the baby arrives.'

'Yeah, that would be nice, Charl. But right now I'm panicking over it all. I just wouldn't know what to do or where to start if the baby *did* arrive.' Suddenly, we heard Sadie call for him from the bedroom. I had never seen my brother look as nervous as he did right there and then as he heard Sadie yell for him. 'Oh my God,' he said as he hurried to the bedroom. 'I hope she isn't having it now.'

I thought to myself, Here's my brother; the brother who shows no fear when it comes to doing daring safe robberies and using dangerous explosives, and yet in this situation of his wife about to give birth, he is absolutely terrified… and I mean terrified!

He came back into the room a couple of minutes later. 'She's OK, kid.' He said with a sigh of relief. 'She only wanted a cold drink.'

I tried my best to console him. Just then we heard Tosh beep his car horn outside. Freddy jumped up shaking, scratching the back of his neck and looking all around with an alarmed look on his face. 'I didn't think Tosh would turn up after last night's events. I thought he might still be suffering with shock.'

'Well,' I said. 'That's him in the car out there so he must be over it.'

'You had better go, kid, and explain to Tosh what is going on in here.'

'Yeah, OK. Are you going to be alright here on your own with Sadie?'

He nodded an anxious looking yes. Just before I left the apartment he passed me the cloth bag which held the money from the safe the night before. 'Give that to Johnny, he will cut it up along with the other bag Keiron has.'

I told Freddy I would catch up with him later as there was nothing I could do to help him with the situation. So I left Freddy's and got into Tosh's motor. I quickly explained to Tosh Freddy's predicament regarding his wife and the imminent birth. Tosh, being the way he was, started to laugh on hearing all this.

'What's wrong with that brother of yours? The way he's carrying on you would think that he was the only man ever to become a dad for the first time.' He laughed again.

'What would he be like if he had had to go through it five times like me with my five kids, eh, Charlie? Now that's going some ain't it kid?' He sounded really proud of himself. I couldn't help but laugh at Tosh and his sense of humour. He was some fella.

After a short journey, Tosh pulled the car up outside Johnny's house and we went in.

'You had better take a look at that!' Johnny said slapping the daily newspaper down on the table.

Tosh and I had only just walked into his house. As predicted, Keiron was already there sitting down at the kitchen table. The newspaper was headlining about the graft we had pulled off the previous night. Tosh picked it up and had a quick look at the newspaper headline and then he passed it to me.

Some part of it read:

The Police say they are convinced it is the same gelignite gang who have carried out this robbery and state that they will not rest until they have apprehended the perpetrators and that it wouldn't be long.

The statement went on to read:

The Police are hopeful an arrest would be made very shortly.

Johnny and Keiron were both looking at us awaiting our reaction. Tosh took back the paper and went on to read a little more. Then he looked up from the paper. 'It's getting pretty heavy isn't it, John?'

'Too right it is!' said Johnny. 'You know how devious those bizzies can be; especially that other bastard, Balmer.'

He was referring to the head of Liverpool C.I.D. Bert Balmer, he was renowned for his unscrupulous corruption. A man who would stop at nothing to make a charge stick, even going as far as to fabricate evidence against anybody he thought may have something to do with the crime. However, worse than that, if a man had a police record and was completely innocent and had nothing to do with the robbery that didn't matter to Inspector Balmer. He would still find the ways and means to implicate. In other words fit you up!

'We will have to start to watch our backs,' Johnny went on. 'In fact it wouldn't be a bad idea if we all took it easy for a while. If you know what I mean?'

Keiron looked perplexed at Johnny's announcement. 'Just what are you getting at, John? Are you suggesting that we should call it a day?'

At first Johnny looked at his brother as if thinking to himself,

Here we go Keiron kicking off with his erratic behaviour again. 'No, Keiron, I'm not suggesting, I'm telling you to just think about it. You know what the bizzies are like and if they start putting two and two together, especially with the reputation our family's got, they have always had it in for the Oates' brothers as you well know.'

Keiron sneered at Johnny and answered him sarcastically. 'Yeah, yeah, I know. You're making a mountain out of a mole hill. Those bizzies have to catch us first. Just look at the way we are working now, look at the improvements we have achieved since we have been operating with the jelly. We can literally open a peter in just a few minutes and that's without really sticking our necks out. Let's face it, you can't get better than that. I'm going to continue while the goings good.' Keiron then turned to me. 'I bet you want to keep on grafting, don't you, kid?' He smiled and patted me on the shoulder. However, before I could answer him he went on, 'Of course you do!'

'Alright, enough said!' Johnny interrupted. 'Let's get this money chopped up.'

Tosh, like me, had just sat there at the table quietly while John and Keiron had been bickering. Moments later things calmed down a little and the two brothers joined us at the table. Johnny began to count the money. Keiron's smile went from ear to ear as he feasted his eyes on the money. Then he looked at Tosh and me. 'How can we stop when the reddies keep coming in like this? No way!'

When Johnny had finished counting the money, he told us it totalled just over two thousand pounds which was less than we had expected but still a lot of money at that time in the nineteen fifties. Nevertheless, we had gone ahead and gambled with our liberty by reverting back to the old way of taking the safe regardless of the risk of being apprehended. So, in a way, I realised that Johnny could be right: we had taken a big risk and it could have come on top for all of us.

Tosh and I got up to go home and Johnny gave me Freddy's

share of the money to pass on to him. By the way, overnight Keiron had held one bag of the money and Freddy had the other one but there was never any doubt about either one of them taking any of the money for themselves. We had complete and utter trust and faith in each other. None of us would ever contemplate taking any of the money dishonestly and ripping the others off. The money taken on the graft, no matter who took it home, would not be touched until the whole group of us reunited to count it up and divide it up between us. Moreover, when the robbery was reported in the local paper, the police would state exactly how much had been stolen and so if at the chop there *was* any less than the amount reported, we would all know who had been deceitful and helped themselves. However, that would never happen in our crew; we were all loyal and had high principles.

CHAPTER 20

A NEW ARRIVAL

As we approached Freddy's house, we could see there was already a car parked outside. Tosh pulled up behind it and as Tosh wanted to see Freddy, he got out of the car with me. The strange car was a brand new 1958 green Morris Minor traveller (estate), with wooden panels on each side.

I looked at Tosh quizzically. 'I wonder whose that could be?'

'It looks like a doctor's car, that, Charlie. It's definitely not a nurse; they always come on a push bike. And I should know all about that lark with having five kids myself. No, that's a doctor. They all use Morris Minors these days.'

'I hope everything's alright in there, Tosh.'

'Don't worry, kid. She's probably had the baby. Come on, let's go in. Everything will be OK.'

It was Freddy who opened the front door to us and he stood there beaming all over his face.

'She's had the baby, she's had the baby,' he said excitedly. 'It's a boy, it's a boy! The doctor is in the bedroom with her now. I thought it may be the nurse at the door because she is on her way around here too.'

'What did I tell you, Charlie? Congratulations, Fred!'

We were all talking in the hallway as we didn't want to go into the bedroom to disturb the doctor attending Sadie.

'Here's your chop of the money,' I said to Freddy as I passed him the bag. 'Johnny asked me to pass it on and send his best wishes to you and Sadie.'

We stood there for a moment as if we were taking it all in

and then Tosh looked at me before holding out his hand to shake Freddy's. 'Me and Charlie will get off now, Freddy. This isn't the time for us to be here, it's a woman's thing this, with the nurse coming and everything, besides, we will only be in the way. I'll catch up with you tomorrow when things have settled down a bit.'

It seemed we left the house just as quick as we had arrived there. I thought to myself, So, my brother now has a son; a baby boy, his first child. He would be dead chuffed.

'This is when it all starts for him now, Charlie. Once you're a dad, this is where all your headaches and worries begin. It is a life changing thing having a kid.'

I went straight home to my mother's and broke the news to her of Freddy and his newborn son. My sister was there too when I arrived and I went on to explain how Freddy was over the moon and especially at it being a boy.

My mother, however, had mixed feelings over the whole affair. 'Well,' she said, 'maybe he will settle down now, it's his first child and it will give him some responsibility for a change.' My sister seemed delighted with it all and was saying how surprising it was and the way you change when a child comes along. My mother, though, was looking concerned and still unsure: 'We will just have to wait and see, won't we?'

CHAPTER 21

TOSH CALLS IT A DAY AND KEIRON DOES A DISAPPEARING ACT

Times were changing rapidly among the criminal fraternity. Safe blowing in England was at its height. In fact at one time it was spiralling out of control. Grafters (people into crime) from other cities were participating in this newfound method of blowing a safe open via the use of gelignite. However, as the saying goes: all good things come to an end!

As time passed things became increasingly difficult for these efficient and professional criminals. The police were becoming more vigilant; operating with higher numbers of police on foot patrol and these officers were becoming extensively more aware. They were now paying more attention to sounds while out on the beat, and they responded instantly to any sound that could be attributed to the explosive bang of a safe being done. They also had their ways and means of gaining information of forthcoming robberies: conducting and building relationships with paid police-informants and any other devious methods of operation open to them.

Due to all of this, things started to take a turn for the worst, not just for our crew, but also others. It was becoming quite clear now, particularly in our area of Liverpool, that the graft we specialised in was getting harder. There were less and less safes to blow open due to the influx of other criminals and not enough safes to go round.

Subsequently, big companies were changing their style of safes and instead of the old key hole in the door of the safe (the most vulnerable part) they were being replaced by combination locks, therefore, making it harder for us to blow; as for a start, there was nowhere to put the gelignite and detonator. As they became more and more security conscious, they began to look towards having new alarms systems installed therefore increasing their crime protection and making it much more complicated.

Other big companies and businesses also took the alternative route of no longer leaving any money in their office safes, preferring instead to leave it securely in the vaults. That was the situation we were all up against. We would have to find other ways.

Tosh, Freddy and I had a meeting to attend at Keiron's place to discuss alternatives. It was decided that we should look into targeting other territories outside of our own area of Liverpool. After we had discussed all the *if's and but's,* even Keiron, although he was still as impulsive as ever, began to realise the real danger of us coming unstuck if we didn't change the localities that we operated from.

'We will have to start grafting out of town,' he said. 'The further away the better. I wouldn't like to get lifted (arrested) by the local plod (Liverpool Police). He paused for a moment and looked at Freddy. *You* should know what that sly rat of an inspector, Balmer is like Fred; an out-and-out devious bastard.'

'Yeah, Keiron, that's true,' Freddy replied. 'I think we all know what *he's* like. We will just have to make sure we don't come up against him, you know; just sort of play it real safe.'

'That's what I mean, Fred, by us all grafting out of town... and I mean out of town... right out of the way!' Keiron began to get excited again now and he spoke with pure enthusiasm. 'We have got everything going for us haven't we? You know, with the jelly and Tosh doing the driving. We just can't go wrong, can we?'

Tosh had been sat quietly while all this talking had been going on. He had not said a word, which was out of character for him as he was always the one with ideas and suggestions. He always added his opinions to the conversation. Suddenly, he interrupted Keiron. 'Hang on a minute,' he said to Keiron. 'What gives you the idea that I will be doing the driving? Or for that matter, doing any more graft?' Keiron was taken aback at Tosh's outburst and so too were Freddy and me. 'I'm going to lay it on the table straight to you all. Firstly, I'm getting sick and tired of all the arguing that has been going on with you, Keiron.' Keiron gave Tosh a scowl on hearing this. 'And don't be pulling a face,' Tosh went on. 'You know what I'm talking about all right. You have even fallen out with your own two brothers!' Tosh gave Keiron a right dressing down. We all sat in silence, even Keiron, while Tosh continued with his tirade. 'You know what your problem is, Keiron? Money, money. That you just blow away on horses, parties and women. That's all you're interested in... *yourself*; just as long as the readies keep coming in for you.' Tosh paused for a moment and then with a softer and more respectful tone he addressed Freddy. 'I've been thinking hard about this, Fred. And it's not because of Keiron,' he said looking across at Keiron. 'I still love him as a friend; even though he *is* a pain in the ass. I'm just stepping down. I'm done.' None of us could believe what we were hearing. No, not Tosh; he was one of the main men of our crew. Admittedly, he was a lot older; maybe in his early forties, but he had the expertise and the ability (if I can put it that way).

Freddy and Keiron looked completely stunned that Tosh, of all people, was bowing out. 'You're not serious are you Tosh?' Keiron asked now sounding humble.

'Oh, yeah, I am. I'm dead serious. And it's not just because of you, Kearn. We all get a bit uptight sometimes in the business that we're in. Nah, I've been thinking about this all week.' Freddy asked him why. 'Two things really,' Tosh went on. 'That last move we did, I was nearly killed; you all saw what happened. That big, steel safe door nearly took my head off my shoulders. I'm lucky to be here now talking to you all. If you remember, I did say to you all in the beginning that using explosives was too dangerous for my liking. But it's not just due to that alone that I'm finished.' He lowered his voice as if in thought. 'I have been at this game a long time and along the way I have been fairly lucky. And as you know, Freddy and Keiron, I have never been arrested *or* done a single day in jail. It is time for me to get out while the going is good. I'm pushing forty now and have made a nice living out of it all and now with my wife and kids, well, I don't want to jeopardise anything. No, I'm going straight from now on. I have a tidy little business and everything, so that's it!'

When Tosh had finished saying his piece, Keiron spoke with more than a hint of sarcasm in his voice. 'What happens when you go broke, Tosh, and your pot's dried up?'

Freddy and I couldn't believe what he was saying and it made us feel decidedly awkward. Tosh though, came right back at Keiron, speaking sharply in his gruff voice. 'That will never happen to me, Keiron. And do you know why?' He glared at Keiron with a look of superiority. 'I can always make a living no matter what. You see, Keiron, *I'm* not a squanderer or a gambler like you are.' Tosh had finally got it all off his chest and stood up ready to leave. 'I'm not being disrespectful,' he said looking around at us all. 'But I've got to make a move. I've promised to take my wife and kids out to the pictures.' He smiled then turned to me and patted me on the back. 'Play it safe, kid.' He then looked at Freddy and Keiron and said, 'I'll see you around.' Tosh then left closing the door behind him.

'What do you think of that, Fred?' Keiron asked in disbelief.

'He sacked everything off just like that.' Keiron snapped his fingers in mid-air as he said *like that*.

'That's his prerogative, Keiron,' my brother replied. 'The man is entitled to change his mind. He can do what he wants for that matter.'

'Yeah, I know but that came right out of the blue. We're fucked now for a wheel man, aren't we?'

'No, we're not,' Freddy said. 'There's still your Johnny.'

'I don't think so, our Johnny told me he is taking a break for a while.'

Keiron quickly turned to me. 'How about you, Charlie, can you drive?'

'Sort of,' I said noncommittally. 'But I'm nowhere near as good as Tosh. *He's* the expert at it. The only driving I have ever done has been with my young pals, and even then some of the driving proved a disaster. There were a couple of crashes along the way in the cars we had stolen.'

'Well, what are we going to do, Freddy?' Keiron wasn't quite his excited, enthusiastic self by now.

'For now,' our Freddy said. 'Absolutely, nothing. I think we should take a leaf out of your Johnny's book and leave the graft out for a while, at least until things have died down a bit.'

Keiron now had a look of complete, utter disbelief on his face. 'What do you mean, Freddy? It sounds like you're following in Tosh's footsteps now too.'

'Keiron, Keiron,' Freddy said. 'Just calm down will you. It's only going to be a temporary thing. You know yourself there's a lot going on in and around the city right now. It's crawling with bizzies. The place is red hot at the moment.

For a few moments there was complete silence. The three of us just sat there no one uttering a word. It was as if we were all caught up in a moment of contemplation.

'Right,' said Keiron suddenly. 'If that's how it's going to be, I'll jump in with Bert and Harry,'

He was referring to the Cannon brothers who I mentioned in a previous chapter. They were notorious for their daring safe robberies. They were supposed to be the best grafters at the business, but not in our league of safe *blowing*.

'Suit yourself, Keiron,' my brother said to him, sounding exasperated. 'Come on, Charlie, we had better be making a move.' We both stood up and made our way to the front door ready to leave. Then as Freddy opened the door he turned to look at Keiron with his last words. 'I'll see ya.'

That was it. That was how the meeting ended.

I went back to my brother's place for a little while. We walked in and were greeted by his wife Sadie with a big smile. She was there with the baby.

'How's he been?' Freddy asked her gesturing to his son.

The child was fast asleep in his cot. They had recently decided on a name; they called him Carl. Sadie was exuding happiness and contentment, in fact so too was my brother. He appeared to have changed somehow. I think it was all down to baby Carl. Sadie left the room to prepare some tea and Freddy began to talk seriously to me. 'Maybe Keiron could be right, Charlie. About me thinking the way Tosh did and following in his shoes. I *have* thought about finishing with the graft.' He paused as if uncertain. 'Not just yet though,' he went on. 'We will knock a couple more jobs off first.' Then Freddy looked at his son snuggled up warm in his cot, sound asleep in slumberland. 'I want to get to know *him* more and bring him up properly. I want to give him a decent life.' It was touching what my brother had just confided to me and the plans he had for his wife and child. It was quiet obvious that he didn't want to jeopardise all this new happiness he had found. 'I have got to be careful kid. I can't afford to come unstuck and get sent down for years in jail. I don't want any more of that. That's the reason I'll be pulling out of the business very shortly.'

'I understand,' I said to him. 'We will just be more careful than ever before. Remember what you told me, Freddy: don't ever do anything if it doesn't look or feel right.'

He nodded. 'Yeah.'

'Well then, we will stick to our instincts no matter what.'

'Ok, Charl,' he said to me with a smile.

Just then Sadie returned from the kitchen with a tray of drinks. She put them down on the long coffee table and set about organising the crockery. Freddy sat back and relaxed. The three of us began chatting; most of which was dominated with talk of the new baby, Carl.

It's funny, but when young couples have their first child, be it a boy or a girl, somehow the topic of conversation always revolves around the baby and what it is they would like the child to be when it grows up. I remember this from my own past experience among other things and I also recall that sometimes it doesn't turn out quite the way you would have planned.

CHAPTER 22

THE UPS AND DOWNS OF THE 1950S

In the year of 1958, times had changed considerably for teenagers like me. The music industry was becoming big business. New singers were emerging on the scene with their own unique and individual style of music. This was phenomenal. One of these singers was Jerry Lee Lewis, he was crazy, the way he played the piano on stage and the antics he got up to with his style of rock and roll was just something else! Other great performers hitting the top of the music charts too were Buddy Holly with 'That'll be the day.' The Everly Brothers and of course the King of them all... Elvis. His number one hit had just been released and was called 'One night with you.'

I recall being in a dance hall having a dance with a girl when this came out. It was slow; like a real bluesy song. All the kids, including my pals, were dancing slowly to it that evening and being all young and full of energy we were having a great time... with not a care in the world!

At this time in the late fifties there were also some new styles of motor cars starting to hit the roads. One that particularly caught my eye was the new Ford Consul. There were others making an impact too upon the buying public that could *afford* them. Another favourite of mine was the MG Sports Convertible, now that to me was the business. It had solid chrome bumpers and chrome wire spoke wheels. I went to see Tosh about buying one with the money he had saved up for me.

'You're not ready for that yet, Charlie. It could bring it on top for you. You don't want the bizzies on your case or anything like that.' What Tosh said to me persuaded me not to go ahead with the deal. I respected him and took his sound advice.

Once when I was out and about on my own I came across one of these magnificent MG convertibles in red. It was parked on the driveway of a house in an affluent neighbourhood, which I just happened to be passing through one day. There was a man who looked a lot older than me, in his twenties, polishing this real eye-catcher of a car. I had stopped to admire the car for a moment when the guy cleaning it looked up and saw me there. He immediately stopped what he was doing and while glaring at me he took the polishing cloth and he threw it down aggressively as if to say, *What the fuck are you doing around here in our posh neighbourhood?* I will never forget that day, and I made a vow to myself that I would have a house and a car like that in the not too distant future.

You see at that time of the 1950s, we had a class system in England. As well as the working-class there was also the middle-class and the upper-class. It's strange but funny that it was always the middle-class people who were the snobs; maybe they felt inferior because they were in between the classes and this gave them a bit of an inferiority complex.

Sometimes when my pals and I (at that time about twelve years old or so) would all be passing through a middle class neighbourhood, they would be the first ones to call the police on us. There has been many a time that I have been pulled by the bizzies and asked what I'm doing around their affluent neighbourhood, even though we had done nothing wrong. *Get back to where you come from*, was always what they ordered us to do; and this was to just a couple of young kids passing through. Is it any wonder we began to rebel?

As I have mentioned, times were rapidly changing in society in the late fifties and it would be just a few years later that the classes, especially the middle classes, would fade out or go altogether. Unfortunately, what we have in the present day are the *haves and the have nots*.

We also had employment booming in that era. Well, employment for the working class people. There was no excuse for anybody to be out of work. That is of course unless you were severely disabled. However, I *did* see some people with severe disabilities working in those days. There weren't the disability allowances the way we have them these days.

I recall an old neighbour of ours who lost his hand during the Second World War. He used to work pulling a school dinner cart around with his good hand. It wasn't unusual to see. I think it was a pride thing with the disabled people really, but it appeared to me that everybody went to work in those days, which brings me back to when I first left school. I started work with every good intention of earning an honest living and of being an upright citizen. Like most school leavers at the time we were encouraged by our parents, who knew no better at the time as they themselves were slaves to the industry, to work hard the way they did. They were kept down to work for some rich capitalist just to make him even richer.

I remember vividly the day I began work after just leaving school. What I saw and learned on that day was what I can only call typical slave labour. Here's what happened on my first day working for an *honest* living.

I left school in the summer of 1955. My friends and I were discussing what we were going to do now. Before we had left school, we were all into petty crime and doing a bit of this and a bit of that. Now though, I couldn't believe what most of them were planning to do. One or two of them were planning to go down the mines and become miners. This sounded like slavery to me but they seemed excited about the idea and thought it was going to be a good job. Another two friends in our crowd, Tommy and Yank, were both getting jobs on building sites carrying bricks and learning a trade, but the rest of us, which was six, out of our little school gang were sent by the employment exchange to work in a place called United Glass Bottles Factory, just outside of Liverpool in St Helens... our first job!

That morning, my friends and I were all sitting on the top deck of a bus, which was leaving Huyton, on our way to work. When we got off the bus in St Helens, we made our way towards the big glass bottle factory and all I could see and hear was a clockwork clonking noise and lots of people walking into the factory to start work. The men wore steel toe cap work boots and cloth caps and the women trudged along in their work trousers and flat heeled shoes. It was like an organised ant march; everybody marching to work ready to clock on and looking forward to clocking off. It all sent shudders up and down my spine and I had a strong feeling of trepidation. My friends however were laughing and jostling along asking each other what they thought the first day was going to be like. I knew already that this life wasn't for me and I wasn't happy about being there with them and becoming a kept-down peasant like most of our forefathers.

On that first day we waited for the yard manager to collect us from the hut we had been told to wait inside. When he arrived he greeted us in his St Helens accent: 'Come on, lads. I've got you all a job here. Pick a truck up each and follow me.' He had pointed to a long row of old, and some rusty, two wheeled trucks which were all uniformly lined up, looking as if they were waiting like little machines one behind the other ready to go to work. To me they resembled the workers we had just witnessed; rows of them behind one another moving almost in unison ready for work to begin. We all picked up one of these two wheeled truck each as instructed and followed the yard manager. We pulled the trucks up the old cobbled factory yard. All of a sudden I heard giggling and laughter coming from a group of women who were pulling the same trucks as us down the hill that we were on the way up.

Their trucks were loaded with big wooden boxes filled with bottles. The women were only in their early twenties some were still in their late teens, but they were all women to us being young baby faced kids and nobody took much notice of them. These women all wore head scarves and they had vest-like sweaters on with their pants or skirts even though it was May and getting quite warm. They pulled their trucks past us giggling between themselves at us; the new gang of kids being brought into the factory and led to their slaughter. I shuddered as I noticed their hairy armpits as they were pulling the trucks. They weren't like the girls of today well-groomed and shaved or waxed. Their armpits had big dark clumps of hair under them. These people we called *woolybacks* because they were from outside of Liverpool. They seemed to have no thought about how they looked and didn't appear to care. They all just plodded on with their work; this was their way of life and always would be.

I knew I couldn't stick at this sort of life and after just three monotonous days of being there I left that predictably grim factory never to return. That last day I just threw my lunch bag over the wall of the factory telling my friends that I'd had enough and this just wasn't for me. They couldn't believe I was going. They really did seem to believe that this was a decent enough job and were shocked that I was throwing it away after just three days. I chose a different path and would not become a drone working day in day out for a wage packet at the end of each week and just scraping a living together.

I am not trying to justify myself by stating this but maybe this is one of the reasons I turned to crime. I was young and ambitious and I wanted to sample the good things in life and there was only one thing that would make it happen... money and plenty of it. It came fast and furious; burning a hole in my pockets. Most of it went on the good things in life that young kids craved like dance halls, parties and drinks, fairgrounds; a kid could spend a fortune on the fair in those days, records and record players; if you had a top of the range record player it was considered dead cool. Also of course the clothes... I remember on many an occasion taking four or five of my friends to get them all rigged out in the latest clobber: leather jackets, jeans and coats etc. These friends of mine were good kids who worked honestly for a living but were always skint (no money) as the wages they were picking up were buttons (a pittance).

The way I looked at it then was that my young life was for living and money was for spending!

CHAPTER 23

THE SOUNDPROOF JOBS

It was now almost two years since I became involved with my brother Freddy and his friends. I had come a long way since leaving school in 1955 and in that space of time I had sampled money beyond my wildest young dreams and I was still only a teenager, not quite eighteen years old.

We were quite aware and had to accept the downside of our safe blowing now as it was becoming too dangerous and risky due to the loud explosive bangs they created so we had to come up with another safer way of doing it. I came up with an idea... picture houses (cinemas). I spent a lot of my money on attending the picture houses, sometimes I would sit in the best seats and would watch the movies four or five times a week; usually with my pals or maybe a girl.

Picture houses were thriving back then. If you went to one of these picture houses on a Friday or a Saturday evening you would see the queues of people stretching from the entrance, down the street and around the corner of the building. They would be so busy that they would have what we called a *two house show*: one showing in the afternoon and one in the evening. At that time it was one of the main sources of entertainment for the public. Whole families would go to these picture houses; they were big business. Which brings me nicely back to the story and our *type of business!*

'Freddy, I have found a way of... well I'm *pretty* sure it will work, how we can blow the safes on premises *without* them being heard.'

'What? How?' my brother asked eagerly. Freddy was excited but I was relaxed with a cool, calm and collected attitude. I was proud of myself and what I was about to explain to him.

'What's it about?' he asked.

'Remember you told me that tragic story about two men you knew: Charlie Connolly and George Kelly?'

'Yes,' he replied.

These two men he told me about were supposed to have held up a picture house and it was stated that George Kelly had shot dead the manager. This tragic event took place around 1950; I must have only been about nine or ten years old at the time so I personally can't recall anything about it. It was a high profile case. Both men were charged with the murder of the picture house manager. They went on trial. George Kelly was found guilty and sentenced to death. Charles Connolly got ten years. Shortly after the trial and after losing his appeal, George Kelly was hanged at Walton Prison. He was just a young man, only in his twenties.

As a post script to this story, the policeman who was in charge of this case was none other than the ruthless Inspector Herbert Balmer! It was proven years later that Inspector Balmer had fabricated evidence against George Kelly and Charlie Connolly. It was found that vital witnesses had been intimidated and it was revealed that this Police Inspector had used other devious ways and means. George Kelly and Charlie Connolly were found to have been innocent men and were completely exonerated and each was granted a Royal Pardon. Though it was tragically too late for George Kelly. As a result of his corrupted ways, Inspector Balmer had caused an innocent man to be hanged!

'That was a liberty and a very sad story kid but what has it got to do with the graft we are going to have off?'

'Well it's like this,' I went on. 'That picture house called The Cameo, where the shooting took place, was situated in a large community. It was practically surrounded by houses; some of them only being a few yards away.' Also, let's not forget that in those days picture houses closed just after eleven o'clock at night.

'Yes,' he said. 'And what?'

'Think about it, Freddy. The shooting had taken place just after the picture house had closed. The manager and his assistant were still in the office counting the takings and yet out of all those people who were milling around outside, not one of them heard a gunshot go off.' I paused and looked at him for a moment waiting to see if he had realised what I was getting at. 'Because they couldn't! And the reason they couldn't is because the inside of picture houses are sound proofed. Look, Freddy, I have thought about this long and hard and I even went to the pictures a couple of nights ago just to test my theory. And it was right! It was a war picture I went to see and while it was showing on the big screen the noise of the bombs and guns going off was deafening inside the place. I got up from my seat while the film was still on and made an excuse to the ushers about needing to go outside for a few minutes. He let me out and I stood there and listened... I could hear absolutely nothing from outside that picture house. So what does that tell you?'

'Oh yeah, kid,' he said, a little bewildered. 'I understand now. They must all be sound proof mustn't they?'

'Yes, they are and I proved it to myself that I was right. We can only have so many of these picture houses off at the most though.' I stipulated this because I knew that it would be all over the papers in no time. The story they would print about targeting picture houses due to the sound proofing would put the bizzies on the alert even more than before.

During this discussion, we talked about the need of a driver; we had to forget Tosh as he was well out of the business now. The only other person we could ask was Johnny, so it was decided that we would pay him a visit and explain the graft to see if he would be up for it. We knew where Johnny would be hanging out so we went to see him.

'How are you doin', Fred? And you, Charlie?' Johnny greeted us with his big grin. 'Long time no see.' He was standing by his barrow which was laden with fresh fruit: lovely rosy apples, pears, oranges and a whole host of other colourful, quality produce. It was an impressive display and all stacked high in uniform rows. Johnny's wife was there with him. She too smiled warmly when we arrived. It was a brisk, fairly cold February day and we were right in the heart of the city. Johnny reached up to the top row of the apples and took one from it. He rubbed it against his dark Crombie overcoat a couple of times and then passed it to me. 'Here you go, kid. Get your teeth into that. They are nice and sweet.'

'Thanks, John,' I said as I took a big bite of the sweet apple.

'Can we have a little chat, John?' Freddy asked.

'Sure, let's go into The Dart.' The pub was just across the street. 'Keep your eye out, love,' he said to his wife. 'I won't be too long.'

The three of us headed for The Dart. It was a chilly day but that hadn't deterred people from getting about their business as there were still plenty of people around. It was lunch time and it was quite a densely populated area at that time of day. We entered the pub and on seeing us the manager nodded a greeting to Johnny.

Johnny turned to Freddy and me. 'Come on, let's get into the back room.' The back room was *the office* where our little get-togethers took place.

'It's quieter in here, Fred. We won't get disturbed.' Just as we sat down a youngish barmaid came over to ask us what we would like to drink. The drinks, she said, were on the manager. Johnny ordered half a pint of Guinness and persuaded Freddy to have one too. I settled for a Coke.

Once we got ourselves comfortable we began the talk. Freddy outlined to Johnny everything that he had put together concerning the picture house and how it could be done without any hassle. 'Our Charlie has come up with a brilliant idea.' He then went on to tell Johnny of how we could make a quick killing at the business we were about to embark on. After explaining it all, Freddy and I sat back and waited to see what Johnny's reaction would be and awaited his opinion of the idea.

Johnny Oates was a straight talker; a man who wouldn't pull

any punches. If he didn't want to know he wouldn't pretend, he would tell you straight to your face. 'I think it's fuckin' brilliant, Charlie. But like you've said, we had better go to work fast on this one. Once it gets out they will all be trying to hit every picture house around.' He was of course referring to the other firms who were now into safe blowing themselves. 'Count me in,' he said.

'That's good, Johnny,' Freddy said. 'But you do know we will be taking pot luck at first. By that I mean we *will* select one of the top picture houses to have off, however, we will just have to chance it and hope the safe is one we can blow open, you know the old key hole job?' Due to the progress of the past year we were all well aware that a majority of big businesses were starting to get modern safes. These safes had combination locks that were practically impossible to blow open. When Freddy had finished speaking Johnny gave a big smile. His broad smile displayed his straight and white teeth; it was no wonder the ladies found him attractive. He had that big white smile with a friendly personality and he was always having parties and playing the archetypal, genial host. However, seeing his broad smile Freddy looked bemused and asked if he had said something funny.

'No,' he said. 'I've just solved the problem for us.'

'How? What do you mean, John?' Freddy asked mystified.

Johnny lowered his voice slightly and spoke in a more serious manner. 'I know someone who works in the best picture house in the city. It's a woman; she's a good friend of the family. She works there as an usherette, and the place is packed out tight most nights.'

My brother and I looked at him in wonderment... trust Johnny to come up with something as good as that! Although on reflection, Freddy became apprehensive due to it being just a young girl. 'What's the woman like, John? You know... if she gets a pull by the bizzies afterwards? Would she stand up?'

'She's as good as gold. Her family and I go back a long way. They are all staunch people. She wouldn't implicate me if that's what you mean, Fred.'

'That's OK then John. Your word goes without saying.'

'I will make it my business to go and have a word with her later on tonight and see what she can come up with.'

'That would be great, John,' Freddy said with satisfaction.

When the meeting about the graft was over the conversation turned to just general chit chat as the pub was starting to fill out with it being lunchtime. While the three of us were conversing on general everyday news, Keiron's name happened to crop up. Freddy explained about his behaviour and how he went to graft with the Cannon brothers.

'I've got news for you, Fred. He has fallen out with them too.'

'Well, that didn't last long,' said my brother.

'That's Keiron for you,' Johnny replied. 'I know he's my brother and I love him and everything but, he is to hot-headed at times. He doesn't take after me or Francie. I've been told he has now gone off to London.

CHAPTER 24

MY THEORY WAS PROVEN RIGHT

'Sunday night is the best time to have it off, Fred. There will be three days and nights takings in the peter and not forgetting all the cigarette money, ice-cream, lemonade, popcorn and all that. Yeah, there's plenty in the safe from over the weekend.'

'That's brilliant news, John.' After saying this our Freddy paused and thought for a moment. 'It's Friday today. We could have it off on Sunday. What do you think?' He looked at Johnny and I for a reaction.

Johnny answered him immediately: 'Can do.' Then I agreed without any hesitation.

'OK, we will hit the place on Sunday.'

This was more than good news. Apparently, the lady usherette, Johnny's friend, gave him some valuable information regarding the inside layout of the picture house.

She had described everything in detail and the peter was exactly our type: a typical Milliners safe with the keyhole in the door and it would be movable had we needed it to be. However, no need for any moving around in this case because we could blow it open exactly where it stood. We wouldn't have the hassle of packing it to deaden the sound either as the place was already soundproofed. She had said that the office containing the safe was situated on the second floor and that its door was secured with a simple Yale lock. So we knew it would be no problem at all to open; a small jemmy would do this in seconds.

Another attribute to our advantage was that there were no bells (alarms). This information sounded like a robbers dream...

unlike the present day. With the progress made in science and technology the police are far more advanced and well equipped today with their high tech security cameras, sophisticated computer systems and even the use of the helicopter. So it certainly wouldn't be today's robber's dream.

As I previously mentioned, the deterrent they had back then, and one that proved to be successful, was the police forces themselves. It was massive, strong and powerful. Come nighttime bizzies could be seen everywhere. They patrolled the streets in twos and most of these policemen were big, fit men who could easily outrun the average man in the street. There were more police than criminals back then and although I have no love for the bizzies they did make the streets a lot safer. There were no lowlife scum intimidating the elderly and women and kids, that sort were never seen or heard of. Yes, the police were efficient in those days and being in the sort of business we were all in, we had to be extra careful!

The next day, Saturday, we decided to go to the movies, thereby giving ourselves the opportunity to check the place out properly.

'I don't think you should come in on the move though, Johnny.' My brother Freddy was looking concerned. He wanted Johnny to have himself placed somewhere else to be sure of an alibi.

'Nah,' Johnny replied quickly. 'There's no need for me to do that. I can trust this woman, Fred. She's dead sound and I can vouch for that.'

'I'm only thinking of your best interests, John. You know we have always worked that way. The person who supplies the information doesn't come on the move.'

Johnny nodded. 'Yeah, I understand that but...'

'Well, how about you sitting off in the car and Charlie and I will go in?'

Johnny wasn't having any of it, he was adamant he wanted to play his part and be one hundred percent involved and after a little deliberation it was agreed that all three of us would take part.

Later on that Saturday evening, Freddy and I ended up going to the pictures together; in fact, we went twice. The first time was during the day, as by doing so we could see what was what, have a good look around so to speak and weigh the place up. The night-time was vastly different. There were lots more people attending so we had to wait in the queue with everyone else. The movie being shown that night was a box office hit called *The Defiant Ones* starring Tony Curtis and the talented black actor, Sidney Poitier. It was a black and white picture and a powerful film.

Inside the picture house there would be an interval every so often and the lights would be brought up brighter. There would be usherettes stood around holding their trays, which were secured with a band around the neck, selling popcorn and other refreshments. Each usherette carried a small torch which would enable them to see properly when the lights were dimmed down during the film.

While this commotion was going on, people milling around during the interval, it gave us the ideal opportunity to take a better look around. Freddy and I took it in turns vacating our seats and checking the place out. Johnny's friend, the lady usherette, had mentioned that straight after the film ended the male staff would open the push-bar doors, which were at opposite sides of the theatre. This was to let the large flow of people leave the building quickly as soon as the film was over. People always wanted to get out as fast as possible at the end... it was always like that and still is today for some reason; I'm not sure what that reason is though.

Freddy and I had gone over the place thoroughly. We had cased the main office and found it just where the woman had said. She was also right about it only having a Yale lock on it. I also took a look around for other rooms on the same floor. There was a small room where lots of cleaning items were stored. This was where I was planning to hide just as the picture house was closing. It would be about eleven o'clock or half past eleven. I would wait until the staff had all left and locked the place up. Then I would come out of hiding and open the push bar doors from the inside to let my brother and Johnny enter. This was all a good easy plan; in fact, it sounded too good to be true!

When Sunday came around all three of us went over everything thoroughly. We would go to the picture house that night to see the last show, which would be from seven o'clock until about ten thirty or eleven. We set off in Johnny's car at around half past six on the night in question; although thinking about it, we didn't *really* need a car as it was only about fifteen to twenty minutes' walk from Johnny's house. After all, we wouldn't exactly be carrying anything heavy that night; Freddy just had a stick of gelignite and a couple of detonators in his suit pocket with a pair of soft black leather gloves. Johnny had nothing at all on him except a pair of gloves and as for myself, I had a small packet of plasticine and a crowbar cut down to about eight inches, which were all discretely hidden away inside my suit jacket... oh and I almost forgot, a small packet of matches! Unbelievable really, don't you think? As opposed to all the heavy tools we used to have to carry along with us when we were taking a safe or trying to crack into one on previous jobs, now we travelled so lightly. The tools only weighed a few ounces and were extremely easy to conceal and yet they were deadly tools capable of blowing open a big strong peter. The town was quite busy that cold February night when we arrived but plenty of pubs were open at the time and looked to be doing a roaring trade as usual.

'Park the car a little out of the way, John. In fact put it among those other motors.' Freddy was pointing to a couple of pubs which each had a number of cars parked outside of them and they were only two streets away from our target.

As we started to approach the picture house, which incidentally, hadn't quite opened yet, John stopped abruptly... 'Will you take a look at the size of that!' He was referring to the queue of people outside the picture house waiting to go in. It stretched from the front entrance to right around the side of the building. The cinema goers were standing in twos waiting for it to open.

Freddy shivered. 'Let's join the queue. It's getting a bit cold out here.' He was stamping his feet to keep them warm. 'I hope we don't have to wait too long.'

Johnny, who was standing behind Freddy and me, leaned forward in between us and spoke quietly. 'Don't be moaning about waiting in the cold, Freddy. Just take a look at all these punters. That's all plenty of money that will be in our safe tonight.' He began to chuckle. Freddy and I looked at each other and began to laugh too. Just as he had finished speaking, the glass entrance doors opened and people began to file in. At last the queue began to move.

Once inside we all knew how to play our part. I was to go and secrete myself in a place that had been suggested by Johnny, via the usherette who had given us the information. I would do this when the main picture was coming to an end. I had already been to look at the place. It was a room not too far from the office that contained of all kinds of cleaning materials like toilet rolls, bleach and disinfectant. It was obviously the cleaner's store room. I had sneaked in there yesterday when I found the door was open. Inside was a kind of big, wooden wardrobe which I could fit easily inside and close the door on myself. Like the girl usherette had said to Johnny, it *was* a good place to hide. Of course we were also told that with the usherette being on duty that same night, she would keep a watchful eye out. I thought to myself, I couldn't have asked for anything better.

Johnny, Freddy and I had settled in our seats to watch the movie which had begun. I was getting a bit bored and restless... this was the fourth time we had watched it over a period of two days and nights. I got up from my seat after a while and made my way to the gent's toilet. While I was in there I had a nose around and noticed it had little oblong windows which were both open about two inches. As I went over to them I was thinking this could be an escape route for me if anything went wrong, but I found that there were steel bars on the outside of them. Well, I thought, they have all the security sorted on the outside but absolutely hopeless on the inside where we would be.

It was planned that when Johnny and Freddy had left the building after the movie had finished I would already be hiding in this cleaning room and would wait there until the whole of the staff had completely gone, particularly the manager and his assistant who, we had been informed, would be the last to leave. To be absolutely sure of them all vacating I would give it five minutes or so before coming out of my hiding place. Then I would go down to the ground floor and wait by the big push bar door that we had selected earlier. I would stand there until I heard a couple of knocks from the other side which would be Freddy and Johnny. Once I knew they were there it was just a matter of me unbolting the top and bottom of the door and then pushing the long steel bar to open it.

'Don't forget,' Freddy said, 'wait until I knock twice on that door, Charlie. Even if you have to wait for half an hour or so just stay put until I knock. I won't come near the place until I know that we are absolutely safe to do so. Alright, kid?'

And that's exactly how we did it. I stayed glued to that door when the place had emptied out. I waited behind it for about ten minutes... then I heard two knocks. I unbolted the door as quietly as I could and pushed the bar while still trying to stay quiet. The door opened and Freddy and Johnny quickly stepped inside. I took a last look around outside and everything seemed OK, not a sound or a sight, so I closed the door again and quietly put the bolts back on.

Closing that door made us feel safe inside the picture house. It seemed weird with it so quiet. You could quite literally hear a pin drop now and yet just half an hour ago it was so noisy and full of life. We all spoke in whispered voices until we realised that we could talk as loud as we liked and nobody could hear us from the outside even if we shouted to each other as the whole picture house was sound proofed. We were going to have to cut across the large foyer to the stairs that led up to the balcony and the manager's office. As I mentioned previously, the picture house had large glass front and glass doors which meant that anybody could see us from outside especially as it was well lit up, so we would have to be really vigilant.

'We will have to be careful here,' Freddy said. 'We have to make sure nobody from outside spots us going across that foyer.'

I suggested that I could creep across the foyer with my back up against the wall. 'I will go and position myself at the front of the foyer and give you the OK to get across and up the stairs.'

'Yeah that'll be good, Charlie,' said my brother.

So I began to edge my way as far as I could creeping along with my back on the wall towards the window until I got to a position where I could get a good view without being seen from outside. I could see the whole street through the huge glass windows and doors. I could see clearly left and right. There was the odd car passing and there were still a few people around, the stragglers making their way home from their night out. When I knew it was safe enough, I shouted across to Freddy and Johnny. 'OK, go now but be quick!'

They both hastily ran across the foyer and began to climb the stairs and out of sight as they headed towards the manager's office. They would be waiting for me as I was the one with the crowbar to open the office door. So I took one final look through the glass front of the picture house to make sure it was safe and then I too disappeared up the stairs after them, running up the steps two at a time. I safely reached the office where Freddy and Johnny where waiting and I took out the small crowbar from my jacket pocket. I began to prise the door where the Yale lock was positioned.

As I jemmied the door Johnny encouraged me. 'That's it, Charlie, go on.' Then he shouldered the door simultaneously as I prised it and the door gave way. We looked at each other with a grin and then we entered the office; me first, followed by Freddy and Johnny.

Surprisingly inside was fairly bright considering it was nighttime. We knew that we couldn't risk switching on a light in there anyway so Freddy took his torch from his pocket and switched it on. He was careful to keep the beam low as he shone it around the room. We found that it was quite a large office with a couple of desks and lots of chairs and filing cabinets; all the usual furniture you would expect in there. The beam of light from the torch searched around the quiet office room into all the nooks and crannies as it sought out our prize. Then suddenly, there in the spot light we found it. It was standing up against the far wall... our prize... the safe! It was a big and strong looking safe that would appear to be totally impenetrable. One would think this was impossible to crack. However though, it's amazing what half a stick of gelignite and a detonator can do...

Freddy bent down in front of the safe looking it over, and after a quick examination he straightened up seemingly satisfied. 'OK,' he said to Johnny. 'I'll start to work on this with Charlie. You whip back down to the foyer, John, and keep your eyes peeled on the outside. This will only take a few minutes and we're out of here.'

'Will do, Fred.'

I interrupted quickly before Johnny moved. 'No, kid.' I said to Freddy. 'I'll shoot down there to keep lookout. I don't mean to be funny or anything but, I know where I can hide myself down there where I can't be spotted from outside.'

Johnny looked at me a little taken aback. 'Are you sure, Charlie?'

Freddy asked me. 'I thought you wanted to have a go at this yourself?'

'I know the score,' I said to him.

'Alright then, kid, you know what to do when you're down there; give us a shout if something's not right.'

With that I left the office and went to the top of the stairs. Then, as mad as it may seem, I went down the stairs on all fours like a cat, just in case someone from outside could see me if I were standing up. They were big, plush, carpeted stairs so it was fairly comfortable doing it, to tell the truth. Once at the bottom of the stairs, I had a good view of outside and could see there were no people around. I kept my back against the wall as I skirted around it to a position where I knew I would be safe from any prying eyes on the street.

I stood watching and waiting. My adrenaline was pumping away the way it always did in a situation like this knowing that my brother would be going about setting explosives and a detonator into the safe keyhole. It had gone almost deserted outside now. There were just the main-road tall streetlights on but nothing out of the ordinary. Now and again a motorcar would pass by but so far I could see nobody about. I still waited and watched.

Suddenly... out of the blue, I saw a movement on the far side of the street. It was a good distance away but I strained my eyes to make sure. I was now positive. There were two figures walking towards the picture house on the opposite side of the road. I had my face up close to the window to get a good look. My breath steamed up the window in front of me. I lowered myself down to where it was still clear as I didn't want to wipe away the condensation of my breath from the window and draw attention to myself. So on lowering myself down I got a better view. It was one of those moments we all dreaded. It was the enemy... two uniformed policemen strolling down side by side. I would know them anywhere; they were definitely two policemen as I could see the tall, black helmets and the movement around their shoulders from the capes they wore, flapping.

Just then my brother shouted from the balcony at the top of the stairs. 'Charlie, we are about to blow this now. It's all set up. I've only got to light it, kid... Is everything alright down there?'

My young mind had to think fast. These two policemen were walking towards us on the other side of the road, only about a hundred and fifty metres away. I was torn between the devil and the deep blue sea. It had been suggested that these picture houses were one hundred percent soundproof and if anything could prove that theory right then it was right now and if the safe did go off and those policemen *did* hear it we would still have time to get away. It was a gamble with my young life and those of my brother and Johnny. What did I do?

'Yeah,' I shouted to my brother. 'Everything is dead sound down here. Go and get it done quick.'

'OK, Charl.' He disappeared.

I was watching the two policemen drawing closer. I could actually see them plainly by now they were chatting to each other looking relaxed as they strolled towards the picture house. I was feeling anything but calm; my nerves were in turmoil, my stomach was churning with anxiety and anticipation. I thought, Have I done the right thing? I have just given my brother the go ahead to blow open a safe with the bizzies outside! Is it all going to come on top because of me? I was looking at them while all this was going through my head when all of a sudden there was an almighty…

BANG!

I'm sure I felt the building shudder from the blast, then... absolute silence! It was all over in that one bang. I looked at the two policemen to see if there was any reaction from them but... nothing! They just kept strolling nonchalant and chatting as before. I was ecstatic and couldn't control myself. I shouted out: 'Yesss!' They were right across the road by now; practically parallel to the cinema but they just carried on quietly past. I was dead excited. My heart was pounding as I took one last look up and down the road. I saw no one and nothing about except for the backs of the policemen as they carried on down the road further and further away from the cinema.

I shot up the stairs fervently to the office where Freddy and Johnny were with the safe. The blowing had been a success. The door from that seemingly indestructible peter was now wide open offering up its valuable contents of which my brother Freddy and a smiling Johnny were only too pleased to accept. They were emptying the safe as I entered the office and I had decided not to tell them about the bizzies walking past. I thought it would be better to tell them later so as not to panic them.

Johnny looked at me with one of his big grins on his face as he was holding cloth bank bags full of coins. 'How are we going to get these away, Freddy? We're going to need a horse and cart with the weight in them,' he said, laughing. They had a couple of bags of paper money too: twenty pounds, ten pounds and five pounds.

Freddy turned around to Johnny. 'Put all the paper money in our coats now.'

After they had stuffed their pockets with the paper money Johnny looked at the bags of silver stacked on the office table. 'What about those though, Fred?'

'I don't know about them, John, with them being so heavy. We can't take the risk just in case.'

'Hang on, Fred,' Johnny retorted, shocked. 'You're not thinking of leaving all that money here? There's easy a few hundred pounds in those bags!'

'Yeah, John, I am. Like I told you, we can't take the chance not carrying that weight with us.'

Johnny shook his head looking defeated. It was heartbreaking to leave those bags of money there but, like Freddy said, if we had taken them, it could have been our downfall and besides, we still had to get out of this place.

'Come on, let's get the fuck out of here,' Freddy said. 'Time's going on and it's getting a bit late.' It wasn't quite twelve o'clock yet, however, even twelve o'clock was a dangerous time; the time when more police were on the streets patrolling. 'Can you go back down, Charlie and give us the OK?'

Again, I went down the wide, plush stairs and into the foyer the same way as earlier and crept to the front entrance. I had another good look through those huge windows, checking up the left and right of the main road outside. It was practically empty except for two or three people at the far end. I could just make out about a hundred metres away. They must have been more stragglers making their way home from town.

I shouted up to Freddy: 'Come on, everything's OK.'

The two of them descended the stairs swiftly and positioned themselves near the push-bar doors which we had entered. I stayed where I was for a moment until Freddy shouted over to me. 'Is it OK now, kid, because I'm going to open this side door?'

'Yeah, go on, it's OK.'

Freddy unbolted the top and bottom of the door and pushed

the bars down as quietly as he could. They made a noise but not enough that anyone would hear. He poked his head out of the door and took a good look around before turning to shout over to me. 'We are going out now, Charlie. Get yourself over here. We'll all go out together.' I quickly made my way over to the door. Johnny was already standing outside with his back against the wall beside the doorway. 'You stand over there with Johnny while I shut this door kid.' Freddy then tried to pull the door to, but it wouldn't close. So after a few failed attempts, we decided to leave it and go up the side entrance of the street.

Johnny was hurrying up ahead of us to get the car started while we followed a few paces behind him. We had to cross over the street at the top end. There were a few people around on their way home but the three of us walked briskly past and out of the way. Johnny finally reached his car and got in to start the engine as we followed and got in with him. Then he gave us one of his big grins and drove us happily away.

We ended up going back to Freddy's place to cut up the readies. It was a nice big chop we each got from just over three thousand pounds in total; again, an absolute fortune in those days and to think it only took a few minutes!

CHAPTER 25

POLICE FIT UP

It is now believed there are several gangs now using gelignite or 'jelly' as it is now known among the Liverpool criminal fraternity. Police have already arrested a gang member and he has now been charged with being in possession of gelignite and is awaiting trial.

The C.I.D. are now out in force including renowned for his successful police work Detective Inspector Balmer. They are determined to put an end to these gelignite gangs or jelly gangs as they are now known.

We all knew the only way the police would be able to achieve this was by using their devious ways and, as I have spoken of before, performing a fit up (fabricating evidence).

'It's a fuckin' liberty if ever there was one,' Francie, Johnny's brother, was saying to us, getting heated. It was a few days after the picture-house robbery and we had arranged to spend a little time together. 'I knew it was only going to be a matter of time before those bizzies would start their dirty tricks, fitting people up!' Francie was raving mad as he explained how a good friend of his had evidence planted on him by the police and how it had happened in his own home.

'How did it all come about, Francie?' Johnny asked his brother. 'It's not like Charlie Rawlinson to make any slip ups; he's too clever to be taken in like that. In fact, all of his circle are very close knit.'

'I know they are, John. They are all clever fellas, but the plod have fitted him right up.'

Francie was talking about another well respected firm who were into the same business as us. They were from the Wavertree area of Liverpool. They were good, real professionals and just like us, nobody could penetrate them.

This is an absolutely true story that I am about to relate to you here: Charlie Rawlinson was a successful safe breaker but he also had a good front: he dabbled in cars which he bought and sold. He was something along the same lines as our friend Tosh. Charlie Rawlinson wasn't flash or anything like that; he was more of a family man. Working at his legitimate business was a messy, dirty job at times, what with tinkering around with all those car engines, so Charlie would wear heavy working overalls. These were something like an all-in-one suit, called boiler suits back then. The bizzies and the C.I.D. knew the reputation of Charlie and his firm: John Mac, Dickie J, etc. These men were all staunchly loyal to one another and tight lipped. The police couldn't get anywhere near them, but the bizzies, who we should never underestimate, knew Charlie & Co were bang at it!

Francie went on to tell us all the story of what had happened to Charlie: The police had called at Charlie Rawlinson's house and after being greeted at the door by Charlie's wife they were politely invited inside. His wife was house-proud and his home spotlessly clean and so every time Charlie came home from his legitimate work and entered the house he would immediately take off his work clothes and hang his overalls on a coat peg in the hallway. There were three or four bizzies and as they entered the house one of the sly bastards, who it appeared was in charge, put a stick of gelignite in one of the pockets of Charlie's working overalls. He was able to do this discreetly as he walked past the garment hanging up in the hallway. Francie stopped at this point for a moment. We could all see he was really choked and angry at what had happened.

'They are wicked bastards, Francie,' Johnny said.

We ourselves were all fuming over it too. Francie composed himself and went on with the story: 'The bizzies had turned Charlie's house over and found nothing inside so about ten minutes later they decided to leave. Charlie was politely leading the way to the front door down the hallway to see them out. The bizzies followed him and he opened the door for them. Just before stepping out of his house, one of them, again the one who seemed to be in charge, looked at his work clothes hanging up on the pegs in the hallway. As well as all the bizzies, Charlie's wife was present too. This detective asked Charlie if these were his clothes. Charlie told him that of course they were and that he had only just taken them off. The detective proceeded to pat down these clothes and then put his hand in the pocket of the overalls. Then, in front of Charlie, his wife and the bizzies there present he pulled out the sealed stick of gelignite! "What's this hey, Charlie?" the detective asked him with a sly smile.'

Our Freddy interrupted: 'I know how you feel, Francie. That bizzie who planted the jelly on Charlie Rawlinson will be a clever bastard in court. He will know all the tricks of the trade alright and the police who were there on the raid with him will have been specially selected. I'll bet one or two of them will be rookie bizzies who have not long been in the force. Most probably honest, new recruits who have joined the police force with every intention of upholding the law but along the way some of them get taken in and tarnished by the older ones with all their corruption, which then becomes rife. That main detective in charge of the raid had deliberately made sure that they all saw him find that jelly in Charlie's pocket; including Charlie and his wife, but nobody had seen him sneakily plant it when he first entered the house. So to those bizzies and to Charlie's wife, it would have looked like a genuine discovery he had made. The evidence on him is too overwhelming, Francie. I hate to say it, but when Charlie goes to trial he's got no chance of an acquittal; not with that evidence stacked up against him.'

Johnny looked over at Freddy. 'You should know, Fred. You've had it done to yourself, haven't you?'

'Yes, I have, John, many years ago and the bizzies who took charge of the case was none other than that hateful, devious bastard, Balmer. He pulled all kinds of strings against me in court and he got me sent down for ten years on a so-called jewel robbery. I was only a young kid of nineteen. I had no form and I had never been in trouble before, let alone been in prison. If the serious crime squad have any inclination that you're at it, they will use their authority to the extreme and, make no bones about it, they *will* fit you up.'

'You're right, Fred,' said Johnny. 'That's why I have always tried to get it across to that hot headed brother of mine, Keiron.'

'Yeah, well, Keiron is Keiron, isn't he, John? But no matter what you think or say about him, he is dead game and has always been loyal to us all.'

'Oh I know that, Fred. I just want him to be more careful and watch his back; especially with all this going on.'

After that heavy conversation we all had the same feelings with regards to the bizzies and their corruptive ways.

CHAPTER 26

COPYCAT GANGS

A couple of weeks later another major picture house was targeted and the usual stories hit the newspapers.

SAFE BREAKERS KNOWN AS THE JELLY GANG BLOW OPEN SAFE

Escape with large haul of cash

Only this time it wasn't us that had carried it out.

Johnny got in touch and confronted us about it, looking bewildered and concerned: 'Hey, Fred, what's going on? I thought you might have given me a shout when you and Charlie were planning to do more graft.'

We explained to him that it hadn't been us and that he should know us better than that. We wouldn't pull a stroke like that, least of all on him. He accepted this and apologised, saying the bizzies and the papers had reported that it was the same gang. 'They said it had all the hallmarks of the last picture-house robbery.'

'There you go, John, never believe what you read in the papers,' Freddy answered. 'I would have thought that a man of your experience would know all that by now. Most newspapers only give secondary information. However, now that you're here, John...' Freddy turned to look at me. 'And you, Charlie. I may as well get this off my chest as it's what I was going to tell you both anyway, especially now, following recent events.' He looked serious and a little hesitant. 'I have decided to pull out,' he looked down at the floor as if he didn't want to see the reactions on our faces. 'I mean, let's face it and be sensible about things. Everywhere is now becoming too hot for our type of graft. You can see what's going on now. There are other copycats blowing safes and if we happen to come unstuck, we would be blamed for the lot, they would throw the book at us... Although, that's not the only reason I am finishing. I'm not using it as an excuse. It's my family, you know, I have a lovely wife and a little boy to consider now... and... well, I want to spend more time with them both...' He paused and appeared to be deep in thought for a moment. 'Every time I go out on a move, I worry about what would happen to the two of them if I came unstuck, especially now with all the corruption and the way that those bizzies can fit you up. So, now I realise that I can't afford to risk it, and knowing my luck if I did get sent down I wouldn't see daylight again...'

I remembered my brother Freddy doing that long ten years. It was a few years ago now and I was only a child at the time but I could vividly recall my mother and sister returning from visiting him at the prison, which by the way, was far from home; they would both return absolutely broken hearted. It was so tough to see my mother with tears down her face crying over him, after all, he was her son, and only nineteen years of age!

I would often hear them talking with older relatives about how he was trying to cope in there and how hard it was for him to do such a long time. Nineteen was no age to be banged up in that hell hole of a place. I used to hear them in conversation saying things like, my God he is still down the block (punishment cell). Due to his youth and the fact that he had never been inside a prison before he was finding it arduous to conform so he was forever breaking the rules and getting into trouble.

When he was down the block he was put on a prison diet of bread and water; incidentally, that was one of the punishments back then, you wouldn't hear of it nowadays; the European Court of Human Rights would have a field day with that kind of mis-treatment! I used to hear a whole manner of things about the terrible ordeal he was going through in there, like drastic weight loss for example.

Freddy resumed talking to us. It was as if he was trying to apologise to the two of us for finally finding happiness but, more importantly, he wouldn't want us to think that his bottle had gone and he was too scared to carry on. In fact, knowing my brother the way I did, he would have hated to think that we thought anything of the kind; he was too proud of a man for that. I agreed and understood everything he said, and that wasn't me being biased at all, just because he was my brother; it was because his words were ringing true. My family and I could see that he had gone through enough during his young life and that so many years had been wasted. I was glad that at last he had found much deserved love, peace and contentment and all the money in the world can't buy you that.

Johnny grabbed hold of Freddy and began to shake his hand. 'If you want out, Fred, that's your choice,' he said smiling affectionately at Freddy. 'Only *I'm* not ready to retire just yet. I'm waiting to have a really big touch and only then do I intend to take a back seat. For now though, like I have said before, I will wait until this heat dies down.' Johnny then turned to me. 'So, Charlie, for me, I'll go back to my little front and work my fruit barrow.' He began to laugh. 'It's a good little earner.'

CHAPTER 27

THE DOWNSIDE WHEN FACING THE MUSIC

How remarkable, I thought to myself, the way Johnny thinks... and for that matter, the way all the other grafters who are in our line of business think. They are all waiting and hoping for the big one to come along, the one that will put them on easy street (make them rich). It's the same predicament that some of those old prospectors were in, always searching for that pot of gold... the one big hit that they could retire on.

Sadly though, they can go on and on hoping and waiting until eventually their lives have passed them by and they have grown old. They realise too late that the golden egg is never going to come their way and that the most precious years of their life has gradually passed them by; some of them having served long prison sentences.

'That's what I plan to accomplish, John... a legitimate front,' Freddy said, smiling for a change. 'I have a little stash put away, and who knows, I might become successful.' He looked at us both, still smiling.

In a way, I was more than happy to hear that my brother was finishing with crime and going straight. There was one sure thing too: my mother and the rest of my family would be pleased to hear it. As for me, no way! In fact, the thought of finishing had never even crossed my mind. I wanted to go on living this fast hard life so that I could have money to burn on the good things that life had to offer me.

For now though, I would have to be a little patient and like Johnny had said: I would have to wait until the heat had died down because at present, in and around the city, there were numerous more police manning the streets, pubs and clubs like never before. So presently, it was just a case of not being silly and of using common sense.

Obviously, there would be some jelly gangs who wouldn't pay any heed to the danger that was lurking around and because of this the police were beginning to make a lot of arrests. Fellas who were known to have been into safe blowing at any time were getting pulled in by them on a large scale, whether they had been at it or not.

Dirty tricks were being played by the C.I.D. and police informants were active in the pubs and clubs that most of these Liverpool criminals were known to socialise in. It was just a matter of time before the bizzies got their results, especially with the way they worked hand in hand with their low-life paid police informants. Some of these despicable creatures would shop their own mothers if necessary.

In my opinion, and that of many others, the greatest liberty at that time was the Charlie Rawlinson case. He went on trial at the high court for being in possession of explosives, namely gelignite, with intent to blow open safes.

Back in those days, unlike today, when a person was taken into police custody for questioning there was no such thing as a tape recorder used. We all know that what is played back and heard on a tape recorder will be the truth. As you answer a question fired at you it is all being recorded there in the room and this is later presented in court. In those days however, there was no tape recorder.

The only time a solicitor was called to assist and represent you was when the police were satisfied that they had finished their questioning and sometimes this could take a few days! The procedure was such that you would have to make an appearance at the Magistrate's Court to answer to the charge. Subsequently, it was then, and only then, that a solicitor was called to represent you and attend court to try to arrange bail and have you released from custody while awaiting trial. However, the majority of the time and especially if you had a police record, you would be refused bail and find yourself remanded in custody.

On the day of your trial, you would attend court with a barrister. The police would give evidence in court regarding what you were supposed to have said to them during questioning and while in their custody. They would falsely claim that you had admitted to things, which you had not, such as, *Yeah, I did it, but try and prove it,* whereas no sensible criminal would ever say that. For instance, they would do such things as to have an orderly say he had overheard you admit to the crime when he had brought a cup of tea to your cell. They had no qualms about using a whole host of devious methods to incriminate you.

You would never stand a chance against the lies told by the police as the public were led to believe that our policemen were the consummate, honest, upholders of the law and would never dream of telling lies in court. So the prisoner trying to protest and telling his barrister that he had never said such a thing was futile. The jury who had been selected by the police and the courts would absolutely, unequivocally believe in the honesty of our police force. The jury in those days always consisted of professional people, the likes of who would own big businesses like factories, cinemas, building firms etc, which had probably been robbed at some time or other. Therefore, as you will realise yourself, these people on the jury would be immediately biased. It is of course totally different now.

The police deviously planted evidence on Charlie Rawlinson. Sadly, he knew and we all knew that when his trial *did* come to the high court he would not have a leg to stand on. He and his barrister protested vigorously and fervently but the police had their witnesses, all *police* witnesses by the way, and Charlie Rawlinson got sentenced to five years. It was the biggest liberty of all time but those bizzies had no scruples so they didn't care and unfortunately, that's how Charlie Rawlinson ended up. Charlie was the first one they brought in and he wasn't the last as he was subsequently followed by many more due to the way the police worked and used their devious methods.

We were all totally shocked at what had happened to Charlie Rawlinson and the undeserved suffering and distress his innocent wife and children were caused. Everyone involved in this business was now on their guard due to the methods the police employed in the so called solving of crime.

Surprisingly, it served as a powerful deterrent to some jelly gangs and we *did* hear that due to the severity of the sentences being imposed and, more frightening than that, the police corruption and the way they were believed giving their evidence under oath, some had completely turned their backs on safe blowing.

CHAPTER 28

BAD NEWS

During the passing of time and while waiting for the OK from Johnny, I used to go back to hang out with my pals and, at the age I was, life was dead exciting for me. In actual fact, when I think about it I now realise that the 1950s were the best part of my youth. There were the girls and clothes, music and dance halls, socialising with all my young friends, and of course, the money I had to spend (which no other teenager in our neighbourhood could even dream of earning).

Whenever I needed more of my money, I would discreetly pay Tosh a visit as he was still safe-guarding my stash. When I was round there at his house, he always took the opportunity to preach to me, *Don't be going mad with it, Charlie. Take it easy and don't draw attention to yourself.* Of course I would always pay heed to what he was saying and try to take his advice as I knew he was absolutely right. Then, however, being so young at the time, I was enjoying myself too much to care. My head was often lost in what I thought was a brilliant way of life and I wanted it to go on forever.

I still regularly used to visit my brother Freddy. Surprisingly, he had started up his own business. He was always a good musician and particularly excellent on guitar. Mostly though he would play jazz which didn't appeal to me at all as my tastes were completely different. I preferred rock and roll. He gave lessons and taught people how to play the guitar. Being a highly intelligent man with extraordinary talents, he even turned his hand to manufacturing his own guitars. He would literally make them by hand and he began to do well at this skilful and specialist business, becoming rather successful at selling the guitars he made. A guitar was a sought after instrument at that time and almost every kid wanted to own and play a guitar. Freddy was in his element with his newfound way of life and so too was I. It made me really happy to see that things were finally working out for him.

One day while visiting my brother's place, who should call out of the blue, but the Oates brothers Johnny and Francie. They both appeared concerned and solemn as they entered. 'How you doing?' Johnny asked as he entered. As I have said before, Johnny usually greeted you with a big smile but today he had a sullen, serious look on his face. 'I don't suppose you two have heard about our Keiron?' Johnny looked at Freddy and I as he spoke soberly. 'We have just been informed that he has been caught bang to rights. The bizzies ambushed a car he was in somewhere in London, along with two other fellas.'

Francie took over the conversation. 'The police have thrown all kinds of charges on them including safe blowing.'

Freddy shook his head in disbelief. 'I'm so sorry to hear that, about your kid. What happened?'

'We haven't been told the full score yet, although up until now, and according to his brief, he is up to his neck in it all. The charge is too serious so they have knocked his bail back. He is up in court next week.'

'This was waiting to happen,' Johnny went on. 'I tried to drum it into our Keiron, told him time and again to have some patience and wait until the heat had died down. But would he listen? No.'

'Well, then there's nothing you can do about it now, John. That's one of the greatest drawbacks of being in this game.'

I was shocked at hearing this. Keiron getting caught came as a bit of a blow; I just couldn't imagine him being out of action. He was his own man. But then like most men, somewhere along the line they have a weakness. Keiron's was that he had no patience whatsoever. I don't even think he was desperate for money as he had made plenty; although, he did spend quite a lot. I think deep down he just loved to be *at it* especially when it came to opening safes; he got a real buzz out of that. For now though, like Freddy said, there was nothing we could do but wait and see what the outcome would be when he eventually went to trial.

As if that wasn't enough to contend with, hearing about Keiron's demise, only a few weeks later we heard that the Cannon brothers, Bert and Harry, were now being targeted by the C.I.D. They were getting hounded.

Being persecuted by the police is a terrible nerve-wracking experience. Once they have you in their sights and they are on your case they will not stop until they get results. So all we could do was hope was that the Cannons didn't make any silly mistakes. They shouldn't do, after all, they were real professionals in every way and they knew all the rules. Yet looking at it from the other aspect, the bizzies were now breaking the rules to suit themselves so what chance had anyone got when things were going that way?

CHAPTER 29

SUSSING THE PLACE OUT

Some weeks later: 'Listen to me, Charlie, you don't need me, you know how to handle it now.'

My brother Freddy and I had just been discussing some really good graft that had come our way. It was considered a racing cert, dead reliable information and plenty of readies inside of the peter. Johnny couldn't come on the move with us because he and his brother Francie had enough on their plates with Keiron and his problems. There was his case to get sorted and all this while they were going back and to on visits down to London. All of this just made it impossible to get anything else done. Their priority was obviously their brother, Keiron.

What my brother was saying was true: I could blow a safe now. I knew exactly what to do and when. The problem was that the fella who had come to see us with this proposition of work was involved with Bert and Harry Cannons' firm and obviously with the police surveillance on them they personally couldn't go on the move. Tony Burns though, was a man who had a good pedigree as well as being game and loyal.

'I understand what you are saying, kid,' I said to my brother. 'Only, they are *insisting* that you come on the move. And as for me, they are thinking I'm just a kid and that I might fuck everything up. You and me know better though. We know that I won't.'

'OK, Charlie, I will have to see them again and explain it to them. Tony Burns is a good friend of mine and whatever he says is dead straight.'

The next day, my brother and I had a meeting with Tony Burns.

We wanted to make sure it was well out of the way of prying eyes and ears so it took place on the outskirts of the city in a place called Kirkby, where Tony lived. Kirkby was a new town which hadn't been built for long, maybe eight to ten years at the most. It was created to alleviate the overcrowding of council houses in the city centre, which were vastly over populated. So we met at Tony's place in Kirkby and got our heads together around the table. His wife was home but she gave us our privacy. She was hospitable and occasionally she would bring us cups of tea for refreshment during our talk.

'I appreciate what you are saying, Freddy, and all this about your Charlie, yeah, I know he's very game and he's good, but you are the expert, Fred. We all know you're the best at this business!' Tony wasn't saying my brother was the expert just to butter him up; he knew, as we all did, that you couldn't try that on with our Freddy. What he was really doing was showing him the utmost respect.

'Can't it wait for a while?' Freddy asked. 'You know, at least until everything has quietened down a bit for Bert and Harry? Then maybe you can all get your heads together again and do it without me?'

'That's just it, Fred. We won't be able to have it. By next week, the money starts to get taken to the bank instead of leaving it in the safe overnight, and believe me, Fred, what's stashed inside that peter is a fortune.' What Tony was saying was quite correct. It was now a well-known fact that big companies were being told by their insurers not to keep large amounts of cash in overnight safes. They were just covering themselves really so that they were less likely to have to pay out due to any big robberies taking place. This was the new way of doing things and it was happening all over the place these days.

As the conversation carried on between us deep down I knew that my brother didn't want anyone to know he had finished with crime. It was kind of a pride thing among the criminal fraternity. It can be an insult to hear anyone say those words: *What's the matter has his bottle gone*?

'What's it to be then, Fred?' Tony asked. 'Are you in or what?'

My brother sat in silence for a moment and then looked over at me. I could tell by his face that he didn't want in. Then amazingly, out of the blue, he suddenly turned to Tony. 'OK, Tony. Count me in. But it's got to be my way or no way.'

Tony grabbed hold of my brother's hand and shook it with delight. 'Whatever you say, Fred. I will let the rest of the crew know that it's on.'

It was a Friday afternoon and the move was to take place on the Sunday night. This was due to knowing that the safe on the premises would then hold a full week's takings. It was an out of town piece of graft and pretty far away in Wales. It was a massive steam laundry employing a large amount of people and according to information it was said to serve many other businesses in and around Wales: places like other large factories, hospitals, hotels, restaurants etc. We were told that it was a thriving enterprise. Freddy had insisted that we arrange to go and look over the place the following day, Saturday.

After the meet, Tony dropped us both off back at Freddy's place. We were having a talk about the graft and I was looking at my brother intently. 'You don't have to come in on this, Freddy, you know. There's no shame in admitting to anybody that you are going straight.'

'I know, but it's just one of those things, kid, isn't it?' My brother was knowledgeable and experienced and he began to speak to me seriously. 'I know we have been told all about the place we are going to have off, kid, but sometimes people tell you things, like about what the set-up is and everything, and I'm sure they do it with all good intentions, but I have experienced, on many an occasion, getting there and finding it is entirely different from the way it had been described. That's why we are going to see for ourselves, to make sure!'

The next day, Saturday, Tony picked us both up from Freddy's place and drove us over to the factory in question. It was in a place called Wrexham and it took just over an hour to get there. Due to it being a Saturday, we arrived to find the town extremely busy. This was better for us as we would look less conspicuous while having a look around. We parked the car and went on foot, mingling with the hustle and bustle of the crowd so that we blended in. As Tony had been to this place before he knew exactly where to head for. Within ten minutes or so we reached our destination. Just as described, we found a huge sprawling factory set in its own grounds out on the far side of the town.

'There it is,' Tony said triumphantly. 'Big place isn't it, Fred?'

'Yeah, it is.'

'The office holding the peter is on the top floor,' Tony went on excitedly. 'But that's no problem. There are no bells (alarms). It's a knocking bet (easy).'

Freddy and I just stood there quietly for a moment carefully observing the site and taking it all in. As it was a Saturday the factory was closed. We began to walk around the perimeter of the grounds. There was a road that went all the way around it. We noticed that some of the windows of the factory were left slightly open on the second floor. It was a three-storey building, probably built around the turn of the century. It all just seemed too good to be true: no alarms, windows open and above all... a fortune in the safe. We knew that we could be in and out of there within five or ten minutes at the most.

'What do you think, kid?' Freddy asked me.

'It looks easy enough.'

'Yeah, I know,' he said. 'Too easy!'

Tony jumped in with: 'You're dead right it is. The info is bang on, Freddy. You know what the people are like that live in these out of town places; they haven't got a clue about security.'

'Yeah, OK,' Freddy said to calm him down. 'What I need to do now is find out where the main police station is situated.' We strolled around the town again, searching for the local police station. We finally located it over on the opposite side of the town which wasn't too bad for us really.

'That's another good thing,' Tony said still full of enthusiasm.

'The bizzie station is well out of the way, don't you think, Fred?'

'Yeah,' Freddy replied noncommittally. 'At least it's not just around the corner.'

Then, still mingling in with the public and not looking out of place or obvious we took another walk around the town. Once we were all fully satisfied with everything we returned to the car. Tony drove us out of Wales and we made our way back home.

I was the first one to be dropped off when we arrived back in Liverpool, which was great for me as I couldn't wait to get ready to go out. I was having a big night on the town with my young pals. Just as I was getting out of the car my brother gave me a warning: 'Don't forget, Charlie, take it easy when you're out tonight, kid. Me and Tony will pick you up tomorrow. Alright kid?'

'No worries,' I reassured him.

CHAPTER 30

HOME COMFORTS

Saturday nights were my most favourite of the week, especially when going into the city centre. It was all going on there and it was certainly the place to be; the atmosphere was unbelievable. My friends and I always had a right blast particularly when it came to chatting up the girls. Somehow though, this particular Saturday night, I just couldn't get into the party mood. My mind was concentrated on tomorrow, Sunday, the night of the graft we were about to have off. Now and again one of my pals would ask me if I was OK; they couldn't help but notice a difference in me no matter how much I tried to enjoy myself. Joey and Yank were two of my best friends and they knew what I was up to with my brother; I mean let's face it, I always had more money than any of them. Although whenever they were skint, I would always make sure that they were alright for a few quid.

Going to bed that night, unsurprisingly, I couldn't get to sleep. I was restless, with the events planned for the tomorrow night churning over and over in my mind. Freddy, Tony and I were about to blow the fuckin' locks off a safe door! This prospect had me excited and yet apprehensive at the same time.

I did eventually drop off to sleep, but it had been a restless night and this resulted in me awaking late on that Sunday morning still feeling drowsy. I had my own bed now though, which was much better when I needed to get some quality sleep. There was no more over-crowding. I could stretch out in whichever position I felt the most comfortable in, having the whole bed to myself versus the earlier years when my three brothers and I all shared a big old fashioned bed.

My brother Billy who was two years younger than me had now moved in with my sister, to keep him out of trouble. This alone though didn't totally alleviate the overcrowding problem, so when the money I was making started to come in regularly, the first thing on the agenda for me was to buy myself a nice single bed, in fact I bought two; one for Jimmy and Joe, my two younger brothers, and one for myself!

On waking, I stretched and yawned sleepily. Then I got myself up and began to get ready. I could hear plenty of activity coming from downstairs. It was happy activity though; the sound of my mother's voice singing would always lift my heart. I could hear the rattling and clattering of crockery and saucepans but rising above all of this I could hear the lovely dulcet tones of my mother singing as she went about her daily chores.

What did really spurn me to get up though, was that I was absolutely starving and I could smell the bacon being cooked in the frying pan. I loved bacon and eggs with hot toast and a mug of tea in the morning. It would give you a kick start for the day ahead. So, after cleaning my teeth and having a quick swill (wash) in the bathroom, I made my way downstairs and straight into the kitchen, where I flopped myself down in front of the big old kitchen table. My mother who stood cooking by the stove turned around and glared at me with one of those disapproving looks:

'Where have you been? And what time did you come home last night... or should I say this morning?' I didn't answer her. I just shook my head.

My old fella was sat there in his usual place. He always reminded me of an old ornament as he never seemed to move out of his chair. I really didn't get along with my old fella. He looked at me and tut tutted: 'He's been gallivanting, out all night.' As he said this, he gave me a dirty look.

My mother looked over at me and shook her head. 'You look terrible, Charlie. Are you alright? You haven't been drinking have you?'

'No, Ma,' I replied. 'I don't drink.'

My old fella tutted again and shook his head. 'Hhhmmm,' he said looking at me.

I just looked over and tutted back at him. 'Hhhmmm,' I mimicked. 'Is that all you can do?'

My mother quickly interrupted just in case an argument developed between us. 'That's quite enough from you two. Do you want your breakfast, Charlie? You *are* hungry aren't you?'

'*Am I hungry?*' I exclaimed to her. 'I'm starving, Ma. I could eat a horse!'

Within minutes of saying this, a large plate appeared on the table in front of me, full of bacon and eggs. I feasted my eyes upon this delicious sight and savoured it for a moment with my mouth watering as I did.

My mother then completed this vision of culinary art when she placed on the table a plate of hot, thickly cut, buttered toast and a large mug of tea. Wow, my stomach was talking to me... *Get stuck in and enjoy!*

CHAPTER 31

GETTING IT SORTED

Later on that afternoon, I went over to my brother's place where we were joined by Tony so that we could go over the plans for the graft that night: details of how we would best organise and safely pull off this big move we were plotting to do in Wales.

'Let's not forget,' my bother Freddy warned us. 'It's not as though we will be grafting in and around Liverpool. This is vastly different from the familiar places we are all used to.' The way he was outlining everything to us was absolutely correct. It was true that we all knew practically every back alley in our hometown and we knew how to disappear if anything came on top.

As Freddy was forewarning us and encouraging caution, Tony appeared to get a little concerned. 'Hey, Fred, I think you are going to the extremes here, mate. I mean, the information we have is one hundred percent and according to *you* we could be in and out of the place in less than ten minutes.'

'I know what you are saying, Tony, but nevertheless we must take precautions no matter what.'

'Yeah, OK, Fred, I understand.'

'Right, let's make a move. We should get up to the farm to see Tom and Bob.' As we prepared to leave Freddy's place, I recall him speaking softly to his wife Sadie, who was stood in the hallway holding his baby son. 'I won't be too long love. It's just a bit of business I am going to see about.' Then he kissed them both before leaving. It was a heartwarming moment.

We arrived at Tom and Bob's farm to pick up the most important part of our working equipment: the gelignite and detonators.

After exchanging pleasantries with the two farmers and having a brief chat, we returned to the car and Tony drove us away.

Bob and Tom were two real good fellas. They kept themselves to themselves and they never questioned what we were up to; mind you, we always looked after them as far as money was concerned; after all, they were taking a huge risk letting us store our explosives on the farm.

CHAPTER 32

THE LAUNDRY CAPER

So, we set off on our journey to Wales. To me Wales was... well obviously, it was another country. To my pals and I, as just little kids, it was a faraway land! In the early nineteen fifties some Liverpool kids, who were a little more fortunate than us in those days, would spend happy summers there with their parents on family holidays and, this was all I knew about Wales at the time.

Tony drove the car, with my brother alongside him in the passenger seat and me sitting alone in the back. As we embarked on this journey, I began to feel a little differently about Wales, a bit uneasy. It had become quite dark now as it must have been around eight o'clock. We had just passed through the famous Mersey Tunnel and emerged on the other side of Liverpool's great river. We were approaching the main road with led into Wales.

It brought back memories to me of coming to these parts on a school day trip. I'm only talking about five years previous, as I was still only seventeen years old, remember. We were all dead happy little kids full of exhilaration and wonder. It was our first school outing and we were thoroughly enjoying every magical moment. As we travelled along, being young boys and girls, we messed about on the school bus singing as we did and taking in all the sights of this new land. At the end of the day, we couldn't wait to get back and tell everyone at home all about our exciting trip out to Wales. Now though, as we drove along and knowing full well what we were about to do, I felt decidedly tense and apprehensive. Out here we were in unchartered territory!

Half an hour or so later we were deeper into Wales and we

finally arrived in the town of Wrexham. The place looked and felt a lot different at nighttime as opposed to the daytime when we had been here to take a look round and I couldn't help but feel a little anxious. Tony drove the car at a steady speed through the town as he headed for the place we had decided was a good position just the day before. It was alongside a local pub and not too far away from our target: the big laundry factory. Tony pulled the car nice and easily into the street at the side of the pub, which surprisingly was open. This was unusual as in those days the public houses in Wales were often closed on Sundays. There were several other cars parked up there so our car didn't look out of place. The time was not far past nine o'clock and a few people were still out and about; not too many though, just a few. For a moment or so, the three of us just sat in the car taking in our surroundings. We had planned to make the rest of the journey on foot as walking steadily it would only take us about eight to ten minutes.

Freddy broke the silence: 'Let's get going.' He turned around to me before he got out of the car. 'Like we have agreed, Charlie, you and Tony follow me and whichever street we take to get there, the two of you stay on the opposite side from me. OK?'

'Yeah, OK,' I replied.

This was a significant thing for Freddy to say. There was a good reason for it. Freddy would be carrying the explosives in his pocket and if pulled and searched by any police out on foot patrol that evening, he would be arrested immediately and for a serious offence. Walking alone, he would appear less conspicuous and therefore less likely to get a pull. Also he was smartly dressed and looked just like any other member of the public out on a Sunday night making his way home.

As for Tony, he too was smartly dressed and was carrying nothing incriminating; just his gloves in his coat pocket and as it was winter time this was nothing out of the ordinary. Me: I had a cut-down crowbar secreted up the sleeve of my jacket, a small torch and a pair of gloves on. Now, if I thought I was going to be stopped by any police, within seconds, I would leg it around a couple of streets and quickly dispose of the crowbar, taking care nobody saw me do it. I would then put myself on offer by quietly and nonchalantly walking back down the street. I mean, what could the bizzies do arresting me? For what charge? These were precautions we had to take and to be prepared for anything. In these small towns, the police knew everyone in their community and a stranger would look prominent.

My brother got out of the car first and began to walk at a steady pace, then Tony and I got out to follow on behind Freddy but on the opposite side of the road, keeping our eyes on Freddy. There were still a few people about but not as many as before; just the odd couple trickling past. They were probably making their way home as people used to get home early on Sundays in preparation for work the next day. As I mentioned previously, jobs were numerous and most people were in employment back then. Tony and I continued to meander through the town about forty to fifty paces behind Freddy, who was still on the opposite side.

'So far so good, Charl. There's not a bizzie in sight.'

'Yeah,' I replied. 'But it's only early yet, Tony.' It was usually about nine o'clock when the plod started their patrolling of the streets. They would check property, ensure there was no public disorder and generally just keep a lookout for any trouble. I continued to stroll along with Tony Burns, and although I had heard good reports of him, he was someone I wasn't at all familiar with. I began to take note of his mannerisms like the way he talked, which was fairly fast and high pitched. I think he was about Freddy's age, late twenties maybe thirties. He was of average build with dark hair which he wore in a side parting. The dark grey suit he was wearing just didn't look right on him somehow. I don't know why; maybe it was just me being a teenager and fashion conscious. He talked quite a lot and he kept turning his head left and right, which in my opinion made him appear suspicious.

'There's plenty of readies inside of that peter we're gonna have off, Charlie.' As he said this he rubbed his hands together. 'I can't wait.'

I thought to myself, This fella is starting to count his chickens before they have hatched. It felt like there was a stranger in our camp. Freddy, Tosh, the Oates brothers and I all worked well together; we were a good team, but something about this fella didn't feel right.

We had been walking for about five or six minutes. It was the usual routine with Freddy leading the way up ahead of us. We had reached the edge of the town by now and looming at the top end of the street just a couple of minutes away was the big old laundry factory. It was dark now as there were no street lights. Taking a good look around, we could see there wasn't a soul in sight. Up ahead of us Freddy turned into the street up the side of the factory and suddenly disappeared from our sight.

'We're here, Charl,' Tony said. 'All ready to go.' Tony was telling me this as if I didn't know what was going on. I was concentrating on my brother so I was well aware of what was going on. I had long since stopped listening to him chattering away. He had a voice that was now beginning to get on my nerves.

When our Freddy had disappeared from view I quickly urged Tony: 'Let's catch up to him.' I began to walk at a faster pace and Tony kept up by my side. We soon caught up with Freddy. The street we were on at the side of the factory's perimeter was dark and there the three of us stood and paused for a few moments

'Forget about us going in the front way,' our Freddy said sternly. It's lit up; it's too risky. We could get spotted.'

'I thought we agreed to go in the front way,' Tony answered back in his infuriatingly grating voice. 'I mean, the door looked easy enough to knock off.'

'Tony, I've told you it's a fuckin' no,' Freddy said with exasperation. 'We will get over this perimeter fence, find a way around the back and break in there, at the rear of the premises.' He said this with a decidedly annoyed tone in his voice. I don't think *he* was too happy with Tony's interference all the time either.

'Oh, alright then,' Tony said. 'Whichever way you think.'

All three of us made our way quickly and quietly to the

perimeter wall at the rear end of the factory. It was like the middle of nowhere. There was a field on the opposite side of the street and everywhere was eerily and dauntingly silent. We all stopped and took a last quick look up and down the dark, deserted street.

'Come on get over and be quick,' our Freddy said urgently. Almost in unison, we climbed over that wall pretty fast and in turn we dropped down on the other side. Once over, Freddy quickly got up and led the way in single file around to the back of the factory. When we got around the back, we were faced with two huge doors and about six or eight tall ground floor windows. We stood and gazed at the two huge, robust doors which appeared, unfortunately for us, big and impenetrable. Just by looking at them, I knew that my crowbar was no match. Surprisingly though, we noticed that two of the factory's tall windows were slightly open. The window frames were made of steel or iron and were really old fashioned in a Georgian style with long window panes. This was unbelievable, it seemed as though this big old factory was inviting us inside. Freddy and I looked up at the open windows.

Freddy shook his head. 'I don't believe this. The security here is so lax. You would never see anything as negligent as this in and around Liverpool.' He paused for a moment, then gestured towards the open window. 'That's our best way in.' We had already looked at the front doors of the factory a couple of days before and we had been confident that we could open them easily with a stick (crowbar), unfortunately though, we had to abandon that way of entry because like my brother had said with the front being well lit we would be putting ourselves on offer gaining entry that way.

I looked at Freddy. 'I'll get through that window and see if there is a way to open one of those back doors.'

'Yeah, OK, kid,' he replied. 'It would be a lot better if you could.'

'Give us a lift up to the windowsill then.' The windowsill was made of old thick stone and was about four foot long and about a foot wide. Freddy bent down and with palms up, he clasped both his hands together. I put my foot onto his hands and as I did so he gave one great heave up and with this help I easily reached the windowsill. The iron window frame was about six foot tall. The bottom half of the window was closed but the top half was slightly open. I grabbed hold of the top half and began to pull the window towards me to open it up wider. This made it wide enough for me to easily gain access.

I climbed through the window and let myself down onto the floor on the other side. I took a quick look around and found that I was in a room full of industrial sized washing equipment. This was obviously the factory floor where all the laundry was boiled and washed. This explained why the windows were slightly open; it was for ventilation when the place was in full swing and filled with steam from the great stainless steel vats that were all around. There were huge extractor fans that must have had to work to full capacity for a room as big as this one. Everything was huge. There must have been hundreds of laundry baskets dotted around too, and great big bags full of laundry, either waiting to be done or waiting to be delivered back to wherever they had come from. It looked to me like the whole of Wales sent their washing here as it was a massive concern. This place must have employed a large work force to man all this equipment

It was fairly dark in there and at first I couldn't see well. So, with my back to the wall underneath the window I had just come in through, I started to edge my way along it until I came to the back entrance door. Then I heard my brother's voice coming from the other side of it: 'Are you OK in there, kid?'

'Yeah. I'm just going to try to open this door.' I began to examine the door to see how I *could* open it. It had a bolt at the top and bottom both of which I proceeded to unbolt but annoyingly, it was still locked. There was a large keyhole lock in the door which, I could tell by the feel of, was a good strong lock. I called to my brother, 'I have unbolted it but it is locked on the inside.'

My brother answered me back: 'That will be a mortice lock. There's no point in trying to force that. It will be too strong and we can't afford to make much of a noise.' Freddy was right; these mortice locks were hard to break open and the jemmy I had with me would be no match for it at all. My brother called again from behind the door: 'Charlie, we will come through the window. It's the only way.'

'Yeah, I think that's best.' I made my way back to the open window and to my surprise, when I got there my brother was already half way through it, quickly followed by Tony. Once we were all on the inside, we stood and took a brief moment to survey our surroundings, get our bearings and take it all in.

Turning to Tony, Freddy broke the silence: 'The safe is on the second floor, isn't it?'

'Yeah,' Tony replied. 'It is.'

'OK. Let's make our way up there.'

Our eyes had now become accustomed to the dark and although there were no lights outside, there was still just enough light coming through the tall windows to enable us to see. This was fortunate because it meant that we didn't have to use the torch, which could possibly have been seen from outside. We reached the far side of the factory floor and came across the huge, wide staircase. The three of us cautiously made our way up the steps. Even though we had had good information and was told that everything would be safe and sound in here, it was still always in the back of your mind that there could be a night watchman around that could find us on our way up to the floor with the safe. We reached the top of the stairs and I'm sure the other two must have been experiencing the same feelings as I was, which was my heart pounding in my chest, adrenaline pumping around my system and coursing through my veins as we were creeping around in the still of night. At the top stairs there was another huge expanse of space and although we were faced with numerous doors to different rooms we quickly found the door to the office. Unbelievably, it wasn't locked! It just had a normal door handle to open it... so we entered the office.

'We will need some light in here,' my brother Freddy said. 'We will just have to use the glim.' (torch)

I thought for a moment and then spoke to Freddy: 'Can't we get one of those laundry sheets from downstairs and put it up to the window? Then we can use the lights to see what we are doing properly. There are plenty of them down there.'

'Yeah, that's good,' Freddy replied. 'We will need to bring some of those up here anyway to pack the safe when I'm ready to blow it.'

In the office, which was typically furnished, we found the safe exactly where we were told it would be up against the wall on the far side of the room and it was a big strong looking one too. 'Fuck... that's a big one!' our Freddy exclaimed.

We all stood and looked at it. Since we had come up here, not a word had been uttered from Tony's lips, which was unusual because he was always gabbing away. Now though he had gone quiet. He stood staring at the safe as if being in awe of it all. Then suddenly he piped up. "There's plenty inside of that,' he sounded almost like he was gloating. 'And it was good info we got.'

Freddy just murmured back to him, 'Yeah, yeah.' He spoke as if to say, *We haven't even opened it yet and there he is saying there's plenty in it. I've heard all this before.* Sometimes nothing was as we had thought; there were occasions when we had blown a safe and found it to contain nothing at all, or certainly not what had been promised. 'Look, Charlie, I'm going to make a start on this. Tony, you get hold of the torch and keep it dead, dead low. I only need to see the front of the safe... nothing else.'

I passed the torch to Tony. 'What about the covering of the windows?' I asked. 'It's foolish to put that torch on yet.' First we tried the torch out by shining it on the floor. It was quite a dim light so in the end we didn't have to cover the window. Tony got even more excited and animated now. He was keen to see what Freddy was doing to prepare the safe. He seemed eager to assist. As Freddy crouched down by the safe and got ready to set it up for the explosives, Tony crouched down next to him shining the torch, which left me just standing there, however, I made a suggestion: 'Look, kid, I think it would be better if I kept lookout on the top windows. I can keep my eye on everything outside then, you know, just in case.'

'Yeah, OK,' my brother replied.

I planned to make my way back to the window where I would be able to observe the back and front of the place. I would just keep down low and look through each window in turn, patrolling and keeping looking out a window at a time. 'You never know, Freddy. I mean there are lots of people around here and it's dead quiet out there.'

'Yeah, OK,' he replied. 'But when I have set this up, we will have to bring some of that stuff up here to pack it.'

On hearing this, Tony, being eager, quickly stood up. 'I'll shoot back down the stairs and fetch a bag of that laundry up now, eh Fred?'

'Tony, get back down here and just concentrate on holding that fuckin' torch still for me, will you?'

'Oh, alright, I just thought it would save time, Fred.'

'No, Tony, just stay put with me. We can get the packing gear after I've set all this up.' I could see my brother was getting really annoyed with him. I also sensed that tensions were beginning to build. After all, neither Freddy nor myself had ever worked with Tony before this and it did seem a bit strange... well, to me it did anyway. I felt uncomfortable with him and I knew my brother did too.

I made my way up to the next floor hoping that the dust would settle between my brother and Tony. I knew Freddy could be abrupt at times as I had seen his tantrums with the rest of our crew on many an occasion, but hey, that's just the way he was made. He just wanted everything done properly and thoroughly; he was a perfectionist and that was that.

I took a look through the first window I came to which was at the front of the factory on the third floor. I vigilantly scanned the area of the street outside. It was deserted at both ends other than the odd car driving past every so often. The time must have been getting on to about half past nine by now and I just hoped that this would only take a few more minutes. I was eager to get the hell out of there.

I don't know why but, I kept getting an uneasy feeling being here in this place. I felt uncomfortable because we were out of our usual area. We knew the streets of Liverpool and the surrounding areas so well. We were familiar with the movement of the police there and the beat their patrols took them on. Whereas, this was totally out of our comfort zone and something just didn't feel right about it. I told myself that I had better snap out of this feeling and concentrate on what I was supposed to be doing. I took another glance through the window and so far everything seemed fine. It was still quiet out there. I contemplated that with the place being so quiet on the outside, we would have to make sure we used plenty of packing around the safe to muffle the sound as much as possible. Any sound would travel in the stillness of the night around there. There was one thing for sure though: there would be no shortage of packing. There were bag upon bags of laundry in this place.

I decided to move over to the back end of the building across the massive factory floor. There were more windows there, similar to the ones at the front. I looked out through the first one and again saw nothing out of the ordinary. The road the factory was on had a street at each end and a huge field opposite the factory building. The streets at each end of the road were deserted and the field opposite the factory was in complete darkness. Just as I was concentrating on keeping lookout, I heard my brother calling me from downstairs. I ran across the floor and down the wide stairs to Freddy and Tony.

'I just set everything up on the peter,' Freddy said. 'We need to get the packing done now, kid. Let's get stuck in and bring those big bags of laundry up.'

'Freddy,' I said. 'I think I should stay on watch on the windows upstairs, you know?' I shot a look at Freddy as if to say *You can never be too sure* but, it was to no avail.

He quickly replied: 'Nah, we need at least a bag each to pack that safe properly. It will take the lot of us to bring them up. So, come on, let's step on it and get it done.'

We all hurried quickly down the stairs to the ground floor where the laundry was all bagged up. Each bag was full to the brim with clothes, towels, sheets etc… you name it, those bags had it in them. We grabbed a bag each and found they *were* heavy alright; they must have weighed nearly a hundred weight (112 lb)!

After us all doing some huffing and puffing, we finally managed to get them up to the office. On entering, I took a quick look around and could see that Freddy had it all prepared. He was a professional, and using his knowledge and skill he had set it all up perfectly. On a closer inspection, I could see the gelignite was packed tightly into the keyhole and that the detonator was set in the centre of it with the fuse left protruding out. It was just the packing to sort out now and because there was plenty of it, it should deaden the sound considerably.

'I want all those bags of clothes emptied,' Freddy said. 'We will try and smother the front of the safe using the backs of a couple of those big office chairs. We can butt them right up to the front of it.'

As Freddy and Tony began to pack the safe with the heavy clothes, I was getting a little concerned. I turned to Freddy. 'Look, I had better get back up those stairs to the next floor and make sure everything is still OK outside.'

He too realised that it was essential I did this. 'Yeah, you do that, Charlie. Me and Tony will sort this out. When we are about to blow it, I will give you a shout, kid.'

So there I was back on the third floor watching and waiting. I was just hoping that everything would go according to plan; I mean this was the main part of the move now; waiting for the door of that safe to be blown. This part of the graft could be nerve wracking at times but because I felt so far away from our own territory, the nerves were much more intense and it became something of a terrifying ordeal... at least for me it did. I had this ill at ease feeling that I *could not* put to the back of my mind. I had to pull myself together and think positively that everything was going to be fine, and that we would be out of there in just a few more minutes from now. I was abruptly shaken from my thoughts by the sound of somebody coming up the stairs. I quickly crossed the factory floor and found that it was Tony.

'Alright, Charl? There's nothing about outside is there?'

'No, everything's dead sound.'

'Brilliant. Only, Freddy sent me up. We are about to blow the peter. He said the minute it goes off, you come right down, Charl. We will be getting off as soon as.'

'Yeah, OK. I know the score, Tony.' He disappeared swiftly down the stairs, seemingly excited.

As I stood lookout at the window, I could feel my heart pounding in my chest and the adrenaline pumping thorough my veins at a pace. I was rooted to the spot, anxiously waiting to hear the thunderous explosion from the peter going off. Then, just as I was contemplating all this...

BOOM!

It went off much louder than I had expected and even though I was waiting for it, it still took me by surprise and I could have sworn that the very ground beneath my feet shuddered!

Coming to my senses, I took a last look through the windows one by one, on both back and front of the building. I couldn't see anybody at all, and so being confident that all was still quiet, I ran across the floor to the stairs. The adrenaline in my system gave me enormous drive and I shot down that staircase two at a time as it pumped and throbbed in my veins. It was only a matter of seconds before I had reached my brother and Tony at the safe.

They were frantically pulling the packing away from the safe. Then to all our shock we found that the door was still intact. The lock had failed to blow as it should have. Panic station was setting in now. We had to get out of there as fast as possible because even though there was plenty of packing on and around the safe it hadn't seem to deaden the sound. It was an almighty bang and somebody outside must certainly have heard it. Tony was kneeling down in front of the safe trying to pull the safe door open. He just wouldn't accept that it was useless and that it was still jammed shut.

CHAPTER 33

BREAKING OUR GOLDEN RULES

'Come on, we have got to get out of here fast!' Freddy more or less shouted at Tony.

One of our golden rules and a rule not to be broken was that if the safe didn't open the first time we didn't hang about. We just got the fuck out of the place as soon as.

Tony stood up from the safe which he had been trying unsuccessfully to open. There wasn't a flicker out of him, unlike me and Freddy, we were on tenterhooks ready to run out of the place. We couldn't understand how he seemed not to care or realise the danger that could be awaiting us if we didn't move fast. 'What's the panic for?' Tony asked looking at the two of us. I couldn't believe what I was hearing him ask. This proved too much for my brother Freddy. He lost it...

'The panic is this... if we hang around here much longer we will all come unstuck. Do you understand what I am saying?'

'Yeah, I understand what you are on about, Freddy but, don't you realise how much money is in that peter. It's full to the brim.' Before my perplexed brother could answer, he went on. 'Look, Fred, that lock on the safe door is practically broken. If we give it one more, quick blow, I know and so do you that it will open.' Freddy couldn't believe what he was hearing from Tony now. Then seeming oblivious, Tony began to almost beg Freddy, trying to persuade him to have another go at the safe. 'Come on, Fred, it will only take a couple of minutes. Think of all the dough inside of it.'

For a moment, I thought it looked as if my brother was toying with the idea, so I gave him a look as if to say, *You are breaking the rules that we have always stood by. Safety comes first.*

'Tony, I couldn't care if there was a million quid in that peter, we are going now and that is it.'

Three or four minutes had now passed since the loud explosion of the safe and that's a long time in this dangerous situation we found ourselves in.

'I'll stay and blow it myself. There's a fortune in there. If you two want to fuck off, well, that's fine by me.'

My brother sharply turned to me and I could see he was absolutely fuming. Then, what Freddy did next shocked me. He actually gave what was left of the jelly and the detonator to Tony. 'Come on, Charlie. Let's get out of here.'

We were about to leave when I had a thought and turned to my brother. 'I'll take a quick look upstairs, kid, and make sure the coast is clear outside.'

My brother looked at me quizzically. 'Charlie, time is running out on us.'

Just as I was about to run up the stairs I saw Tony actually bend down in front of the safe to try to set it up again. Oh no, I thought to myself, This is mad, everything is going crazy here. I ran as fast as I could up the stairs. I had never experienced anything like this before. My mouth was dry and my body was trembling. I could still feel my heart beating fast and loud going ten to the dozen in my chest. I reached the top of the stairs and headed straight for the front windows. Just as I approached them I thought I saw a flash of light outside. I stopped dead in my tracks. I froze and thought for a moment. No, my mind is playing tricks on me here. Still, cautiously, I looked out of the window. Then... I saw them!

Two uniformed policemen wearing tall helmets outside the factory. They both carried torches. My young heart beat like a drum and came up to my throat; it felt as if it were in my mouth. I immediately pulled away from the window hoping and praying that they hadn't seen me. I stood there for what felt like the longest minute. The beams from their torches flashed intermittently around the walls of the large room I was in. They were obviously looking around outside the building using the torchlight in the pitch black of the night.

This can't be happening, I thought frantically. It's like a bad dream… a nightmare! Desperately, I shouted down to Freddy and Tony from the top of the stairs: 'It's the bizzies, it's the bizzies! They're outside of the factory now!'

The two of them came running to the bottom of the stairs.

Freddy began shouting to me: 'Come on, come down. We will go out the back window.'

I went running down those stairs as fast as possible to Freddy and Tony. Tony's whole demeanour and attitude had changed dramatically by now. He looked totally shocked; now it was *him* who was panicking.

He spoke sheepishly to Freddy in a hoarse voice: 'What the fuck? What can we do?'

'Head for that back window,' Freddy replied quickly. 'The way we came in.'

All three of us hurried to the back window but when we got there we found that there were even more police outside by now – even around the back. I suddenly noticed the presence of a Black Maria (police van), with its lights on. It was parked in the street between the factory and the field. As well as all the police outside there were also local people beginning to gather around. They were obviously here to see what the commotion was all about. I looked at my brother, and somehow I knew what he was thinking and how he was feeling... how had it all come to this?

'That's it,' he said, looking at all the activity outside. 'We're finished. They have got us bang to rights.' I knew my brother was never a defeatist, but with the situation we now found ourselves in, there was really nothing we could do *except* admit defeat.

I had an idea and it could be our only hope, our last chance. I shook Freddy's arm. 'Hey, kid. I'll shoot back up to the top floor. There may be a sky light or an opening we could get through. You know? Maybe a drainpipe we could climb down? There could be a way out here.'

Freddy looked at Tony and I. 'OK, let's go up there.'

The three of us quickly dashed up the stairs. We passed the second floor and carried on up the next flight of stairs to the third floor. All three of us must have been thinking the same thing because before we did anything else we ran to the windows and looked outside. What we saw and heard out there made my heart sink.

There were even more police surrounding the factory now and from the window we had a good view out along the main road where we could see a long black police car racing to the scene. The bell on the top of the police car was ringing like mad. Incidentally, they didn't have the sirens that we have today on modern police cars; primitively they had an actual bell on the roof. The car arriving was a black 1950s Austin Westminster, a big, powerful, solid motor. It pulled up screeching to a halt at the front of the factory. Only high ranking top bizzies drove around in cars like that, so we knew full well that the detective inspector and his cronies had just arrived.

We stood and watched in silence as all four doors opened simultaneously and out they stepped... dressed in plain clothes, suits, coats and hats. One of them who seemed to take charge appeared to be instructing the uniformed policemen and barking orders at them. These were obviously the detectives of the C.I.D. They were all after a piece of the action. This was a disaster we were watching unfolding before us. Tony looked like he had already given up the ghost; he had a bewildered expression on his face, saying nothing and staring blankly out of the window.

Freddy shouted to him to keep well back from the window as we hadn't been spotted yet. We urgently began to rush around from place to place searching for a way out. It was no use; everywhere we looked we could see policemen so it became quite apparent to all three of us that we were totally surrounded. It gave us the impression that the entire Welsh police force were out there surrounding the factory that night. They had us completely trapped, unequivocally cut off. With a sinking feeling I knew now and so too did my brother and Tony that there was no escape!

I really felt for my brother and what he was going to have to face once again. There was a quick discussion between us about what to do next. Freddy broke the deathly silence in a sombre tone. 'This is it. We'll just have to hold our hands up and face what's coming to us.

I looked back at him. He was totally downhearted by it all. 'Kid,' I said to him. 'Maybe you could hide somewhere in here while me and Tony front up to the bizzies. You know... we'll convince them that there is only the two of us.'

I shot Tony a quizzical look. 'You will go along with that, Tony, won't you?'

'Of course, Charlie,' Tony replied. 'That goes without saying.' He went on to apologise to my brother.

'Honest to God, I'm dead sorry, Freddy. This is all down to me. We should have got out of there after that first blow.'

'Tony, forget it. What's done is done.'

'Yeah, but...' The look to kill on my brother's face shut him right up.

'Besides, the C.I.D. would go over this place like a fine toothed comb if I tried to hide in here. I might have stood a chance if it was only the uniformed police but the C.I.D. they are meticulous with their investigations.'

So that little plan was abandoned and we decided to go back down the stairs and face our arch enemy... the police! We had almost reached the ground floor when we heard the back door being unlocked and opened; the very back door that we couldn't break through earlier on.

Then we heard a loud voice shout out, 'Hey, you lot. Come out now and give yourselves up. It's the police. We have the place surrounded.' Then there was silence for a moment or so before the voice shouted again. 'Can you hear me? We know you're up there. Come on be sensible and come down.'

For another brief moment we all stood frozen to the spot upstairs, then Freddy shouted down to them. 'OK, we're on our way down.' The three of us cautiously walked down the stairs. Freddy was at the front with Tony and I behind him.

As we reached the bottom of the stairs, the police were waiting for us. There was about six or seven of them and a man in plain clothes who must have been the manager of the factory as he had the keys to the place and had obviously unlocked the secure solid back door that had been impossible for me to open. The door was wide open and all were stood inside almost forming a circle. We could also see that there were quite a few more standing outside. I had never in my life seen this many bizzies all together in one place at one time. We were quickly surrounded and they began to put on the handcuffs. After they had checked that the cuffs were on properly, they led us to the door.

The one who seemed to be of the highest ranking, spoke to us: 'OK, boys. Is it just the three of you?' We all nodded solemnly. 'Right then, let's go.'

We were led away in single file: Freddy once again at the front, me in the middle and Tony at the rear. We each had a policeman leading us out by the arm. We were led around the side of the factory towards the front entrance, where the Black Maria waited ominously. To get to this police van we had to walk past the crowd of locals that had gathered outside. They swarmed around and looked us up and down. This crowd wasn't hostile at all but we were being closely inspected as we were escorted past them towards the parked up Black Maria. We could see the policemen smiling as they mutually congratulated each other on the successful apprehension of catching safe blowers as they were actually in the act of blowing a safe. For the inhabitants of this small town of Wrexham, this subjugation was obviously a huge event. For the local police force it was a real feather in their cap.

We were driven straight to the police station where we were put through the usual procedure of being searched asked our names and addresses etc. I was the last one to be processed. It was the uniformed desk sergeant who took down our particulars. Freddy and Tony had already been escorted to their cells. It was my turn now. The uniformed desk sergeant was a heavily built fella who looked to be in his forties and had a big red face, looking like he spent more time outdoors than here behind a desk inside the police station.

He looked kindly at me. 'How old are you, son?' I told him that I was seventeen; not quite eighteen. As he took down my details, he made no attempt to intimidate me at all; in fact, he did all he could to put me at my ease. Actually, he spoke to me in a soft fatherly manner: 'You're just a kid, aren't you? What on earth are you doing mixed up in this sort of thing?'

I didn't answer him. I just stood looking down at the floor. He took me to my cell and unlocked the door for me. I walked in silently. Then before closing the door, the police sergeant stopped and looked at me. 'I'll get you an extra blanket, son. It's cold in there. I'll get you a mug of hot cocoa. That'll soon warm you up.' With this he closed and locked the cell door.

The cells holding us were on a corridor just off from the main part of the police station. There was just a blank tiled wall opposite the cell doors, so there was nothing to look out on. They were really quite isolated. Each door had a square hatch in the centre, so that, if they needed to pass anything in to you like for instance a drink or food, this hatch made the task easier to do.

My brother Freddy was in the cell next to mine. He popped his head out of the hatch in his cell door and called to me. 'What's going to happen now, Charlie, is the C.I.D. will come to interview us, separately of course.' Having been through this sort of thing before, Freddy was something of an expert on the procedure. 'It won't just be the local C.I.D., there'll be others coming from different parts of the country where safes have been done. They'll ask you to T.I.C. them (take into consideration) basically; what they'll offer is for the three of us to admit to other jobs done in the past. And that is a definite no! We know nothing of the other jobs so don't fall for any of their flannel 'cause they haven't got a thing on us; if they did, they would have been on to us sooner. They'll be bluffing. What you say to them, and keep saying to them, is that you want to see a lawyer before you speak. Obviously, we won't get a brief straight away. They'll probably keep us here for a couple of days.'

PHOTOS

FRANCIS

KEIRON

At the beginning of my life of crime these men were my mentors.

I found them to be men of decency and principles.

I would also like to point out that no violence of any kind was ever used during the safe-blowing crimes we committed.

JOHNNY

TOSH

CHARLIE

CHAPTER 34

VISITORS FROM DIFFERENT PARTS OF THE COUNTRY

Freddy was dead right about all this. The next day police officers came to visit us from all over the North of England and The Midlands. They wanted us to admit to other jobs done in their areas. Most of the jobs in these places that they tried to pin on me were in parts of the country that I had never even heard of let alone visited. I just stuck to my guns the way Freddy had advised me to. I adhered to another one of our golden rules that if I was ever picked up by the police for questioning I would keep my mouth shut and admit to nothing, even when caught red-handed the way we had been here, and that's exactly what I did. This obviously really annoyed the detectives who wasted so much of their time questioning me.

I recall two in particular who came into my cell. We had the good cop, bad cop. The bad cop tried to intimidate me by pacing around, whereas, the good cop looked calmer and spoke softer.

I was sitting down in my cell when the bad cop spoke to me first: 'You're Charlie Seiga, aren't you?'

'Yes.'

'Right, well now I want you to listen carefully to what I have to say.' His voice and attitude were intimidating. 'You know and we know there have been numerous safes being blown by you and the gang you operate with. We are here to clear a few of those safe robberies up and it would be in your best interest to co-operate with us.' He stopped for a brief moment. I think he thought that because I was just a young kid I would be an easy touch. So he went on: 'Do you understand?'

They were both towering over me. I looked up at them as I was sitting on the bed in the cell.

The good cop interrupted: 'Hello, Charlie. I am Detective Sergeant Jones,' he said mildly. 'My colleague and I have come to ask you a few questions. It's about a certain picture house where a safe was blown. It happened quite some months ago now in our vicinity. You see, Charlie, these safe blowing robberies that have been taking place have similarities. We have to ask you these questions, Charlie, as we believe it was your gang who carried this out. There is one picture house in particular that I want to question you about. When the explosion went off boxes and boxes of cartons of orange juice were splattered all over the place. I remember it was a right mess. Some of us were slipping on the orange juice and getting covered in it.' He smiled, and I sort of smiled back at him as I recalled so vividly that move we did with the orange juice and everything, it was such a crazy night.

The bad cop saw me smile and immediately sprang into action. 'Come on! Admit to it. We know it was you and those others in there.' He was alluding to Freddy and Tony of course. He was looking down at me and glaring now. 'Come on, you little bastard! I'll wipe that smile from your face.'

I just replied to him in my young innocent voice, speaking soft and low: 'I think you're mistaken officer, it wasn't me. I know nothing about it at all.'

His face was red with rage and his two hands were clenched into white knuckle fists. If I had been in custody in his vicinity, I would know what was coming next. Most Liverpool bizzies at the time were renowned for violence on prisoners in their cells but because I wasn't in his jurisdiction, he knew and I knew that he couldn't do anything heavy with me. Besides, there was a uniformed policeman outside of my cell all the time that I was being interviewed. After all, I was in custody of the Welsh police and they were responsible for my welfare.

'OK,' he said sarcastically. 'Play it your way, smart-arse. But remember, we are coming back to charge you.' With this he stormed out of the cell closely followed by the good cop.

Then I heard my brother's voice calling to them from the cell next door to mine and I quickly put my head through the hatch in the door to listen. He called to the bad cop. 'Excuse me, officer.'

'Yeah, what?' the bad cop asked.

'He's a good kid in there, isn't he? Freddy replied. 'A real good kid.'

'Yeah,' the bad cop retorted. 'You have him well tutored.'

He walked away down the corridor in a huff. Then I heard Freddy shout to me from his cell next door: 'Are you alright in there, Charl?'

'Yeah, dead sound,' I reassured him.

Then Tony shouted to me, 'Charlie, Charlie, can you hear me? That cop who just interviewed you, he was a right bastard, wasn't he? The other one was alright though.'

'Yeah, he was, yeah.'

Then Tony went on: 'The bad one was grilling me quite a lot himself. The first thing he asked me was, "Come on, Tony, what do you know about this jelly?" I just said to him, the only jelly I know is Hartley's!' (Hartley's was a firm that made jelly and jam in Liverpool). 'Do you get that, Charl? Hartley's jelly?' he said laughing. 'He didn't like it at all and he just pissed right off out of my cell. I never uttered another word to the bastard.' I had my head out of the hatch in my door and hearing Tony laughing made me laugh too then Freddy joined in.

During our stay at this police station, we often got some of the bizzies coming into our cells to stare at us through the hatch in the door. Most of them wouldn't say anything; they would just nod and smile, whereas others simply stared. We could hear them chatting among themselves as they walked away from the cells. It was like the circus had come to town. However, for us this was no joke; this was real! It was as if we had become famous overnight. I thought to myself, Is this what fame is all about? Because if it is, you could keep it! I was sure by then that this was the biggest thing that had ever happened in the little town called Wrexham.

After the lengthy questioning we had endured by the police

forces from other parts of the country, we were eventually charged with safe blowing by the Welsh police. The following morning we made a brief appearance before the local Magistrates Court. We had been in custody for two long days. My worst fears that morning in court were not about the court itself with the magistrates and the police; although that alone was intimidating enough to a young kid like me, but no, my worst fear was the presence in court of my mother and sister.

The court room was absolutely packed out. It was standing room only. I think the whole population of the city of Chester must have been in there. They had all come to see the three safe blowers that had made the news. After all this was a high profile case and they all wanted a front row seat at the proceedings.

The atmosphere was tense and I remember standing in the dock, alongside Tony and Freddy, and not hearing a word that was being said. I was taking hardly any notice of what was being said or the proceedings taking place. The only thing that I could think about was my mother and how ashamed I was of myself for bringing this trouble to her door. Every time she looked over at me, I just hung my head in shame. I knew though, that she would blame Freddy for all of this, just the look on her face told me so every time she looked across the packed courtroom at him. Some of Tony's family had travelled over to make an appearance in court too so we were all well supported... for all the good it would do!

Our representation conducted the procedure of our defence to the best of their abilities, and although my solicitor tried his best to get bail for me, due to the seriousness of the charge it was all to no avail. All three of us were remanded in custody to Her Majesty's Prison Walton, Liverpool until the next court appearance which could take up to two or three weeks.

CHAPTER 35

MY FIRST TIME IN THE BIG HOUSE

I had never seen the inside of a prison before and what a revelation when I first walked in there. It wasn't the conditions that shocked me so much as the prisoners themselves. Walton Prison had a notorious name at that time due to the number of hard cases, tough villains and gangsters that were housed there. What astounded me was that instead of the young, tough men I had expected to find in there I discovered that the majority of the prisoners were dregs. I couldn't believe how, so called, hardened convicts could sacrifice so much of their self-respect and go creeping and crawling around some of the screws. Some even went so far as resorting to snitching on one another, and personally, I found that despicable. I did however find some of the fellas doing time in there to be OK, but they were few and far between. Those types though retained their pride and dignity. I don't want to talk too much about prison life as it sounds so tedious and to me the stories you hear about the prison life all sound the same.

We were all getting regular visits from our families most days and on one of these visits Johnny Oates came in. He broke the news about Keiron's trial in London. He said Keiron was found guilty and sentenced to seven years. It was a blow to us all. I just couldn't imagine Keiron being locked away for so long and to me, because I was only just a kid, seven years was like an eternity.

After a couple of weeks in Walton Jail had passed by Tony, Freddy and I were hauled back to Wales for a hearing of how we were going to plead. We each decided to plead guilty. We had no other choice really; after all we were caught bang to rights.

Besides, what was the use of pleading not guilty? It would only serve to provoke the courts. Being so young, and having no previous convictions, I was granted bail that day, procured by the good work of my defence team. All three of us were sent for trial at Chester Crown Court. My brother and Tony were escorted back to Walton Jail while I had to wait in Wrexham police station until somebody came to bail me out. Eventually my old fella and a good neighbour of ours called Frank came for me. I was dreading the reception I would receive when I arrived home, especially when it came to fronting up to my mother. I just knew that all hell would break loose.

On arrival home though, the anxiety and worry I had put myself through during the journey had been totally unnecessary. It turned out that the anticipation of what to expect from my mother was much worse than what actually happened. Instead of the hostile reception I had expected she literally threw all the blame on our Freddy. 'I know, Charlie, son, that he encouraged you. He put you up to it all. He's a bad influence.'

How could I possibly answer to that? If only she knew the truth: that only I were to blame not my brother. In fact looking back on it all, it had all been down to me. It was all my idea about the jelly, the explosives, for safe blowing. Maybe if I'd never mentioned it to Freddy and the rest of our crew, we wouldn't have been in the regretful predicament we found ourselves in. What was done was done though, and all the ifs and buts and maybes wouldn't change a thing.

CHAPTER 36

THE TRIAL

Sat with my brother and Tony in the dock of Chester High Court that day in 1958 was tense. All three of us had thrown ourselves at the mercy of Lord Justice Castles by pleading guilty. It was approaching lunchtime and following my lawyer speaking with the Judge, the court proceedings had come to an abrupt halt. The Judge had decided to adjourn until two o'clock and on our return to court we would be sentenced.

We were led out of the dock and down into what appeared to be the cellars of the court. We were locked together in a huge cell that resembled a dark dungeon from the olden days. The names of prisoners from days gone by were scrawled on the cold dank walls. God only knows what fate awaited the poor convicts of those days. This was an old building we were confined in which dated back hundreds of years.

After being locked up for about five or ten minutes, two prison guards came and unlocked our cell. They gave each of us some food and drink after which our lawyers came in to have a final word with us. It was mostly about the sentences we would receive, which, by the way they were talking, didn't sound optimistic, especially for my brother and Tony. Their lawyers told them that unfortunately they could expect long sentences. My lawyer though, appeared more positive; he had plenty of confidence, mostly about the Judge not being too severe with me. This gave all three of us at least some consolation if nothing else. The lawyer went on to tell us that the Judge's wife and young daughter, who was about my age, had been sitting in the public gallery throughout the whole trial and he smiled at me as he went on to say, 'So let's hope he has a change of heart in your case, eh Charlie?'

Two o'clock finally came around and we were led back up from the dungeons and into the dock to hear of our fate. I quickly glanced around the court room and it was absolutely packed to the rafters with the curious, viewing public. The court buzzed with the hustle and bustle of everyone returning to their seats and their places in the court room.

Mr Justice Castles entered the court room and regained his prominent seat in the high chair above the full court. This restored a hushed calm across the room. He sat stony faced as he regarded the three of us stood in the dock. He waited until everyone was settled and it went quiet among the court officials. Just the rustle of papers from the lawyers and the odd juror trying to stifle a cough could be heard and it was then, and only then that the Judge commenced his speech. He began by outlining the case which was one of the highest profile cases in the land at that time. It was also the most dangerous as it involved the use of explosives.

'The crown prosecutor was right,' the Judge said, 'when he said that neither of you showed any concern for safety precautions. It could have resulted in someone being seriously hurt or even worse, killed, by the use of these explosives.' The judge went on. 'All you cared about was your greed for money. I am not dealing here with petty criminals. You three individuals, especially you two... Frederick Seiga and Anthony Burns, you are both active professional career criminals. With regards to me passing custodial sentences, I will deal with you first Frederick Seiga. It is said by the police and the prosecutor that you were the brains behind this crime of safe-blowing.' He paused for a moment and the courtroom seemed to be suspended in deathly quiet. 'I sentence you to five years.' Then he looked across at Tony. 'Anthony Burns, I am not going to waste much more time with words on you. I sentence you to five years.'

He then gestured towards the dock as he ordered the police who were guarding us. 'Take them down. I will deal with the youth separately.'

My brother and Tony were led quickly and silently down from the dock and out of the courtroom. This left me to face the wrath of the Judge alone. Again there was a dramatic pause and I noticed that before speaking to me the Judge took a quick glance across at the public gallery, in which every seat was taken and so now it was standing room only; it was absolutely packed out.

'Charles Antony Seiga, it is said you have no previous convictions and I am told that as you are only seventeen years of age there is a possibility that there could be some hope for you. According to your defence council, this whole episode has been quite traumatic for you and that given the chance, you want to turn your back on this type of behaviour. He also says that you have someone willing to employ you in their company. This is all included in your mitigation. I am assured too, that you didn't play a major role in this crime. I am asked by your council to take all of this into consideration.'

The Judge then took a poignant pause and it felt like the whole courtroom held its breath. He then he went on. 'Well, that maybe so and it all sounds very promising doesn't it; that you will turn over a new leaf? Yet how can I be sure that you won't be tempted again? You are young, like a young lion that has had his first taste of blood and it is this I also have to consider.' He had another one of his theatrical pauses. I remember noting that he had a pen in his hand and he tapped it a couple of times on his desk top before leaning forward and looking at me as if he were thinking, Can I take a chance with this kid?

I stood there looking up at him. My body was rigid with anticipation and strangely I found that both my thumbs were tucked tightly between my forefingers and middle fingers of each hand. I could feel my toes firmly curled up in my shoes; they were also stiff and tight. It was a thoroughly nerve wracking experience; standing in the dock awaiting the outcome on such a serious crime. I had never felt anything like this before. It wasn't like the buzz I got when seeing a safe being blown open. No, this was truly daunting and scary.

Once again I saw the Judge look over at the public gallery. It was believed, as my lawyer had pointed out, that his wife and young daughter were sitting there. He turned to face me again and began to speak deliberately and clearly. 'I am going to place you under probation, supervision for a two-year period. If you break or abuse that position, in any way, shape or form, take heed: you will be brought back here to this very court to face me again. And I will not hesitate to send you to prison. Do you understand that?' He appeared menacing as he stared me square in the face and awaited my reply.

I coyly replied, 'Yes, sir. I do.'

'Well, be off with you,' he said finally. 'And try to lead an honest life.' I'm sure that I caught the hint of a smile as he once again looked across at the public gallery. I hurried out of the court dock. I couldn't believe it. I was, in a way, technically free after standing trial for safe blowing. It was then that, at the age of seventeen, I was to become known as the youngest safe blower in England!

For a short time, I did have a go at mending my ways and living honestly, but it was not to be. I still recalled the trial at the Chester High Court and the stern warning coming from the Judge, but it was to no avail. What did stay etched in my mind, however, was his quote: *The boy is like a young lion who has had his first taste of blood.* He was one hundred percent right about that one; I did have my first taste of blood and I wanted more. How could I give up this exciting fast money-making life? So, I went bang at it!

CHAPTER 37

THE PROMISE

I did fulfil the promise I made to my brother Freddy – but somehow things don't always go according to plan; no matter how hard you try, and promises do get broken.

At first everything ran smoothly. I would routinely visit his wife Sadie and the baby boy Carl to make sure they were well looked after with regard to having enough money for bills, food and clothes. I also took her to visit my brother on a regular basis. Although this was a burden to me, I could handle it due to the way I was progressing with crime. Also, surprisingly, even my mother and some of the older family members cared for Sadie and the child too, so everything seemed to be working out well. I will always remember Freddy's last words to me as we stood in the dark cells of the Chester Crown Court after sentencing. 'Do your best for me, Charl, for my wife and kid. You know I will be out of here in just over three years' time.'

Three years was a long time to a young kid my age and it was for his new wife. Unfortunately, being taken to visit Freddy in prison every month proved too much for his wife and it didn't last long. Freddy had served just less than twelve months of his sentence when his wife Sadie packed her bags and took herself and the baby back to her home town in Scotland. Sometime later, she filed for a divorce never to return.

This really took its toll on my brother's morale and he would never be the same man again, even when he was finally released from prison. Losing everyone and everything he loved and cared about rendered him no longer interested in anything.

CHAPTER 38

A GOLDEN OPPORTUNITY

It was 1960 and I was still *at it.* I was grafting with Johnny Oates. We chose our work carefully now and we didn't step out of line by taking too many chances. And through progress and advances in security, safe-blowing was getting played out. In the criminal world times were changing rapidly, especially for the Jelly Gangs. The old reliable peters, such as the *Milliners* with their big key-holes that were easy to blow, were being rapidly phased out and replacing them were the modern safes of the day, the likes of the Chubb's and other well-known safe companies. These new ones were much more difficult to work on regarding the use of the jelly and the dets. These modern peters had no easy access of blowing them. Combination locks replaced the key hole and other secured means were now adapted to fit these strong powerful safes. The 1950s had come to an end and so too had the safe-blower. However, the safe on this new graft we were about to do was just up our street really as according to the information we had been given it was an old style one with a keyhole. It was 1960 and this would be the last safe I would blow open. Two London guys had come to see Johnny a couple of weeks earlier with a tasty piece of graft. I hadn't met these two guys yet and so had no opinion of them. It was a jeweller's they wanted us to have off and according to the information we had acquired the peter held a large amount of gold jewellery.

Now, due to the changes and the security advancements of these modern day safes we too had to move with the times and adapt our tactics to suit. As I have previously mentioned these new peters were difficult to break into, in fact virtually impossible. Much progress had been made by the safe manufacturers. These safes could no longer be blown open. Also, unfortunately for us businesses now preferred to put their money in banks which meant that most safes no longer contained cash. We had always preferred money as the prize because with jewellery, gold and other commodities we would need to involve someone else as a means of selling the jewellery or gold on.

I can vividly recall this last piece of graft we did... Johnny and I were having a heated discussion about this particular jeweller's that we were about to pull off. 'Charlie, you know as well as I do, there are no readies left in peters these days. Plus the ones that have money in them are impossible to open now.' He was referring to the new safes.

'I know what you mean, John.' I told him. 'But it has always been our policy to only take money. That way we have no hassle about selling the goods on and having to deal with people we don't really know if we can trust.'

'What other choice do we have, kid? Come on, Charlie, think about it. These two friends of mine are sound fellas. This move is worth plenty; in fact, thousands is what the pay-out will be. They have even got a top London jeweller boxed off. He is waiting to take the gold once we have the place off.' I suppose Johnny was right in a way, but still at the back of my mind, I would have preferred cash. These two Londoner friends of Johnny's didn't blow safes themselves; it just wasn't their game, so it would be down to me and Johnny to take care of that part. The graft was a piece of cake really. The jeweller's premises was adjoining another shop which was an old, established, bespoke tailor's in an affluent area. The tailor's was going to be our way in.

This move we were going to have off was a lot further away from where we were used to; by that I mean it wasn't like grafting in our own localities here up north. We were told the place was a large affluent town down south, not too far away from London. This meant that it would take us several hours if we were to drive down by car and no doubt it would be a tedious journey too. I didn't fancy being cramped up in a car for hours on end and neither did Johnny. So rather than go to all that inconvenience we both decided to take the rattler (train) down there instead. We chose the London Express which would mean roughly a four hour journey to London. Johnny had booked us both into first-class so that would mean a much more comfortable and relaxing voyage.

Since being a kid, I have always loved train journeys. I remember as a small boy my pals and I used to go to the Lime Street Station in our city of Liverpool to look at the big steam engines. To us they resembled big powerful rockets. The polished brass, the dark green and black paintwork; all of the sights and sounds of the steam engine that remain in your memory forever once you have experienced the majesty of one of these muscular vehicles. Their massive iron wheels were well oiled and the numerous strong steel pipes would be bursting and hissing with steam. There was something majestic about the smoke bellowing from the funnels on the top of the engine as it sent grey puffs of smoky cloud up into the sky above.

We would often be startled by the deafening sound of the engine's whistle as the driver pulled the chain to signal that the train was about to depart. Then as the huge well-oiled wheels of this impressive piece of engineering began to turn we would prepare to set off running alongside the engine at the front as it left the station. Hissing and puffing it got faster and faster and we would all try our best to keep up with it for as long we could before giving up and watching it puff away into the distance leaving smoke clouds in the air behind it.

Sometimes, we would get up to more devilment – and I mean devilment! We would dare each other to run across the tracks when the train was in sight. We didn't realise with being so young and silly, that our lives were in danger. Today, when I hear about some kid being killed on the railway line it makes me look back and think of how lucky we were and just how dangerous it all was.

At the time it had all been so exciting for us little kids and embarking on our train journey today had brought all those fond memories flooding back. It's funny that getting the train now was no big deal... but back then, to a young boy, it was magical!

I was now twenty years old; this was 1960 and I was sitting in a first-class train carriage with my friend Johnny. We were both dressed smart in our suits and ties and we mingled in well with the numerous other passengers. As long as we kept our voices down, so as not to reveal our scouse accents, we would not appear at all conspicuous among the others on the train. Everything would be just fine; we could both relax and enjoy the pleasant journey we were about to take.

Most of those alongside us were prominent looking businessmen. I smiled to myself. If only these people knew who the two smartly dressed guys were that sat with them today. Of course we knew who they were; honest, working men, some of who would be on their way to a plush office probably to make plenty of money pulling off some big deal. Mind you, were they working honestly? To me they always seemed to be ripping each other off and back stabbing one another.

Anyway, similarly to them, we too were on our way to work; only our occupation was slightly different to theirs. Yes, we were going to work alright. Johnny had his briefcase on the seat beside him as did many of the other passengers but in this briefcase, instead of having paperwork and other items for the office, we had our working tools which consisted of a pair of gloves each, explosives of gelignite, detonators and a crowbar and hopefully our business of the day was to steal thousands of pounds worth of gold... that's providing we could pull it off. Yes, we would certainly reap the rewards. Now, that to me was a good business deal!

However, there could be a terrible downside to our type of employment... meaning it could easily be an utter disaster. If any of these *honest Joe's* fucked up on their work, or messed up a deal or some such, their degree of disaster would be an instant dismissal or maybe a stern reprimand as they were told they were fired. If we fucked up on the graft we were about to pull off, our punishment would be much more severe. They at least would get to go home to what was probably a nice cosy house and family; which really, in the scheme of things, was not that bad. They could always find another job. Whereas, take us... like I said, if we made mistakes in our line of work and came badly unstuck, we wouldn't be going home, we would be going to prison – and for a long time too! That's the reason we had to always try to stay one step ahead of the police. Mind you, even then you couldn't easily predict what was going down. In the business we had chosen to be in, especially while doing something heavy like this move, in the back of your mind there were always the questions: *Am I going to pull this off?* or *Am I going to come badly unstuck?*

I glanced across the table at Johnny sitting opposite and I wondered if he thought the same way; but of course he did, we all knew we were taking big risks in this game. Johnny looked relaxed and was dozing with his eyes half closed. We had just enjoyed a nice hot lunch which had been served to us by one of the waitresses. This was another nice touch when travelling by train in the luxury of a first class carriage. The staff are attentive and make sure you are well looked after. We had ordered drinks after the meal; mine was a glass of lemonade with ice and Johnny had settled for a pint of Guinness.

The young waitress approached us with the drinks and set them down on our table. She was pleasant and smiling at us both. 'Would that be all, sir?'

Johnny nodded and pulled some money from his pocket to pay for the drinks. 'There you go, love.' He passed her a five pound note.

'Oh,' she said surprised. 'I will have to get some change.'

'Nah, you keep the change, girl,' he said, smiling.

'Thank you *very* much, sir,' she said gratefully.

Let's not forget that this was over fifty years ago and the price of those two drinks we had ordered would only have come to about fifty or sixty pence in today's money. So the tip Johnny had given the girl was nearly a week's wage to her.

When the girl had left Johnny turned to me and said, 'Always give a good working kid like that a decent tip, Charlie. They don't get paid much for all the work they do.' I suppose he was right. I had noticed how hard the staff worked on that train journey and particularly for the passengers travelling first class; they got the best service, and some of those travelling snobs let the staff know they expected it too!

Finally our journey came to an end at Euston Station in London and we disembarked. Johnny's two friends were there awaiting our arrival. As mentioned earlier I had never set eyes on these two men before now. I would describe them as being in their late thirties, smartly-dressed and both wearing warm-looking overcoats. It was November and the weather was decidedly chilly that day.

'This is Charlie.' Johnny said introducing me. I nodded in acknowledgement.

The first guy who was fairly tall offered his hand out to me. 'Hello, Charlie. I'm Eddie,' he said shaking my hand.

'And this is Vinny.' He gestured to the other guy who also shook my hand.

'How was your journey?' Vinny asked me.

I told him it was fairly good. This was how you were introduced to others who were at it, like us. You didn't introduce yourself using surnames in those days; that didn't matter, we used first names only. It was just the done thing.

The two Londoners had a motor waiting nearby not far from the train station, so the four of us headed off to where it was parked. The whole place was crowded with people going about their day. They were scattering in all directions and we had to weave our way through this hustle and bustle of the crowd to get to the waiting car. When we finally got to the motor, I saw that it was the latest 1959-60 Ford Consul. This model had not been out long and was impressive at the time. Getting in I immediately noticed that it had the column gear change which was on the steering column below the wheel. It was in the typical American style and me being a young kid, I was in complete awe of it. It was the first time I had seen one of these new cars. I thought to myself, I've got to have one of these motors. After all, I'm not a kid anymore. As we drove away, it was suggested by one of the fellas that we should all get around the table and finalise our plans. We eventually stopped outside an elegant looking apartment block and after parking the car we all went inside. The pad we were led to was plush. Providing all went well and we had successfully pulled the gold robbery off this is where John and I would stay. I think it belonged to Vinny. Once we were settled with a nice hot cup of coffee we got down to business.

It was several hours later and we had all agreed and finalised our plan. The time seemed to have gone by really fast and it was now dark outside. So, it had been decided that tomorrow would be the time to go to the jeweller's shop to look the place over to case it thoroughly. Once we were all satisfied with the plans and arrangements we concluded our meeting.

Vinny and Eddie wanted to take John and I out for a meal that evening, they had even offered to bring a couple of women back for us. They seemed to be going overboard in their efforts to treat us well but, we knocked it all back. After all, we had been up early that morning and spent hours on the train journey to get here so we were both shattered. Besides, we wanted to have a clear head in the morning when we went to look the place over. We were going to need to concentrate. We bid goodbye to Vinny and Eddie after arranging that they would pick us up the next day: Friday the 4th of November.

I was up bright and early after a good night's kip. It was a two-bedroom pad we were in with all the mods and cons. I got myself a nice hot shower and after sorting myself out I was ready to face the day but not before I had had something to eat. With being so young and fit at that time, I was absolutely famished. John was already up and about and he had made a pot of tea for us both.

'Did you have a good sleep, Charl?' Johnny asked as he poured me a cup of tea.

'Yeah, John. Only I'm starving. Is there anything to eat in here?'

'Nah, I've looked. Not a fuckin' thing. Typical, isn't it? A big posh pad like this and no fuckin' food in the larder! Never mind, we'll go and get breakfast when the other two call. You'll be alright then, Charlie.'

We finished our tea off and some ten minutes later Vinny and Eddie called to pick us up. They both greeted us warmly. 'Are we all ready then?' Eddie said. 'The place we're going to is a twenty minute drive away.'

'Yeah, OK. But before we get off,' said Johnny as he gestured towards me. 'The kid here is hungry, and so am I.'

'That's no problem, John,' replied Eddie. 'There's a nice cafe just down the street. We can get something to eat there before we leave.'

After a hearty breakfast down us and a big mug of hot tea, Johnny and I were now more than ready to get on with the day. During the twenty minute car journey to the premises in question we all discussed and went over the plans again. Firstly, and this was my idea, which was unanimously agreed to be a good one, we were to blow the safe on the Saturday evening, which would be the 5th of November, bonfire night. This would be perfect for us as not only would there be a lot of activity going on with people around and about but at the same time our two friends here, Eddie and Vinny, could play their part by setting fireworks off, particularly bangers that made a great deal of noise. This would help to drown out the sound of the safe being blown.

The trip *did* only take twenty minutes or so. We had arrived at a small affluent looking town; you could tell from the design of the buildings and shop premises that this was the sort of place where people with money come to spend and buy their goods. Vinny, who was driving, turned the car onto the main street. 'Our place is just half way down, John.' He said as he drove a bit slower.

We slowly passed by some real upmarket shops. There was one in particular that caught my eye – a high class furrier's displaying all kinds of ladies expensive fur coats in unguarded glass windows.

As I glanced at that shop, I smiled to myself and thought, That fur shop wouldn't last two minutes back in our city Liverpool. The windows of that place would be done right away and the fur coats removed. In the nineteen fifties and sixties, fur coats were well sought after and in high demand, particularly mink.

'We're coming up to it now, boys,' Vinny said over his shoulder to Johnny and I sat in the back of the car. As he pointed out the jewellery shop to us he gently put on the brakes and we took a good look at it as we slowly drove past. It was an expensive looking jeweller's with the bespoke Tailor's shop next door, adjoining.

'Don't go too slow,' John said to Vinny. 'We can have a proper look at it when we've parked up.'

Vinny moved along the road a little faster and after turning a couple of corners he parked up. Another asset for us back in the day was that there were no pay and display meters or double yellow lines to contend with. Funny, when I think about it; if you owned a car in those days, you had no hassle from the authorities. A car could more or less be left anywhere you wanted, even on high streets and along shopping parades. There was no such thing as getting a ticket off a traffic warden; it was unheard of. The laws were so lenient with regard to cars and traffic; there were no M.O.T.s or worn tyre regulations.

Once the car was parked up the four of us just got out and walked away without even locking it. There's no chance of doing that in this day and age. That was one of the many good points of being young in the nineteen fifties and sixties. We went on towards our target: the jeweller's. It was located further up the high street. Eddie and Johnny decided to walk on in front. Vinny and I followed a few paces behind. It was a Friday and the high street of this town was busy. There were lots of people going about their business, many of who were shoppers. The area had a pleasant, congenial feel about it and although there was a bite to the cold air most of the people appeared relaxed and happy.

As the shop came into view, Vinny and I slowed right down and started to browse in the windows of the shops a few doors away from the jeweller's. I glanced up the crowded street and saw that Johnny and Eddie had both stopped outside the jeweller's and were looking in the window at the display of their wares. They didn't look out of place doing this as other people were also looking at the jewellery on display too. We were also reasonably dressed so that we didn't stand out in this affluent area – we mingled in nicely!

I know that I keep repeating myself about the past but there were no security cameras then either. It's hard to believe but that's the way it was. However, one may think everything was easy for a robber in those days, having read the way I have described it all. It must sound too good to be true for a criminal around at that time, but there was a dark side, a down side that proved a great deterrent... the police!

In every town and city all over the country the policemen were there to be seen. They were everywhere. Day and night there were more bizzies than villains back then. You would see them out in pairs patrolling the streets, mainly on foot, especially at nighttime when the shops' premises were all locked up. That's the time when the police would be out in swarms. I have actually seen, on many an occasion, at least four bizzies patrolling on just one street, two at each end. They would be plodding along on opposite sides of the road checking doors and windows on the various properties. Unlike most of the bizzies these days driving around in cars, overweight and sitting on their arses. *Bizzie* is a Liverpool slang word for being *busy* and that's how the police were in those days... very *busy* at their work. Hence the word *bizzie.*

The police in those days had to be six foot tall and they were fit... the majority of them could out run you easily. I know this because some friends (who I grafted with) and I, on many an occasion have experienced it first-hand. Whenever the occasion would arise, and it does happen, when something has come on top and gone badly wrong, we too had to be able to run because if a copper is on your heels he won't give up on the chase unless of course you are faster than him, but that was rare because then the police had some bottle and they were definitely fit.

I knew and so did the others that this town we had just come into was going to be teaming with bizzies later on that evening. Was it any wonder that these streets were going to be well patrolled, I mean looking at all these high class department stores with their expensive goods displayed in unguarded windows for all to see, said it all. On this move we were hopefully about to pull off successfully, we would have to be extra vigilant.

Vinny and I eventually caught up with Johnny but Eddie was nowhere to be seen. Johnny looked at us and gestured for us to cross over the road with him. Once on the other side of the street, Johnny told us that Eddie had gone for a bit of lunch with the guy who owned the bespoke tailors next door to the jeweller's. I asked him what that was all about but before John could reply, Vinny quickly interrupted. 'There's no worries, kid. The tailor is a good friend of ours and with his shop being your way in, Eddie will be getting it all sorted to make sure that everything will be OK for tomorrow night.'

On hearing that the tailor himself was in on it, Johnny and I felt even more confident about the job.

'Come on,' John said pointing to a cafe. 'We'll have a coffee in that cafe on the end of the block. Eddie said he will catch us up in there later on.'

After our coffees and a chat Eddie *did* turn up, on his own, which I was glad about really as I didn't want to see or meet the tailor and neither did Johnny for that matter, it just wasn't necessary. Apparently, the tailor had outlined everything about both properties; that is the jeweller's and the tailor's. Eddie now relayed all this information to us.

Firstly, the front and back doors of each shop had ringers (alarms) which of course John and I fully expected. According to the plan though, we were not going through any of the doors; our entrance would be via a window at the back of the tailor's. It was an old wooden, sash window, the kind where the bottom frame is lifted and pushed up to slide the window open. The building itself was old. Both premises looked attractive from the front, like the old Tudor style. It was painted in the traditional black and white and because both shops were adjoined, I thought they resembled a pair of large cottages. They were both single story and the roof was all in one and was high pitched. According to our information, once we had gained entry to the tailor's there would be a hatch in the ceiling which lead up into the loft. The loft space extended across the top of both shops and the only thing separating both lofts, so we were told, was studded plasterboard. Armed with this good information we knew that this was the way that we could get to our prize: the safe containing all the gold. Obviously, next door would also have a hatch in the floor of the loft which would enable us to drop down through the ceiling and into the jeweller's below. The peter would be situated in the back room of the jeweller's, which was identical to the back room of the tailor's.

When I heard all of this I felt inspired and raring to go and I could see that Johnny was too. Time was moving on and by now it was late afternoon. We had done an awful lot of homework on the town and of course the jeweller's; at one point while we were there Johnny and I had gone to take a closer look at the back of the premises. As I said previously, this was the way we were to make entry. There was a fairly long lane at the rear of the premises with various buildings opposite. One of these buildings was directly facing the back of our target. I thought it looked something like an old library.

It was almost four o'clock by now and after checking all we needed to and doing a thorough rec on the place it was time to leave. Personally, I would have stayed a while longer; at least until the shops had closed up, just to see what the activity was like at nighttime and to scrutinise any bizzies that may be knocking about. However, Vinny and Eddie needed to get back; they said they had other business to take care of.

On the drive back to the Vinny's pad, Eddie announced, 'Oh, by the way, I almost forgot to tell you. There is going to be a big event tomorrow night: a firework display will be taking place at the top end of the high street.'

Johnny and I looked at each other and then he grinned at me and said, 'Well, that has put the icing on the cake. That's really good news.' Then his tone changed completely. He turned to Eddie, with a quizzical look he asked, 'How come you forgot to tell us about that, Eddie?'

'Sorry, John, the tailor told me earlier on and it slipped my mind.'

Johnny looked at him shaking his head in disbelief. I knew exactly what Johnny was thinking as I was thinking the same, How could something so significant almost pass us by? Especially on something as major as the gold job we were about to do. This was big... and I mean big. There was not just a lot of money involved here; when this goes off it will be considered a serious crime and if we were caught doing this we would lose a big chunk of our lives. We would serve long sentences in prison if caught and *that* we could well do without. Being in this *serious* business we had to know and be made aware of everything, right down to the last detail to pull this lot off successfully. We could not afford to make any mistakes. So if the graft that we were about to do didn't look right, for example, the information received was not genuine or something didn't feel right we would have to walk away and sack it all in. Our top priority in this business was our liberty. Fuck the money, our freedom came first.

When we arrived back at Vinny's pad the four of us had another little confab. We just talked about how the day had gone and more importantly, the arrangements of the meet tomorrow evening. It was arranged that Eddie and Vinny would pick us up at six o'clock and we believed that the firework display started at about seven o'clock.

We finally called it a day and Eddie and Vinny prepared to leave the pad. Johnny looked a bit apprehensive at Eddie. 'Is there anything else me and Charlie should know? Because I'm a bit concerned about that inner dividing wall up in the loft.'

'Why's that, John?' Eddie replied.

'Well it's like this, Eddie. When we do get up there, I don't want to find that the wall in the loft is made of fuckin' brick and not as you say... just wood and plasterboard. Because if it is made of brick, we might as well get geared up properly with some heavy tools: a lump hammer and a chisel, because I'll tell you now, Eddie, once we are in that fuckin' loft we won't be coming out until we have had a result, if you know what I mean?'

'No, John, there is no need. It is definitely a studded out wall, plastered on both sides. Our friend the tailor told me that it has been that way for years.'

'OK then, Eddie. That will do me.'

We then confirmed the six o'clock meet for tomorrow evening and said our goodbyes. Vinny and Eddie left the pad and Johnny and I talked for a little while longer. 'You know, Charlie, this move we are doing is gonna put us right on our feet if it all goes well. We're talking thousands here.'

Listening to him I was starting to get a buzz about it all. I was becoming over anxious now and more eager than ever because that good news regarding the firework display, which would start at seven that night, was also working in our favour. Then there was the entrance to the place being through a ground floor old window and to cap it all just a plaster wall was all that would divide us from the prize... a big old peter full of gold. Then I thought about the gold jewellery. I asked Johnny, 'Won't we need a big case or a bag to put the gear in?'

'Charlie, that brief case of mine is big enough. If we fill that up we will have more than plenty.' He laughed. He was right, the big briefcase was big enough and it was wide at the bottom. I do remember that. I had looked at that briefcase several times when we had gone out on graft. Johnny was never without it. 'Besides, if there's any of the jewellery over we can always fill our pockets up.' He laughed again.

I looked at him questioning. 'Fill our pockets up?'

He began laughing again. Soon I was laughing with him. He then became serious and told me that if we did have a good touch he was thinking of getting out of the game. 'I'm almost forty now kid. I'm not like you. You have years ahead of you yet.' Then he looked solemn. 'Don't waste those years, Charlie. You know what I mean don't you?'

I nodded in acknowledgment. 'Course I do, John.'

'Yeah,' he continued. 'I would like to get myself a couple of fruit shops, get them off the ground and take things easy. I have a young son now, Charlie, and my wife, who is a good mother and loyal and true; she's had so much worry over the years about me. You know every time I go out on a move, she is always worried sick wondering if I'm going to come home or end up in jail. It's hard for her when I think about it.'

I agreed with him. 'That's the way we all feel at times isn't it, John; always hoping that we never come unstuck? That thought keeps us on our toes and keeps us one step ahead of the bizzies.'

'Yeah, that's right, kid,' he replied as a slight smile crossed his lips.

I then thought to myself, I wonder what I will be doing when I'm his age? Would I still be at it, like him? Personally, I didn't think he would ever retire. Not yet anyway, Johnny liked the good life too much. Like the old saying goes: wine, women and song.

He got up stretching and yawning. 'We had better get our heads down, kid. It's a big day tomorrow.'

We bid each other goodnight and went into our separate bedrooms. Within just a few minutes of getting into bed, I had completely crashed out.

CHAPTER 39

GOING OFF WITH A BANG

It was Bonfire Night Saturday 5th November 1960.

I remember waking up nice and early the next morning. After having a quick shower and sorting myself out, I walked into the dining room kitchen. Johnny was already up, which surprised me. 'Morning, kid,' Johnny said as I walked into the room. He had the radio on. It was playing Elvis Presley's number one hit, *It's Now or Never.*

As I listened to the words Elvis was singing - *it's now or never* – I thought to myself, That says it all considering what we were planning to do that very day!

Johnny had made a pot of tea and poured out two cups, then he passed one to me saying, 'Here you go, get that down you. Afterwards, we will take a walk down to the cafe and grab ourselves a bit to eat.'

I nodded in agreement. 'Yeah, OK, John. I'm starving.'

He looked at me and laughed. 'Yeah, I know.'

When we had finished our cups of tea, we left the pad and set off straight for the cafe which was only a few blocks away. It was fairly quiet in there when we arrived, but as it was a Saturday morning and only half past eight as suppose this was only to be expected. I ordered the works from the menu: two eggs, rashers of bacon, sausage, beans, fried hash potatoes and a big plate of hot toast. I began to wolf it down and Johnny watched as I devoured it all.

'Fuck me, Charlie. You can't half eat. Where do you put it all?'

As I finished mopping my plate up with the last round of

toast, I smiled across the table at him. 'Well, you know how it is, John, being young and fit.' Then I swilled it all down with the half mug of tea I had left.

'Yeah.' He laughed.

After a big hearty breakfast I was ready to face the day. We both decided to have a stroll around the area taking in some of the scenery. As much as possible we avoided getting into conversation with any of the locals, due to our heavy scouse Liverpool accents which didn't go down too good in out of town places so we hid it as much as possible. Of course sometimes we would have to converse with people so when that case *did* arise we just had to pretend not to be scousers. We spoke clearly and pronounced our words properly, like sounding our 'h's and at times this was hard to do naturally. We were well aware that once the business we were to have off this evening were discovered, all hell would break loose with regard to the police forces here and in the surrounding areas. Also there was sure to be public outcry with this being such a high profile crime.

After our little walkabout and keeping as low a profile as possible we ended up back in the pad. Vinny and Eddie were to phone us there to confirm everything for that evening. Since being here John and I had decided on another significant rule: we were not to use the phone in the pad, especially to make any outgoing calls to our home town of Liverpool. It was vital that we stuck to these necessary precautions as grave mistakes have been made in the past through the use of a phone. Also, it had always been a golden rule among our circle never to let anyone know where you were or what you were doing, not even your wife or girlfriend, no matter how loyal they may be.

Say for example Johnny and I got a pull by the police and were roped in, this is after we have done the move on the jeweller's, as long as we had nothing incriminating on our person such as breaking and entering equipment – crowbars, gloves etc., and of course the gelignite and detonators – the police would have to prove that we had committed the crime. Obviously, it would be quite different if we had been caught doing the job, they had us bang to rights, so that would be another story and we would have no chance of being found not guilty in court. On the other hand, if they had a good idea that we had committed a crime, and more so if they knew that we were active villains, the police would then go to any lengths to get a conviction, even as far as using devious methods like fitting you up, for example, planting evidence on you. However, if you were a professional criminal and as I mentioned previously, you had got rid of any incriminating evidence, they still would not give up. They would just take their underhand methods to the extreme, for example, they would call on your wife, your family or your girlfriend and they would ask them, especially the women, where you were on the night in question. Some women, if they were gullible, would think that they were helping you out and that it was all in your interest if they were immediately to say that you had been with them at the time, whereas, in actual fact, they would be jeopardising you because at the other end of the line you may be relaying a different story to the bizzies. Therefore, if they did not know of your business or whereabouts, especially if you had briefed them previously they knew not to say anything at all if questioned by the police. That way they couldn't put you in the frame.

Johnny and I had been discussing the best and easiest way to get through the dividing wall that was up inside the loft of both shops. We now knew that it was cladded with plasterboards and more than likely it would be on both sides. At first we had planned to smash our way through with a hammer but then thinking about it with all the mess and everything, we came up with the idea of using a good sharp Stanley knife. We could cut a large square section of the plasterboard out making a perfect entrance through to the other side. It wouldn't take long, a few minutes at the most plus doing it that way would be far easier. The Stanley knife, small and light, could be discreetly slipped into your pocket weighing next to nothing and not looking bulky. Again, as I have said previously, the tools that we carried on any graft with were all far lighter than any other workman's tools of the trade and they were easy to disregard when the business was completed.

After sorting out that little hiccup, I noticed that the time was getting on: it was two o'clock. We were waiting for the phone call now from Eddie and Vinny. When the phone *did* ring, Johnny answered it and found that it was Eddie on the other end. He confirmed that they would come to pick us up bang on six o clock. Johnny kept the conversation brief but he told Eddie that we were going to need a good sized Stanley knife. He stressed that it was vital for the job. Eddie agreed that he would pick one up for us on the way along with a small glim (torch).

After the phone call, the two of us just sat and chilled out in the pad. We had a chat then we watched a little television. I think it was a show called Perry Mason who was a detective in a wheelchair but I couldn't get into it so we just sat and chatted, going over the plans for later that evening. We would be moving out in a couple of hours from now. Every time we talked the conversation would come back to the robbery. It was always on our minds like this prior to it actually taking place. Most of the time thinking about the outcome would get me geared up inside as I asked myself what was the outcome going to be: would it be successful or would it be a disaster? I started to convince my mind that nothing would go wrong. It would be just like the other moves we had done in the past, a cinch. No worries at all. Then I would come back to reality: who the fuck am I kidding? I got real again.

After all this apprehension and waiting the time had finally come around. It was just approaching six o'clock. It was dark outside and this November night had turned cold. Eddie and Vinny arrived having been true to their word and precisely on time. The four of us had a brief discussion and went over everything meticulously. If all went well, Johnny and I would be driven back here to the pad. We would then keep our heads down before moving out first thing on Monday morning to catch the train for our journey back home to Liverpool.

'Are we all done then?' Johnny said getting off his chair and standing up. Eddie and Vinny nodded in agreement and like me they got up ready to make a move. 'Come on, Charlie,' Johnny said seriously. 'Let's go and get this fuckin' graft done.'

The four of us left the apartment in silence and got into the car. Eddie was going to drive. I noticed that the car was different this time; it was a new Vauxhall Cresta which was a big comfortable powerful motor. It was a ringer (down to nobody, phoney plates etc), which it had to be for what it was about to be used for. Back then a car could be plated up (stolen) and could be used for months before it came on top. The traffic police were vastly limited; much further behind with regards to tracing stolen cars. They didn't have the sophisticated equipment that they have these days. Today a traffic cop can see all the details of you and the vehicle at the touch of a button and can trace you in seconds.

Right now, we knew we were fairly safe in this car. On the drive to our destination, Eddie drove sensibly; not too fast and not too slow, and twenty-five minutes later we had arrived in the town. It was full of activity as we drove down the main street. There were a lot of younger people like me milling about. It seemed that everyone in the area was in good spirits. The whole atmosphere was cheerful. According to our calculations, the firework display was to begin at half past seven. Not only was this ideal for us but it gave me and Johnny enough time to make our entrance into the tailor's.

'Drive back down the street, Ed,' said Johnny. 'I want to take another look at the lane at the back of the tailor's.'

Eddie drove the car back down the street and returned to the lane again. This place was much quieter than the main street had been.

I mentioned to Johnny that I hadn't seen any bizzies yet. 'Where are they?' I said. 'They've got to be around here somewhere.'

'Oh, they'll be about alright that's for sure,' he replied. 'Especially when that firework display kicks off.'

There was about half an hour to go, which gave us enough

time to break into the tailor's. As the car drove along the lane we *did* see one or two people here and there. With the direction they were walking in you could tell they were heading for the high street where it was all happening.

Johnny must have been thinking the same because suddenly he told Eddie to turn around again at the top of the lane. He told him that if there was nobody in sight when we got to the tailor's shop, he would drop us right off. Johnny then turned to me: 'If everything is OK, Charlie, we may as well go right in. I mean, we would be safer over that wall and into the tailor's yard out of sight. Then we can perform.' A few moments later, the car pulled up at the back of the tailor's. Before getting out, we glanced up and down the lane. There was nobody in sight, it was perfect. 'Let's go, Charl,' Johnny said.

The two of us got out of the car quickly with Johnny carrying the briefcase. The car pulled away nice and easy and disappeared down the lane. The backyards of all the shops had brick walls each with an entrance door in the centre. The tailor's had a strong looking wooden one which was obviously bolted from the inside; we knew this because it was all part of the good information we had received. We both took another quick glance up and down the lane; it was still perfect. There was no one about. The wall was only about seven or eight feet high; we knew exactly what to do next, and it had to be quick. Johnny immediately put his briefcase down, then, as was usual in these situations, he clasped both of his hands together to form a step for me to put my foot on and hoist myself up. In no time, I reached the top of the wall and was over it in seconds. When I dropped down on the other side, Johnny spoke to me in a low voice through the door: 'Everything, OK?'

'Yeah,' I replied. Then I began to unbolt the back door and I opened it up for Johnny. He took another cautious glance around before he was in the tailor's yard with me. I then re-bolted the back door and the two of us were locked in.

For a brief moment, we both just stood still in the dark yard, listening for anything. I don't know why but we did. I think it's just a natural reaction that you feel at first. After all, here we both are equipped with high explosives: gelignite and detonators. Not only that, but we were about to do a big gold robbery. So with all that we were bound to feel that way. Was I buzzing and excited by it all? Was I fuck! It was the complete reverse. I started to get butterflies in my gut and was so tensed up I thought I could feel my heart pounding in my throat. I knew that John had the same kind of feeling too, so did the rest of our friends who we had grafted with on past moves, yet we would never reveal these feelings to one another. Instead, we would always put on a brave face showing that we had plenty of bottle for doing a heavy move like this.

I have heard and read stories about some gangsters who have written in their books – sorry I'll rephrase that – books that have been written *for* them, that when they have been committing a heavy crime, for example a bank or an armed robbery – but, then again, that's if they have ever done one – some of them have stated how exciting and thrilling it all was when performing these robberies. I have even read or heard on interviews that a couple of them have said that it had been so exciting that it had given them a hard on and a real buzz. I'm sorry but to me that's all lies! No normal man, in my humble opinion, would feel that way and if they did they must be plain fuckin' stupid or something's wrong with them.

After we were both satisfied that everything seemed OK we cautiously walked down the stone yard to the big old window frame. It was next to the outside entrance door which we knew not to force open as it was definitely alarmed. Alarmed doors were the only protection for properties in those days. There were no security cameras or inside alarms but, as I have mentioned previously, the most reliable security, and also a strong deterrent, were the police! That is why we would have to quickly start to perform on this move because we also knew that the police in most cities and small towns, particularly like this one, came out in droves by nine o'clock to check property. This strong routine deterrent goes on all through the night, until the next morning.

We finally checked the old window over and John began to prise the bottom sash with our crowbar, having been told that it never got used and so had not been opened for a long time. Of course, we could tell that just by looking at it. John started to prise it again and eventually it moved but it made a bit of a noise. We both stood silent and still for a moment at hearing this. I whispered to Jonny to suggest that I go back down to the bottom of the yard and take a quick peek over the wall, just to reassure ourselves that no passers-by had heard anything.

There was an old fashioned steel dustbin out there so I quickly got up on top of it and took a good look over the wall to make sure there was no one about. After reassuring myself, and then Johnny, that everything was OK, we went back to work on the window. After a couple more pushes it began to open. We prised it again and pushed it up and open. I climbed in. Johnny passed the briefcase through the window to me and then he climbed in too. Then cautiously we pulled the window back down to close it. John pulled out a small glim (torch) from the briefcase and switched it on keeping the beam down low towards the floor and we had a quick look around to familiarise ourselves with the place.

It looked exactly as it had been described to us by Eddie. This back room we were in looked like it was the stock room. Against one wall there were wide wooden shelves and on the far side of the wall there were rolls and rolls of cloth that were suit lengths of many types. I noted that there were tweeds, pinstripes and checks to name but a few. Johnny was also looking at all these cloth rolls and he chuckled after examining a couple of them. 'There's all our packing material for the peter next door, Charlie.' He was pointing to the rolls of expensive material.

I have got to give it to Johnny though, no matter how serious the predicament, he would always find time for a little bit of humour. It's funny though how the mind can switch right back to normality and seriousness. Before we entered the place we had both been on edge and nervous but now that we knew that we hadn't been sussed out and the danger of being seen had passed without any problem, we were more relaxed and chilled. As well as the rolls of suit cloths in this room there were also some expensive looking overcoats and suits hanging up. I looked a little closer at the overcoats; some were real cashmere and some were 'Crombies' (a trendy much sought after name in those days). Johnny looked at me as I examined the coats. 'Come on, kid,' he said. 'We haven't come for them. Let's get up into the loft.'

He shined the torch up to the ceiling and we saw that the entrance to the loft was not too far from where we were standing. We looked around the room for something to stand on so that we could reach the hatch and gain entry. There was a kitchenette and a toilet cubicle on the far side of the room and a door to something else next to the toilet door. We were intending to pull a table away from the wall to stand on but then curiously I opened the door next to the toilet and found that it was a tiny room that looked like an office. Inside, luckily for us, there was a posh type of ladder made of polished mahogany. It was just what we needed. I brought it out of the room and took it to just underneath the hatch where Johnny was waiting.

'That's dead handy, Charlie. That saves us standing on that stupid table.'

Everything appeared to be going well. It was almost as if it was being handed to us. I manoeuvred the step ladder and opened it right underneath the hatch in the ceiling. It was perfect. I began to climb the ladder and when I was almost at the top I could reach to push the hatch open. It did this so easily. I took two more steps on the ladder and was waist high inside of the loft. It was big up there and it had a high roof. I asked Johnny for the torch and he passed it up to me. This time I climbed inside the huge loft and shone the torch around. Only being a small one it didn't give out much light but it was enough for us achieve what we had come to do. I heard Johnny start to climb up the ladder. 'Here, Charl. Grab the briefcase.'

I leaned down and took the briefcase from him as he climbed

up. We could both hear the noise of people and children outside. They would be some of the revellers passing by on their way to the big firework display. It would be starting shortly just a little further down the high street. We could rest assured though that our two friends, Eddie and Vinny, would be keeping a watchful eye on everything. They both knew exactly what their part was to play outside as we had all agreed that after they had parked up the motor they would both split up and take it in turns to pass the jeweller's premises every so often, just to keep watch while Johnny and I carried out the work inside.

Inside this big old loft we were in, and I *mean* big, it had a high-pitched roof with thick old oak support beams. We now turned our attention to the dividing wall, the one that would lead us into the jeweller's next door. We both examined it closely and began to tap on the wall with our knuckles to reveal that it was hollow. Just as we had been informed, it was only a studded plasterboard partition which obviously had been plastered over.

'I think this is the best part to start on,' I said to Johnny pointing to a section of the wall that was in line with the hatch that we had just climbed through. I was speculating that the hatch on the other side of the wall would be in exactly in the same position as this one, all in line with each other.

'Yeah, OK, Charl. Let's make a start.'

I asked him to pass me the Stanley knife and then I began to scour the plaster. We only needed a hole about four foot high and three foot wide so that is was just big enough for us to get through. It was tough going at first due to the wall being plastered but we took it in turns. After all, the plasterboard was less than half an inch thick. After just a few minutes, we started to push it and felt that it began to give way. So I kicked the bottom part of this section and it broke away eventually, making a rough looking square. We reached through the hollow part of the wall and did the same scouring to the plasterboard on the other side, which was a lot easier to scour with the Stanley knife as this side of it wasn't plastered. Once again, it was only a few short minutes before we could push the cut-away board forwards and into the loft on the other side, making the same sized hole as we had on the tailor's side of the partition wall. This was all achieved making hardly any noise at all. We stepped through the make-shift entrance and that was it... we were in the jeweller's loft!

I was getting excited now and wasn't as nervous as earlier. I went in first and Johnny followed right behind. We both stood up on the other side and silently looked around. I was still holding the small torch and with its low beam I found that the hatch down into the jeweller's was in the exact position that I had speculated it would be, just like the tailor's shop hatch next door. We stood over the closed hatch at first and looked down at almost in contemplation. We knew that directly below us was the room with the prize... the safe that was holding the gold!

I looked at Johnny as I bent down to inspect the last obstacle to overcome. I just hoped that the hatch wasn't locked from the inside. The gloves I was wearing were soft black leather and a nice tight fit. My heart was racing now as I felt the hatch top with my gloved hands. It moved. I cautiously pulled it open just a few inches at first. I saw that it was on hinges just like the one in the tailor's. I then pulled it right back to fully open. I looked down into the room. It was more or less the same size as the tailor's only designed a little different. It was some kind of an office and work room from what I could make out because as well as an office desk there was a little work area where they repaired and adjusted jewellery. I did notice one good thing that was in our favour though: directly below the hatch I was looking through there was a long office desk. This was ideal for me as I could drop down onto that dead easy. I explained to John who was now looking through the hatch, 'I can get down easily on that table below, John. What do you think?'

'I know you can, Charlie. But I think we should fetch the ladder from next door first.'

So that's what we did and with me back down in the tailor's shop we began to get the suit rolls into the loft. I passed them up through the hatch in the tailor's ceiling to Johnny who was stood by the loft hatch reaching down to grab the rolls that I was hoisting up.

After quite a few of the rolls were put up there, I climbed back up the ladder and into the loft. Once back up there, I leaned down through the hatch to grab the ladder and hoist it up and into the loft. When we were both sorted with the ladder and the cloth I dropped down through the jeweller's loft hatch and onto the large table in the office below. I then moved the table slightly away from the hatch above and Johnny passed the ladder down to me. Then I fixed it into position so that he could come down onto it after throwing down the rolls of suit cloth.

Now that we were in there, it was so far so good. Obviously, the first thing we looked for was the peter. It was there alright: a fairly big one standing up at the side of a filing cabinet. Just as we had been briefed, it was our kind of safe: a big strong looking Milliner's with its brass key hole and its famous name on a brass plate.

Time was moving on a bit now and we could hear more activity coming from outside on the high street. We were ready for the next part of our plan. As discussed, once we had gained entry into the back room of the jeweller's, I was to make contact with Eddie or Vinny outside. There would always be one of them positioned as an onlooker outside the jeweller's; they would take it in turns changing positions so as not to draw attention to themselves or the shop. It didn't matter which one was there when the time came.

'I'll open this door a bit, John, and take a look which one is out there.' Before Johnny and I had broken into these two places we had stressed to Eddie and Vinny that it shouldn't take any longer than fifteen minutes to get everything done right up to actually preparing the safe. It had been about that long now so hopefully, if going according to plan, at least one of them should have been there on the front when I pulled the door open.

Cautiously and slowly, I pulled open the door inch by inch. I would only need to open it about two or three inches at the most. I looked through the gap in the door expectantly. I could see a figure at the front of the shop... my heart was pounding now. I just hoped to God that it *was* either Eddie or Vinny. I had no need to worry... it was Eddie. He was looking through the shop window but his eyes were fixed intently on the door and he had spotted me immediately... this I could see. I quickly gave him the OK through the opening to indicate to him that we were ready to make a move on the peter (blow the safe). He got onto it right away and so I closed the door shut again.

Johnny was already making preparations when I returned to the safe. He was busy unwrapping the gelignite from the protective paper that surrounded it; as I said previously, it comes packaged just like plasticine. I took the unwrapped gelignite from Johnny and with a pencil I began to pack it into the large keyhole of the safe. I made sure that there was plenty in there due to the huge size of the safe. We wanted to make sure it was done in one blow; we didn't want to take any chances on this not going off first time. John sealed around the door with putty. Once I was satisfied there was enough gelignite in the keyhole, and this only took a couple of minutes, John passed me a fused detonator. I carefully pressed it into the keyhole making sure it went right in so that just the fuse protruded out. We were all set ready to blow it.

Before Johnny lit the fuse we got the rolls of suit cloth we had brought from next door and we packed them all over the front of the safe, making sure we were still able to get to the prepared fuse. Then we pushed a chair that was in there right up to the rolls of cloth tightly as this helped to stabilize everything. We had just finished this dangerous preparation when, talk about more luck... the firework display down the high street kicked off. We could hear people cheering and laughing as it got started. It was getting louder and louder out there. Rockets and all kinds of fireworks were being set off. I quickly went back to the door again and opened it exactly like before. It was Vinny who was there waiting this time. I gave him the signal to begin setting off those firework bangers they had on them. I closed the door again and returned to the safe. The fuse was ready and waiting. John carefully set it off with his lighter. This was it!

We both got into the recess where the toilet was. The noise from the fireworks outside was all we could hear now, banging away out there and precisely at the time the safe went off. It went off with a real big noise but we were confident that the fireworks would drown it out. We both rushed over to the safe... it had been a perfect hit and the door-lock was blown right open. This is when panic began to set in. We had to control ourselves here and not get ahead of ourselves. We could still hear the fireworks going off outside that Eddie and Vinny were responsible for and this came as a great relief to the two of us!

Johnny had got the big briefcase wide open and we opened the door to the peter. There was no problem with doing that either because it almost fell open. We started to throw all of the contents of the safe into the briefcase. Moving as fast as we could we filled it with the small boxes and cloth bags which according to good information would be full of gold!

We completely emptied the whole safe... but then, something we had not been told about was that in the bottom half of the safe were two locked solid steel drawers. These had not blown open as they had strong locks on them. We tried to prise them open with the crowbar we had with us but we knew that it was impossible; they just wouldn't budge. Johnny was effing and blinding then he turned to me looking annoyed. 'I bet there's a fortune in those two fuckin' drawers.'

We both knew now though that we had to get out of there as fast as possible so we made a move, hurrying, as we had to get out the same way we had come in up through the loft and back into the tailor's shop next door. I carried the briefcase and it was quite heavy. Johnny followed on right behind me. We knew it was gold; we had seen some of it in a couple of the parcels we had thrown into the case. I started to go up the ladder to the loft above with Johnny still behind me. This was the most dangerous part for us now.

Time was of the essence. Who knows, somebody might have heard us blowing the safe from outside or a bizzie could have been nearby, all kinds of crazy thoughts run through your mind at a time like this but you have to stay in control. At one point I was thinking that the police could be on their way here to ambush the two of us. This all goes through your mind doing something like this. We knew full well that we were nowhere near out of danger yet.

We came to the last leg of our escape route: the loft hatch into the tailor's next door. It was only then I realised that with hurrying too much we had made a mistake... we had not brought the ladder from the jeweller's with us. I looked through the hatch down into the tailor's back room. As we hadn't got the ladders, we would have to drop down onto the floor below and we were fairly high up here, about ten or twelve feet. I knew I could drop to the floor below quite easily, I had no problem with that, but it was Johnny I thought about. I didn't think he was as agile as me. I asked him, 'Will you be OK dropping down there, John?'

'Yeah, I think so kid,' he replied.

So I dropped first by lowering my body down through the hatch feet first and then hanging onto the edge of the hatch with my hands to get my feet closer to the floor before dropping down. When I hit the floor, it gave me a bit of a jolt, but otherwise I was OK. Johnny leaned down through the hatch to pass me down the briefcase. Obviously, I couldn't reach it from below as it was about twelve foot above me and he couldn't just let it drop down as it was too far below him. The problem was that it was dead heavy and if he just let it fall it would probably burst open and the contents would go everywhere. Luckily, there was a chair nearby which I grabbed and put underneath the hatch then I stood on it to reach up so that the briefcase didn't have as far to fall. With doing this I managed to catch the case when it dropped which wasn't easy due to the weight of it. I then had to move the chair away so that Johnny could drop down.

It was a hard floor he was going to land on and when *I* did it, it had given me a jolt in my ankles like an electric shock. So just as Johnny was about to prepare to come feet first through the hatch to drop down I told him to hold for a minute. I started to grab a few of the rolls of cloth from the shelf nearby and placed them all around the floor beneath the hatch to cushion his fall.

'OK, John,' I said. Take it easy and you should be OK.'

He carefully dropped down and landed on all the rolls of cloth. He fell over off balance a bit but hey, he was fine and he got up. We then turned our attention to the outside window. We opened it again easy enough then Johnny got through first and when I had passed him the briefcase I followed him through. Once safely outside, I carefully closed the window behind me. We then went cautiously down the small yard to the bolted outside door. Just before we unbolted the door though, I climbed up onto the old bin and peered over the wall. I could see there was nobody about except, and with great relief, our car. It was parked up on the other side of the lane waiting for us.

'You go first,' I said to Johnny as I unbolted the door. I let him out and then I closed the door shut again and re-bolted it from the inside. I glanced around the yard and at the window we had made our entrance through and once I was satisfied that everything looked as we had found it I got up onto the bin again and quickly climbed over the wall... I was over there quicker than a cat would be! Johnny and I looked up and down the lane and then at each other before steadily walking towards the car. As we did this we heard the sweet sound of the engine being fired up. The car turned around and pulled up by the side of us to let us get in.

'Everything go OK?' Eddie asked as we got comfortable in the back.

'Yeah, yeah,' Johnny said.

Then Eddie turned to Vinny who was driving: 'OK, Vin, let's do one.'

Vinny drove away nice and easy. I knew we were OK so far, as the place had not been sussed out yet, so I relaxed and sat back as

Vinny, steadily and keeping in line with the speed limit, drove us away heading back to the pad.

On the drive back we didn't see anything out of order: no road blocks or police cars racing to the scene of the robbery. Eddie mentioned that there was no strong police activity around. 'I don't think they have discovered the break in yet, John'

'They won't have,' John replied. 'I think it'll be Monday before it'll come on top and that's only because we locked everything up before we left.' Then he turned to me, 'Didn't we, kid.'

'Aw, that's just brilliant isn't it, Eddie?' Vinny said sounding impressed.

We finally arrived back at Vinny's pad without any problems whatsoever. Once we got behind closed doors it was straight down to business between us. The first thing on the agenda was the gold. Johnny laid it out on the table so that we could all look it over properly and what a sight it was to look at. Just absolutely brilliant! I had never seen anything like it. It consisted of gold coins, some were Kruger Rands, and there was lots of gold jewellery, thick bracelets and chains but, for me the best out of it all were some solid gold bars. There were nine in all: eighteen carat and about half an inch thick; approximately four by two and a half inches, all carefully packed into one of the boxes. They were just stunning to look at; especially knowing that on the table in front of us was worth thousands of pounds, which was a hell of a lot of money in 1960. I had been at this game of blowing safes for the past three years and this was the biggest move we had ever pulled off. We were all feeling remarkably pleased with ourselves over it all.

Now, here is the difference between the befores and the afters of crime. As I have mentioned previously, a natural, normal person like us involved in this sort of business does feel the stress and the strain of carrying out a big robbery like this, which I have already admitted, but afterwards following the crime, especially if it has been successful... well then... that's the time that you really get your excitement and feel on top of the world. There are feelings of elation it's so good, and let's face it, who wouldn't? At right that minute, that's how I felt and so did Johnny. I could see how relieved and happy he was and knowing too that he was going to retire and settle down into some kind of legal business.

After we had all looked over the gold which was still spread out on the table it was time for questions and answers among us all. Johnny was the first to start the ball rolling. He was dead serious and so was I. Looking straight at Eddie and Vinny, he pulled the two of them. 'How come me and Charlie weren't told about the two locked drawers at the bottom of the peter?'

Eddie and Vinny looked a bit puzzled then Eddie spoke. 'Look, John, I did.'

I cut him dry before he could finish what he was saying. 'Yeah, and how come there were no stones, not one diamond among that gold there?' I said pointing to the table.

'I know, Charlie, and I can give you the answer right now... it's because they were inside those locked drawers.

'Is that right, Eddie? Or you, Vinny? Why no stones?'

'Alright, alright take it easy,' Eddie said to Johnny. 'I'll tell you why.' Then he went on to explain it all to us.

However, in my mind, straight away I thought, Is there something devious going on between these two?

They began to explain that apparently the diamonds weren't in the deal. It was stipulated that only the gold would be taken. This high class jeweller's shop was a family business and it was a member of the family who had marked the card on it (set it all up) to Eddie. But like he stressed to us, only the gold would be taken. If the diamonds were taken it would wipe the family business right out. Eddie went on to tell us that it was the son of the family, of all people, who had set it all up and also, according to Eddie, was up to his eyeballs heavily in debt. He lived in the fast lane: the nightlife, clubs, gambling, women and he drove expensive sports cars.

Then Eddie turned to Johnny: 'You know what the deal between us was, Johnny. You was brought in on this move to blow the safe to get us the gold and nothing else, and your cut was twenty grand. Am I right, John?'

'Yeah, alright, Eddie,' John retorted. 'I wasn't getting out of order with you. It just surprised me knowing that we had left those stones in that peter and knowing that they were most probably worth a fortune.' John shook his head in disbelief.

'Hey, John, look at it this way: it's been a nice touch we've just done and we will all make plenty out of it.'

Eddie turned to look at me with a smile. 'Won't we, Charlie?'

I suppose Eddie was right really; I mean, to me if a deal has been made and is agreed on by both sides, well that's final as far as I'm concerned. Providing there was no skullduggery going on afterwards; and really, I think that's what John, (and myself actually) was implying at first. Trust and principles were essential in situations like this, which will be proven later on.

On leaving the pad, Eddie and Vinny had temporarily left the gold with us. John and I carefully collected the gold from the table and put it all back into the briefcase. We put the radio on and listened to the local news bulletins but there was no mention of the robbery. The television news had nothing to report about it either.

Johnny and I began to chill out now following the night's events. Earlier on Johnny had bought some food from the local deli just down the road from the pad and he now prepared a big plate of thick ham sandwiches and a pot of steaming hot tea. 'Here you go, Charlie, get those down you.' He said passing me the sandwiches. Johnny knew I had a good appetite. He watched the television, drinking his tea while I sat at the table devouring the thickly cut sandwiches one by one and finishing them off by swilling them down with two mugs of tea. Johnny was a good fella and I respected him rather like a father figure. We sat and chatted for a while, mostly about what we had done earlier on that evening. Then the conversation came around to the subject of Eddie and Vinny.

'I had to pull Eddie and Vinny, you know Charlie,' said Johnny.

'Especially over those two locked drawers inside the peter. But then, after Eddie explained it all to us well, I was OK about it then. If you know what I mean?'

'Yeah, John,' I replied. 'But isn't this all about trust?'

'Yeah, kid, you're right, it is all about trust. '

'Well, then, if you think about it they have got to trust me and you now.'

'How? What do you mean, Charlie?'

'Well, take a look at that, John,' I said as I pointed to the briefcase on the table. 'What's inside that is worth a fortune and Eddie and Vinny know it, and so do we, but they have trusted the two of us with it. Now if we were a pair or rip-off merchants we could easily both fuck off with all that gold, but we haven't and we won't.'

Johnny looked at me as if he hadn't thought about it like that.

'And do you know what... that had never even crossed your mind had it, John, to pull a stroke like that?'

He looked at the briefcase and shook his head. 'No, it hasn't.' Then after a moment's pause he began to laugh. 'Shall we fuck off with it all now then, Charlie?' Obviously, he was only joking. The man lived by a strict code of honour and possessed good principles. After all they were paying us out twenty grand which is the equivalent in this day and age of about five hundred grand or there abouts. That is what you call some money in 1960!

We had a laugh and sat talking for a while. It was getting late now, well past midnight. The four of us had had a productive evening, but now it was time to get our heads down, as there was to be another busy day for us tomorrow. I don't know about Johnny but I ended up crashing out on my bed like a log.

I woke up fairly late the next day, past twelve o'clock. It was a Sunday. My body must have really needed that sleep. I could hear the sound of the radio coming from the lounge of the apartment. That will be Johnny, I thought, already up and about as usual. It's funny how younger people can sleep for hours on end and yet older people always seem to be up bright and early. I had better make a move and get up. I got up out of bed and shivered. It was November and the weather was getting decidedly colder. I shivered again as I went into the bathroom for a nice hot shower. Following my shower and getting dressed and ready, I felt wide awake and full of energy.

I heard Johnny call me from the lounge, laughing: 'Come on, lazy bones. I see you're finally up, eh? It's about time too. Come on I've got your tea poured out and a couple of rounds of toast ready. Hurry up before it gets cold, Charlie.'

I smiled to myself when I heard him. Johnny was always there for me no matter what. He was one of my many older mentors, just like my brother Freddy and Tosh, Francie and Keiron.

I went into the lounge and found Johnny sitting at the table reading the Sunday morning papers. Incredibly, he must have been out and about to buy them earlier on. 'There you go, kid,' he said pointing at the tea and hot toast.

'Aw, thanks, John,' I said, about to get stuck in to the hot toast and tea. He mentioned that Eddie and Vinny would be calling shortly. He went on to say that they would be transporting the gold to some downer (buyer) and this was of course when Johnny and I would get paid. I was dead excited at the thought of it now. Wow all that money! All kinds of nice things were starting to go through my young head, including a new car. After all a brand new Rolls Royce or a Bentley then only cost five and a half to six grand. Now they are over two hundred grand or thereabouts; not that I would be buying a Rolls Royce back then; they were for old rich men not a young kid like me.

Eddie and Vinny arrived not long afterwards. They both looked dead chuffed as they came inside. We were all buzzing for that matter! The four of us gathered around the table to discuss what the next step would be. Vinny and Eddie went on to explain how they would get the gold to the buyer. Then they stressed that when they *did* deliver the gold to him, the buyer would have to go over it carefully to work out the true monetary value of it all. After all, none of us knew how much it was worth. The only clue we would get as to its cash value would be however much it was reported to be worth on the news or in the newspapers. That would be the only way we would have any idea but as yet it was not on the news. We knew it was worth a fortune and we were all now convinced that that robbery wouldn't come on top until tomorrow morning, Monday, by which time Johnny and I would be on our journey back home to Liverpool.

Johnny was annoyed. 'What are you telling us now, Eddie? Is it that me and Charlie won't get weighed in until all this is sorted?'

'Well, yeah, in a way, John, but the buyer has got to go over every item in that briefcase. We all know it's worth a lot of dough, there's no doubt about that, but put yourself in his place, John.'

Johnny suddenly looked gutted and I felt the same. It's not that we thought we were getting ripped off or anything, it was just that we hadn't been prepared for this to happen.

'Alright then, Eddie, how long is all this fuckin' about going to take?'

'Two to three days at least, John,' Eddie replied. 'And I know you and Charlie are travelling back to the Pool tomorrow. But, I mean, you can both stay and hang out here for a few more days if you want to, but on the other hand, the man (the buyer) has pulled up a big lump of dough for you to be going on with, as a good will gesture.'

Eddie then turned to Vinny. 'Show them, Vinny.' Vinny smiled as he pulled out a big wad of money from his overcoat pocket and put it firmly down on the table in front of us. 'There's five grand up front if that's any consolation for you, John. And not forgetting that once I pass him that case it will be well out of our hands.' Eddie paused looking concerned. 'It's all business. I will personally guarantee you that you will be paid out in a few days from now.' He appeared to be sincere in what he was saying and the way he explained it.

John turned and looked at me. 'What do you think, Charlie?'

I was in a world of my own thinking about the parcel of money on the table. I thought, Five grand, that in itself is an incredible amount of cash. I got excited and had butterflies in my stomach just thinking about it.

Johnny asked me again, 'Charlie, what do you think of that?'

His voice brought me back to my senses. 'Yeah. Yeah, I'll go along with that.'

'OK, Eddie,' said Johnny. 'If that's the way it has to be we will leave it at that.'

It was touching around half past four by this time and beginning to get really dark so we began to make a start on things. The gold was transferred into a suitcase of Vinny's. We also told Vinny and Eddie that we wanted to travel back tomorrow with no incriminating evidence on us whatsoever. Vinny assured us that this wouldn't be a problem. He said he would get shut of our work tools the next day without fail, including the most important tool of all: what was left of the gelignite. There was just one stick and two detonators. We all shook hands with each other and after they reassured us that Vinny would come and pick us both up in the morning, Eddie and Vinny both left with the bounty of gold.

So, true to his word, Vinny picked us up the next morning, Monday, and he dropped us off at the train station as arranged. Johnny and I boarded our train on time and travelled the few hours home to our city of Liverpool.

CHAPTER 40

BACK ON HOME GROUND – LIVERPOOL

A few days after arriving home, Johnny called to see me. He had bought himself a nice motor and as usual he was immaculately dressed.

'I'm having a party tonight, Charlie. You and your friends are invited if you fancy it?'

'Yeah, John, I'm up for that.'

'You know, kid, I thought we could celebrate after us pulling that good move we had off.'

This was the way Johnny lived, always in the fast lane... parties, women, to him it was easy come, easy go. He spent money like there was no tomorrow. But then, who am I to talk? I had already been living it up myself with my friends over those past two days and at that time in my young life, money came in fast and it got spent fast. So, really, I wasn't dissimilar to Johnny, except of course, I always tried to make sure that my priority, my family, got looked after, especially my mother. Also, if any of my friends were having a hard time, regarding money, I would always help out. Talking about loyal friends, I grafted with most of them when we were kids and obviously some of them are still at it, but not in the league I was in. Money was still tight back in the late fifties and early sixties.

After the celebrations at Johnny's and the hectic partying, we came back down to reality and set our feet firmly on the ground. We needed to make a phone call to Vinny and Eddie. The reply that came back was from Vinny telling us that it would take a bit longer to get things sorted at their end. Johnny asked Vinny to put Eddie on the blower but it just so happened that Eddie wasn't there as he was away sorting some other business out.

It's funny how you sometimes get a sense about things, like sussing a situation or a person out. You can get a gut feeling that something isn't quite right. This is how I felt about the situation we found ourselves in with Eddie and Vinny. I knew something wasn't quite right and alarm bells began to ring. I became suspicious on hearing of Vinny's reply and especially when being told that suddenly Eddie wasn't about to talk to.

Another week went by. Once again Johnny and I were on the blower to them but the phone just rang out this the time without a reply. Johnny had become agitated over it all now too. I put it to him that one of two things could have happened here: 'They might have come unstuck dabbling with that gold and associating with the buyer, Johnny,' I said to him diplomatically. 'Or, and you mightn't like what I am about to say, John, but I have got a gut feeling about this... we have both been had by the two of them!'

Johnny was taken aback by this. 'No, Charlie. It can't be. Not Eddie. He *will* make contact. I'm sure there has got to be a good reason for this.' I knew that he was really trying to convince himself of this and I was sure that deep down he just didn't want to believe what had happened.

Two days later, my suspicions were confirmed. We made another call to Vinny's pad and this time the phone was answered by a woman. She told us that it was *her* apartment and that she didn't know anybody by the name of Eddie *or* Vinny. Her line was that she had rented out the pad while she had been abroad for six weeks. Furthermore, she was reluctant to talk and so had put the phone down on us.

'That says it all, John. Doesn't it?'

'Yeah, it does. We have been truly fucked by that pair of rats.' Johnny was completely raving mad over it all. 'I'll kill them,' he shouted slamming the phone down. He wanted to muster a few of the boys together and go down there to sort them out. In reality though it would have been a wild goose chase. London is a big place and travelling up and down there would be like looking for a needle in a haystack. Those two pricks could be anywhere by now. Maybe abroad, who knows? We had to admit defeat and accept it. Besides, it was not the time to cop for them but that would come later, years later. That experience did one thing for me though: I would find it hard to trust anybody again, especially outsiders.

Johnny and I split up after that last safe blowing move we did back in 1960 and we went our separate ways, still on good terms though. We both knew and so too did other friends of ours, particularly the older ones, that crime was changing at the start of the 1960s.

CHAPTER 41

THE END OF AN ERA

I had come a long way since that day in 1956 when I was just a sixteen year old kid. I had joined up with a gang of older men one of whom was my brother. They were notorious safe crackers and how they toiled and sweated opening those safes using sledge hammers, rail bars and hacksaws was to me both time-consuming and primitive. I had come up with an idea that I tentatively put to them, which I had gleaned from watching an old black and white film about Jesse James, the outlaw. I had explained to them about how over a hundred years ago Jesse James and his gang used explosives to blow open safes on trains. I knew this would be quicker and more successful.

At first they had laughed at the idea and embarrassed me. One of them said in a sarcastic manner, 'Listen, kid. You are talking about a cowboy movie, set over a hundred years ago.'

'Yeah,' I replied. 'It might be over a hundred years ago but they were more advanced than you are here and now.'

When I outlined my progressive plan and put to them that the best way forward to successfully blow open the safes was to use gelignite, they agreed. To which end, we went ahead and became professional safe blowers. Once we put my plan into action and got started there was no stopping us. Using this high explosive called gelignite, we were hitting places up and down the country then the inevitable happened: other criminals began to use this way forward of safe blowing. In the 1950s, it did at one time become an epidemic. Our crew eventually got pulled in by the police for questioning and one particular detective who was interviewing me at the time asked me, 'What do you know about all this jelly?'

I don't know why but that word *jelly* that the police used when interviewing just stuck with our crew, and we became known as *The Jelly Gang*.

Safe blowing crimes eventually became a thing of the past. In essence it was the end of an era.

CHAPTER 42

WHAT BECAME OF THE JELLY GANG?

TOSH'S STORY: He decided to quit at the right time in his life, being at the age of forty plus. He knew that if he had carried on, at some point, he would have eventually come unstuck and be sent away to prison for many years. For Tosh, what would hurt him the most would not be the fact that he was to be locked up in jail but the thought of him being parted for years on end from his loving wife and children. That would have totally broken his heart.

No, Tosh could visualise those dangers and as he was wise to it he got out while the going was good. He ended up with his own successful, legitimate business and lived happily ever after together with his wife and family. It has been over forty years since I last set eyes on Tosh and I never heard of him again until being given the news that he had died peacefully, still in the loving embrace of his close family. To me he was a real kind hearted man. He never did any serious harm to anybody. His only weakness? Robbing safes of course!

FRANCIE'S STORY: The younger one of the Oates brothers. He too could see the writing on the wall. Really, we all knew it was only a matter of time what with the bizzies breathing down your neck and their harassment; not knowing when or where they will cop for you. At that time if the police had any inclination that you were active and still at it, they would with all their devious methods set you up without a second thought.

Francie though was a smart and clever fella and he was still only young; in his late twenties at the most. He knew it wasn't wise to hang around for too long. He went out to the States and settled in New York and did well for himself. He got himself involved with the right people. He too owned a legitimate business, operating honestly and living the good life until his death just a few years ago still over in America. I will never forget him.

FREDDY'S STORY: I think right from the beginning he was just unlucky and when it came to crime it was no exception.

Having served two prison sentences, the last one being for safe blowing, and having two failed marriages, crime didn't really pay for him. At first in his criminal way of life everything was just fine; things were going right and the money was coming in thick and fast but, having been divorced on his last sentence for the second time and losing the love of his wife and child, he was absolutely devastated. We, that is, the family and I, all thought he would get over it but as luck would have it not long afterwards he was crossing a main road in Liverpool and a fast speeding car smashed into him. It severely injured the back of his head. He was rushed to hospital where the staff there fought to save his life. He was even given the last rights by the hospital priest but due to the skilful work of the brain surgeons he finally recovered. Unfortunately, though Freddy would never be the same man again.

He started to wander aimlessly around the city and his appearance became increasingly dishevelled and unkempt. He also began to drink heavily and he eventually became an alcoholic. Now, it's not as though he never received any help because he did and believe me it was plenty. My whole family, especially my mother, all tried our best to assist him in trying to get his life back on track but it was to no avail, and it got so bad that at times it became embarrassing.

He would wander around dressed like a tramp, and under the influence of drink he always ending up drunk in a police station. Various members of the family would take turns to go down there to rescue him. Everywhere he went to live he would invariably get kicked out due to his drunken behaviour. It seemed though that we were all fighting a losing battle, until one day, after several years of him abusing his body with alcohol and neglect, it came as no surprise to us when one freezing cold night he was found by the police huddled in a shop doorway in the city centre of Liverpool, dead.

To think, he was my older brother, who at one time was one of the smartest looking well-dressed fellas around. He was highly intelligent and well respected by the rest of the criminal fraternity of safe breakers. However, we all knew it was due to his skull being smashed in during that terrible accident; it had caused something in his brain to change and the man he used to be was no longer there. There was an inquest carried out and a small write up was reported in the Liverpool Echo: *Man found dead, etc. Was known to the police as a professional safe cracker in his day.*

KEIRON'S STORY: When he came out of prison after serving his seven stretch I met him in town one day. He seemed slightly withdrawn. I had always visualised him as the smartly dressed and carefree man I had known, who was always so full of life. Prison had obviously taken its toll on him. It was rumoured that he had become paranoid and was terrified of going back into prison. I believe he did try his best to settle down and stay out of trouble. Eventually, he *did* go straight and he became employed by the local council and for a short period of time all was well with him then, a tragedy happened. In fact what happened to him was a living nightmare.

Johnny, Keiron's older brother was still bang at it, which to me was unbelievable for a man his age but, nevertheless, he was still active in crime. Instead of bowing out like most fellas do when they know they are really past it, and let's face it Johnny had had a good life over the years and had made himself plenty, what does he go and do... only an armed robbery of all things, and it was a serious crime.

To come unstuck in the 1960s on something like that meant that the sentences would be severe. You could be looking at ten to fifteen years. Before Johnny was charged with the violent robbery, he had always stayed in contact with Keiron. Being the older brother, Johnny would often call to visit Keiron just to check on his welfare, since he seemed vulnerable after his sentence, and so he always went to check on how he was managing. Keiron at the time had no inclination whatsoever about Johnny and company doing an armed robbery but, somewhere down the line and through information received, the police arrested and charged Johnny with the offence. They knew that there was more than one person involved in that crime so the police then arrested Keiron, who had nothing at all to do with it, nevertheless, they said he was implicated.

By this time Keiron had gone to pieces through the fear of going back to prison. He was completely innocent. His brother Johnny knew this and so did all their associates, friends and the whole community around at the time but, worse was that so too did the police themselves. Their motto though was *Once a thief, always a thief* and if Keiron had reformed, so what? They were just *putting things right for what he has done and got away with in the past.* They didn't care; they just went out of their way to make sure that he was found guilty of this violent robbery along with his brother.

Eventually, the two of them stood side by side in the dock at Liverpool Crown Court. Both pleaded not guilty but it was a kangaroo court from the word go. The evidence against Keiron was so weak it was pathetic. At one point in the hearing, Keiron was asked to put a nylon stocking over his head in front of the jury. According to the police, this was supposed to be how he had been identified, with a nylon stocking over his head. Keiron was advised by his legal team to refuse the request but because he had nothing to hide and thought that this would prove his innocence he insisted that he went ahead and did it. The police witness had apparently picked him out dressed like this and had unbelievably claimed that they could identify Keiron just by the contours of his facial bone structure being visible shaped through the mask of the stocking. It could have been anyone under there; we would all look the same under a nylon stocking. It was impossible to get the true identity of anyone in this way. Well, if that's not a liberty I don't know what is. The trial was a shambles from the beginning to the end!

Sadly, Keiron was found guilty along with his brother. The court was packed with the public and a tense atmosphere descended as everyone waited to see what sentences they were going to receive from the Judge. As was usual, the Judge asked if they had anything to say before he passed sentence. Johnny spoke emotionally to the Judge as he asked him to have mercy on his younger brother: 'My brother had nothing to do with this. My brother is an innocent man. He shouldn't be standing here in the dock with me.'

After Johnny pleading in earnest to the Judge, there was a pause and a hush fell over the entire court. It would have been the same old story in the Judge's mind: *Why didn't he proclaim this earlier on?* Except how could he when he himself was pleading not guilty? Earlier on knowing that the evidence wasn't all that strong, he thought he had a chance of been found not guilty.

Unfortunately though when he made this plea of his brother's innocence it was far too late. The judge looked at them stood together in the dock then spoke with a voice of ice. 'You have both been found guilty of this violent crime.' Then he pronounced their sentences. Keiron got sent down for ten years and Johnny got twelve years. Can you imagine what Keiron Oates mind must have been like after he knew in his own heart that he was an innocent man? He had been determined never to go to prison again and now there he was about to begin to serve a long sentence. Ten years of his life to languish away in a prison cell.

Through the first three to four years of his sentence friends and family regularly went up to visit him. His health rapidly deteriorated and so too did his mind. Prisoners who had served their time in prison with him and had since been released said they found it terribly sad to watch him. One local fella who used to try to console him in there stated that Keiron used to huddle up in a corner of his lonely cell like a frightened animal and that he wouldn't talk to anybody. It was just so sad. Eventually, the years had gone slowly by and Keiron, by now, was a broken soul. After all the years of his sentence he had served in there and only having but a few weeks left to do, Keiron hung himself in his cell.

I often wondered what must have been going through his messed up mind at that time when he knew he only had a matter of weeks to go. Maybe he thought: *What's the use when they (the police) might fit me up again and send me back in here.* Because after all, he had been unquestionably, entirely innocent of all charges last time!

I will always remember Keiron and what a thoughtful and kind man he was. He would always be the first to help any old man or woman who might be having a hard time. He had a lot of respect for the elderly. His character was amazing. He was always full of life and for him to end up the way he did was not only a waste of a life but a heartbreaking tragedy.

JOHNNY'S STORY: He eventually came to the end of his long prison sentence. He never went back into crime, his days were well over. The last time I set eyes on him was years later. It was the beginning of the 1980s. I remember seeing him just staring out of a cafe window as I was passing by. He seemed to be deep in thought, he looked lost, just sitting there gazing out through the window. I went into the cafe to see him.

'Hello, Johnny,' I said as I entered. He looked up at me as if he didn't recognise me at first then he gave a faint smile. 'Hello, Charlie, kid,' he said in one of those vague voices.

I sat down and joined him and we had a little chat together, but all the spark had gone out of him. The joviality he had been known for had all gone. I could tell by his mannerisms and his whole demeanour that he had lost it. I don't think he ever got over Keiron. He probably blamed himself for what happened all those years ago. I did hear that some of his family had ostracized him because of it. The last I heard of him was when he died of cancer just a few years later.

EPILOGUE

I can categorically state that those older guys who I grafted with in the safe blowing business never once used any kind of violence and I'm not stating this in an attempt to justify what any of us did but, it was absolutely true. Those fellas committed the crimes when times were rough and money was hard to come by. It was solely for the purpose of providing for their families; their wives and children... and yes of course it did better their own lives too and enabled them to sample some of the good things in life that otherwise would have been unattainable.

There is one thing for sure: as a kid I had learnt quite a lot from them, they were my mentors, those old safe robbers. Not only did I glean criminal knowledge and organisational skills but I also had instilled into me good qualities and values, each of which those men certainly possessed. They were all staunch men right to the core and I carry those same intrinsic and honourable virtues with me until this day.

They knew how to make money and above all how to live; sampling the best that life could offer them. To think, I played a great part in this activity just through seeing Jesse James in that movie. The whole idea of blowing safes open using gelignite came from him and so too did the reason that we became known as *The Jelly Gang*.

As for myself I was still only a young man with many years ahead of me and so I continued in my chosen way of life. But then, that's another story...

Charlie Seiga 2013

If you have enjoyed this book, you will love Charlie's interviews on Shaun Attwood's podcast on YouTube, and we appreciate your Amazon reviews.

ABOUT THE AUTHOR

Bestselling author of
Killer, The Hyenas, A Liverpool Streetwise Kid
and **A Killer Vigilante**

In 1952, quote from Charlie: 'My life of crime began after I had a vicious street-fight with another kid. He was the local hard-case bully; he and his gang used to waylay me and my two friends. My friends and I were good little earners at that time, and because they couldn't make anything themselves, the hard case bully used to force us to hand over any gear that we had on us. It was like a sort of mugging that goes on today. He was bigger and older than me; aged 15, but I fronted him up and made a mess of him. That gained me the respect of all the local street kids, and I became a gang leader; I was just 12 years old!'

At the age of thirteen he meets his mentor a woman of thirty-eight years old, her name is Winnie. With Winnie, Charlie progresses further, she has him well-groomed and dressed as an office boy wearing a blazer and shirt and tie and she teaches him how to steal expensive diamond rings from under the noses of high class jewellers. This was well planned out, displaying real classic cases of robberies which were highly rewarding.

In 1954 at the age of fourteen and with his daring young gang they pulled off robberies that would put a professional criminal to shame, and he became one of the richest teenagers in the city of Liverpool, where they operated from.

1955. At fifteen years old he eventually gets caught for a jewel heist and even though he is a juvenile he still gets severely treated and interrogated. Police methods were ruthless in those days. He was taken outside in the freezing cold winter rain and handcuffed to a cast iron drainpipe for hours all because he refused to sign a confessed statement. Eventually he was remanded to a juvenile remand home, where he witnessed the sexual abuse of young boys, by their carers, who liked to be called Master or Sir. Charlie rebelled over what he had seen, and due to the subsequent uproar he caused in the remand home he was finally released on bail and, ironically, all charges against him were dropped.

Quote from Charlie: 'Before arriving at Woolton Vale juvenile remand home, I had heard all kinds of stories from kids on the outside about what went on there. Some of the staff were beasts. At night in the dormitory it would sometimes happen. One of the staff would come in pretending he was just saying goodnight and then select one of the little kids and the filth would start. Some of those kids were only about nine or ten years old. The beatings I witnessed were terrible too. How these people got these jobs was beyond me. Those days, forty-five years ago, everything was 'hushed up' and it would be twenty years before the outside world faced up to the problem and accepted that for decades it had been the kids telling the truth and the wardens and staff who had been lying. I knew then that nobody would believe the kids if they complained. I was fortunate nobody tried anything on me... maybe it was because I was bigger and older and could handle myself.'

1956, aged sixteen Charlie turned more and more into a young gangster; but a gangster with a difference. One who will grow to live by his code of honour. He hates women beaters and child molesters. His presence becomes a constant challenge to the lowlife that prey on those who cannot defend themselves.

1957, at the age of seventeen, he mastered the art of safe blowing; which at the time was considered the pinnacle of excellence amongst the top criminal fraternity; and they gave him their respect. He was eventually arrested and remanded to an adult prison. As the crime was serious and high profile; high-ranking police officers from different parts of the country where safe-blowing crimes had taken place, came to interrogate him, (which in those days, was severe), but he refused their requests to talk.

At the High Court in the city of Chester, he stood charged with this serious offence. The right honourable Mr Justice Castles; who presided over his case, was quoted as saying: 'He is like a young lion who had tasted his first blood.' But through a legal and a technical point at the trial, the seventeen year old Charlie Seiga walked out of the court free, and made history for being the youngest safe-blower in Great Britain!

In 1964 at twenty-two years of age, he served a prison sentence of two years in Walton Prison, Liverpool. It was alleged he was dangerously armed with a shot gun; it is said he kept a gang of men including a police officer at bay, while his gang escaped.

Quote from Charlie: 'To be honest when I entered the prison I had acquired a massive reputation, it gained me respect amongst the top cons, so with a bit of pull here and there I was given a cushy job.'

He was appointed work on the prison reception. One of his duties was to serve meals to the last person in Britain to be hanged! He recalls seeing the condemned prisoner (his name was Allen) arriving back from court having been sentenced to death, being taken to the condemned cell, and being the last person to speak to him.

Quote from Charlie: 'I remember saying to Allen "You'll be ok, you'll get your reprieve." He seemed confident because six months before; a man named Masters was in the same condemned cell and he got reprieved. Also at that time in 1964 capital punishment was about to be abolished.'

Allen though was unlucky... he was hanged!

On the morning of the hanging all the prisoners in Walton Prison went from uproar to complete silence. We all knew that he was dead. After about an hour all our cells were unlocked; a friend of mine who was a cleaner told me he had been ordered to clean out the condemned cell; he told me it had been in a terrible mess there were blood stains on the walls and some of the furniture was broken. Later on one of the screws told us that Allen had put up a ferocious fight. I believe what used to happen was that if the condemned man struggled or tried to resist there would be a gang of screws as a back-up, who also assisted the hangman.

In the late 1960s and 70s Charlie became one of the most successful villains of his time. Police believed he was the brains behind the major firms involved in bank raids, wage snatches armed robberies and other serious crimes involving hundreds of thousands of pounds, but they remained unable to convict him; he became known as the 'Houdini' of the criminal underworld.

In the 1980s and 90s, crime had rapidly changed, the old school type gangster had almost disappeared, a new breed of criminal had emerged; and the vast majority of these became ruthless in their activities. The gun became, and still is, the weapon of choice. Gangster wars had broken out amongst the criminal fraternity!

In 1998 he went on trial for murder; he was accused of pumping three bullets into the head of one of these new lowlife breeds. He had also been questioned over other killings which were swift, brutal and brilliantly organised.

Quote from Charlie: 'It is quite true that I have been accused of killing other men and questioned about unsolved contract killings; the Liverpool Murder Squad, in their eyes still believe I was responsible. But they are wrong.'

Quote from the trial judge: 'This is a classic case of a contract killing.'

He was acquitted. No one has ever been convicted of the murder.

CROWN COURT

Regina V Charles Seiga

Particulars in Support of Reg. 9 (5) (B)

This was all in all as gruelling and hard-fought a murder trial as any I can remember in my 27 years at the criminal bar, in which time I have defended in literally dozens of important murder trials. This was a trial which demanded long hours of preparation at nights, weekends and in the early mornings in my hotel room to prepare for cross examination.

It was a dramatic and even a thrilling case. Nobody present will ever forget its atmosphere or the scenes of pandemonium in the public gallery which accompanied the final not guilty verdict.

This trial lasted 19 working days in all and I have to say I under-estimated both its length and factual difficulties at the outset. This was, in summary, in the very top league of contested murder trials in this country.

Jonathan Goldberg
3/11/98

CONFIDENTIAL POLICE MEMO

Liverpool Police Force 1998

Charles Antony Seiga - D.O.B. 7/4/1940

Charlie Seiga had a reputation for being a violent character. Intelligence was constantly being received of shootings being perpetrated by this man, but rarely would anyone come forward to complain about him.

He was known to be a careful planner and always seemed

to provide a back door for himself when he knew he was to be arrested. He would often disappear after such events, and when the heat died down, would calmly walk into a police station and give himself up, knowing full well that the complaint had either been withdrawn or that the complainant, through fear, had been bought off.

He would vent his violence on other criminals who harmed or tried to bully his family or friends.

Having left the police force and now retired, it came as no surprise to me when I read about Seiga being arrested for a contract killing. How he got out of that one I do not know, and the secret of that job, along with many others, will no doubt be carried with him to his grave. The police are not looking for anyone else in relation to this matter and, in my experience; they must be more than satisfied that they had the correct man in the dock.

He was commonly known as Charlie Seiga, but we had another name for him - Killer!

Charlie Seiga became the longest reigning gangster in Great Britain; stretching from the 50s right up to the late 90s. He retired from a life of crime a few years ago; he is now reformed and a successful crime writer.

His books are still selling strongly today; as they will never date, and they are relevant to today's society.

Charlie Seiga has always been an enemy of and hates the lowlife in society who perpetrate such vile acts as rapists, women beaters and child molesters.

A script is currently being written based on this unique, eventful and powerful life story!

JUST A NOTE: All these hard hitting true stories and more can be read in Charlie Seiga's book titles:

KILLER
A LIVERPOOL STREETWISE KID
THE HYENAS
A KILLER VIGILANTE
LIVERPOOL'S NOTORIOUS JELLY GANG

A BRIEF SYNOPSIS OF CHARLIE SEIGA'S OTHER BOOKS

KILLER

By Charlie Seiga

Charlie Seiga was one of the most dangerous faces of the criminal underworld. There were many unsolved killings which were swift, brutal and brilliantly organised. The victims - liberty takers and sadists - were all hard bastards who dealt in the most vicious kind of violence. Many times the police marked him out as the vicious contract killer.

He was also one of the most successful villains of his time. Police believed that he was the brains behind major firms involved in robberies on banks, security vans, lorry hijacking, safe breaking and many other serious crimes. He lost track of the times he was arrested and questioned about various jobs, but he always had an alibi - a witness to say he wasn't guilty of the crime. He was the Houdini of the criminal underworld.

His story is a shocking tale of violence and crime; but it is also a story about one man's fight against the scum who break his deadly code of honour. He hates women beaters and child molesters.

His presence was a constant challenge to the low life that preyed on those who could not defend themselves.

It is an incredible autobiography of one of the most notorious figures in the history of British crime.

'... LIKE WALKING INTO A SCENE FROM THE GOODFELLAS' LOADED
'CHILLING AND COMPLETELY ABSORBING'
SUNDAY PEOPLE

A LIVERPOOL STREETWISE KID

By Charlie Seiga

Times were hard in the 1940s and early 1950s. Kids went hungry and food was rationed. Some families had to beg, steal or borrow to survive. There seemed no way out for some kids, but Charlie found his own way out. On a routine basis he and his child gang plundered every shop they came across, robbing them of their food to put on the family table and their goods to sell on.

At the age of thirteen and always bunking off school, he went on to make further progress in his way of life. With his baby face and dressed as an office boy in blazer, shirt and tie, he was darting in and out of the office buildings in the city centre of Liverpool, raiding their cash draws and safes.

Quote from Charlie: 'We had one of the best little firms in Huyton, we got up to all kinds of things; fighting, robbery, you name it. Nobody could stop us or so I thought. I was scared of nothing and of nobody; especially the bizzies (police). In 1954 and at the tender age of fourteen I was earning more money than a professional adult. I was the richest, poor teenager in Liverpool.'

A Streetwise Kid is a brilliant combination of narrative writing, memoir and biography. A true story of a childhood villain and his young gang growing up in war torn Liverpool.

A KILLER VIGILANTE

By Charlie Seiga

A major breakdown in society has descended, and everything is spiralling out of control on council ghettos across the city. The police don't have the ability to deal with it and are demoralised. The streets are lawless. Marauding gangs are committing the vilest acts imaginable: rapes, violence against old people, arson attacks on family homes and gun crime. Unfortunately, decent hard working people live amongst it all. It is an unbearable existence for them, until John Christian, who was born and bred on the council estate many years before, comes up with a solution to the problem. After recruiting and forming his own crew; their belief was that the low-life scum who terrorise the women, kids, old and infirm should be terrorised themselves in a more frightening manner than they could ever 1mag1ne.

Their presence on the streets becomes a constant challenge to the lowlife and when the team happen to capture any of these vile yobs, the justice they inflict on the scum is swift, brutal and brilliantly organised.

They become known as vigilantes who sheriff their own community. This book contains violence in the most graphic detail.

REVIEWS OF CHARLIE SEIGA'S OTHER BOOKS

'A Liverpool Streetwise Kid'

After reading Charlie's first book Killer I couldn't wait to get my hands on this new title. I read it cover to cover without stopping for breath. The life story of Charlie's childhood years growing up in Liverpool and learning his criminal trade was both fascinating, funny and sad. This book left me crying and laughing at the true stories he tells page after page. I highly recommend this book as a must read!

Fred, Amazon UK

A brilliant combination of narrative writing, memoir and biography.

Kevin Bryan, Publisher, Cumbria

Wow! What a read! After reading Charlies first book Killer I couldn't wait to get my hands on this new title. I read it cover to cover without stopping for breath. The life story of Charlies childhood years growing up in Liverpool and learning his criminal trade was both fascinating, funny and sad. This book left me crying and laughing at the true stories he tells page after page. I highly recommend this book as a must read!

Sarah Johnson, St Helens

Fabulously real narrative! A Kid's Review! Charlie's childhood could never be described as dull and ordinary. He and his family found themselves needing, and Charlie went out there and provide...any way he could! This book is a true gem. The descriptions of the environment in war torn Liverpool will ring bells for many others who suffered and lived through the hard times of yesteryear. And those who were lucky enough not to will get a unique insight into the true way it was! It is sensitive, moving, funny and truly entertaining. This wonderful book is a social history as well as an autobiography; real page turner and a story you can read again and again. It is not unlike a modern day Oliver Twist! Any money spent on buying this book will be money well spent. If only all autobiographies were this honest and raw straight from the horse's mouth. FABULOUS BOOK FABULOUS AUTHOR!!

A. Customer. Amazon UK

Fascinating! The early years autobiography of Charlie Seiga, one of Liverpool's most notorious criminals and author of 'Killers' and 'The Hyenas'. This fascinating book tells how his life of crime began and is in turn sensitive, moving, funny as well as spelling out his villainous ways, always with a strict code of honour. A very scarce book.

Godfry Books

The huckleberry fin of Liverpool! This book is such an unusual narrative for these days, as it is of a 'child' gangster for the want of a better word. Charlie Seiga was just 12 years old when he turned to crime to provide food and other basics for the large family he was from. He starts off just stealing food and sweets but then after meeting his mentor; a thirty odd year old woman who teaches him all she knows about blagging and thieving on a more lucrative level. Charlie Seiga writes about his younger years after writing his first book Killer and getting asked to write in more detail about his childhood. And so as requested here is A Liverpool Streetwise Kid...all the ups and downs, and sad and funny tails of the 'Huckleberry Fin' of (too many line spaces here Jane)Liverpool. Highly recommended. Buy it and read it, you won't be disappointed...5 Star!!!

A Customer

'A Killer Vigilante'

A KILLER VIGILANTE is an exciting read and would make a good film. It is interesting and well written. Some scenes even show off Charlie's sensitive, emotional side. It is written in a very gripping, vivid style, and what impresses me most is the visual power of Charlie's narration; I can really visualise the places, people and situations - it is almost like being there!

Prof Tomasz Pobog-Malinowski
- Professor Emeritus, Media, Edge Hill University
- Visiting Professor, Film Production, University of Lincoln
Producer-Director Flying Brick Films

Gripping! I had to sit and finish this book once I started it as I just couldn't put it down. Well written, and totally gripping. I can't wait to read his other stuff1

Laura C *from Newton-Le-Willows*

Masterpiece! This is another masterpiece by local author Charlie Seiga. It is a fantastic gripping story which I read in one day as I could not put it down. A real feel good story knowing that the bad guys got their just desserts. I would actually say that this is my favourite book by Charlie (and I have read them all) and I hope that he brings out a sequel as I would love to read that too. His writing is gritty and sometimes quite gruesome but true to the story. I have recommended this book to many of my friends and bought several as Christmas presents and the response has been great. Everyone loved it. Keep the good work up Charlie.

Lynch

Surprisingly philosophical! Charlie doesn't only tell a good story but he is very philosophical about things. He highlights the turmoil of the country, very topical at the moment with the current rebellions and the like. He talks of how the people in power let our countrymen down. Charlie Seiga's books and Vigilante in particular were recommended to me as I study social behaviour and the deprivation of some of society, and having read it; I now have no hesitation in recommending this book to everyone.

Roger Emmington, London

Excellent! Gripping, realistic and graphic! This is by far the best crime book I have read in years! Charlie Seiga will be the next big Crime writer of this decade! Great read from an ex pat here in Australia!!! This is a must read!! I have read his other true crime books and this is another hit!

Paul Mc from Australia

Powerful Story! I wasn't sure if I would like this book as it said it was very graphically brutal but it was recommended to me and I thought I would give it a go. It was a great story that kept me interested right to the end and that must be good because usually I start a book but don't finish it as I am not a big reader. It is really, really brutal but only the scum bags get hurt and right from the beginning you are on the side of John Christian. It is shocking to think that in some areas of the north-west these things are actually going on; on a daily basis. The Vigilantes do all they can to even the balance in favour of the victims and I wouldn't be surprised if this story made people think about standing up for themselves and beating the bullies at their own game. It is definitely a book that will get people talking and debating, I would highly recommend 'Vigilante' to everyone old or young, man or woman, you will be hooked from the start. I hope there is a sequel to this title and it would make a brilliant film.

Sammijaz From Cheshire

Good Work Charlie! It's a rare thing when after finishing a book you immediately go back to the beginning and start again. That was the case with Charlie Seiga's Vigilante. I never wanted it to end, so it earned itself a second read, which was exactly what I did. I've read some of Seiga's books before, Killer being one of my favourites, but Vigilante is up with there with the best of them. What makes it stand out from others is how real and robust it is. Nothing is left to the imagination and it's clear that Seiga has experienced firsthand what goes on in its pages. Not since Paul Schrader and Martin Scorsese teamed up to make the all-time classic Taxi Driver has a book of this type grabbed my attention so much. It was 1976 when De Niro hit our screens with his unmistakable portrayal of Travis Bickle. That was then and this is now, now is the time for Vigilante. Get it bought and get it read. You won't be disappointed.

Russ B from Gloucestershire

Violent... But Riveting Took this book home to Egypt and started and, finished it on the plane. It is riveting from the start. Vigilante is a brutal but truly compelling story about hitting back at the low life that are a blight on the lives of good, honest and decent people. The scum though get their just desserts. The good guys going after the bad guys; we could do with more of this to sort out and re-claim the streets and housing estates in England! Although a 'fictional' book about Liverpool vigilantes; it sounds very true to life to me!

KB from Hurghada, Egypt

Impressive! I read Charlie Seiga's new release Vigilante; it is certainly an impressive piece of work; totally convincing and up to a point the reader can empathise with John Christian. The violence although vividly described, is a necessary part of this story. However, the narrative is not all about brutal violence; it is also a good descriptive read.

Bert H from London

Awesome! I haven't read a book cover to cover for two years, despite trying several different ones every week - they simply did not hold my attention and grip me enough to want to finish them. Vigilante, however, I read within two days - I can only say that it is absolutely awesome! It is certainly close to the bone in parts, and not for the squeamish, in terms of the violence; but throughout the story, the reader is told why it is being dished out! If you are a fan of crime and thriller books, this is simply the best out there. In short if this is the genre you are into, you simply MUST read it! You will not be disappointed. Charlie Seiga has written a crime novel that will become a classic - I doubt if it will ever die out.

JR from Formby

Vigilante which I received a couple of days ago .... can't put it down!! The story is infectious and gripping.

Scott Cameron, Liverpool

OTHER BOOKS BY GADFLY PRESS

By John G Sutton:
HMP Manchester Prison Officer: I Survived Terrorists, Murderers, Rapists and Freemason Officer Attacks in Strangeways and Wormwood Scrubs

By Lee Marvin Hitchman:
How I Survived Shootings, Stabbings, Prison, Crack Addiction, Manchester Gangs and Dog Attacks

By William Rodríguez Abadía:
Son of the Cali Cartel: The Narcos Who Wiped Out Pablo Escobar and the Medellín Cartel

By Chet Sandhu:
Self-Made, Dues Paid: An Asian Kid Who Became an International Drug-Smuggling Gangster

By Kaz B:
Confessions of a Dominatrix: My Secret BDSM Life

By Peter McAleese:
Killing Escobar and Soldier Stories

By Joe Egan:
Big Joe Egan: The Toughest White Man on the Planet

By Anthony Valentine:
Britain's No. 1 Art Forger Max Brandrett: The Life of a Cheeky Faker

By Johnnyboy Steele:
Scotland's Johnnyboy: The Bird That Never Flew

By Ian 'Blink' MacDonald:
Scotland's Wildest Bank Robber: Guns, Bombs and Mayhem in Glasgow's Gangland

By Michael Sheridan:
The Murder of Sophie: How I Hunted and Haunted the West Cork Killer

By Steve Wraith:
The Krays' Final Years: My Time with London's Most Iconic Gangsters

By Natalie Welsh:
Escape from Venezuela's Deadliest Prison

By Shaun Attwood:
English Shaun Trilogy
Party Time
Hard Time
Prison Time

War on Drugs Series
Pablo Escobar: Beyond Narcos
American Made: Who Killed Barry Seal? Pablo Escobar or George

HW Bush
The Cali Cartel: Beyond Narcos
Clinton Bush and CIA Conspiracies: From the Boys on the Tracks to Jeffrey Epstein
Who Killed Epstein? Prince Andrew or Bill Clinton

Un-Making a Murderer: The Framing of Steven Avery and Brendan Dassey
The Mafia Philosopher: Two Tonys
Life Lessons

Pablo Escobar's Story (4-book series)

By Johnnyboy Steele:

Scotland's Johnnyboy: The Bird That Never Flew

"A cross between *Shawshank Redemption* and *Escape from Alcatraz*!" – Shaun Attwood, YouTuber and Author

All his life, 'Johnnyboy' Steele has been running. Firstly, from an abusive father, then from the rigours of an approved school and a young offenders jail, and, finally, from the harshness of adult prison. This book details how the Steele brothers staged the most daring breakout that Glasgow's Barlinnie prison had ever seen and recounts what happened when their younger brother, Joseph, was falsely accused of the greatest mass murder in Scottish legal history.

If Johnnyboy had wings, he would have flown to help his family, but he would have to wait for freedom to use his expertise to publicise young Joe's miscarriage of justice.

This is a compelling, often shocking and uncompromisingly honest account of how the human spirit can survive against almost crushing odds. It is a story of family love, friendship and, ultimately, a desire for justice.

By Ian 'Blink' MacDonald:

Scotland's Wildest Bank Robber: Guns, Bombs and Mayhem in Glasgow's Gangland

As a young man in Glasgow's underworld, Ian 'Blink' MacDonald earned a reputation for fighting and stabbing his enemies. After refusing to work for Arthur "The Godfather" Thompson, he attempted to steal £6 million in a high-risk armed bank robbery. While serving 16 years, Blink met the torture-gang boss Eddie Richardson, the serial killer Archie Hall, notorious lifer Charles Bronson and members of the Krays.

After his release, his drug-fuelled violent lifestyle created conflict with the police and rival gangsters. Rearrested several times, he was the target of a gruesome assassination attempt. During filming for Danny Dyer's Deadliest Men, a bomb was discovered under Blink's car and the terrified camera crew members fled from Scotland.

In *Scotland's Wildest Bank Robber*, Blink provides an eye-opening account of how he survived gangland warfare, prisons, stabbings and bombs.

By Michael Sheridan:

The Murder of Sophie: How I Hunted and Haunted the West Cork Killer

Just before Christmas, 1996, a beautiful French woman – the wife of a movie mogul – was brutally murdered outside of her holiday home in a remote region of West Cork, Ireland. The crime was reported by a local journalist, Ian Bailey, who was at the forefront of the case until he became the prime murder suspect. Arrested twice, he was released without charge.

This was the start of a saga lasting decades with twists and turns and a battle for justice in two countries, which culminated in the 2019 conviction of Bailey – in his absence – by the French

Criminal court in Paris. But it was up to the Irish courts to decide whether he would be extradited to serve a 25-year prison sentence.

With the unrivalled co-operation of major investigation sources and the backing of the victim's family, the author unravels the shocking facts of a unique murder case.

By Steve Wraith:

The Krays' Final Years: My Time with London's Most Iconic Gangsters

Britain's most notorious twins – Ron and Reg Kray – ascended the underworld to become the most feared and legendary gangsters in London. Their escalating mayhem culminated in murder, for which they received life sentences in 1969.

While incarcerated, they received letters from a schoolboy from Tyneside, Steve Wraith, who was mesmerised by their story. Eventually, Steve visited them in prison and a friendship formed. The Twins hired Steve as an unofficial advisor, which brought him into contact with other members of their crime family. At Ron's funeral, Steve was Charlie Kray's right-hand man.

Steve documents Ron's time in Broadmoor – a high-security psychiatric hospital – where he was battling insanity and heavily medicated. Steve details visiting Reg, who served almost 30 years in a variety of prisons, where the gangster was treated with the utmost respect by the staff and the inmates.

By Natalie Welsh:

Escape from Venezuela's Deadliest Prison

After getting arrested at a Venezuelan airport with a suitcase of cocaine, Natalie was clueless about the danger she was facing. Sentenced to 10 years, she arrived at a prison with armed men on the roof, who she mistakenly believed were the guards, only to find out they were homicidal gang members. Immediately, she was plunged into a world of unimaginable horror and escalating violence, where murder, rape and all-out gang warfare were carried out with the complicity of corrupt guards. Male prisoners often entered the women's housing area, bringing gunfire with them and leaving corpses behind. After 4.5 years, Natalie risked everything to escape and flee through Colombia, with the help of a guard who had fallen deeply in love with her.

By Shaun Attwood:

Pablo Escobar: Beyond Narcos

War on Drugs Series Book 1

The mind-blowing true story of Pablo Escobar and the Medellín Cartel, beyond their portrayal on Netflix.

Colombian drug lord Pablo Escobar was a devoted family man and a psychopathic killer; a terrible enemy, yet a wonderful friend. While donating millions to the poor, he bombed and tortured his enemies – some had their eyeballs removed with hot spoons. Through ruthless cunning and America's insatiable appetite for cocaine, he became a multi-billionaire, who lived in a $100-million house with its own zoo.

Pablo Escobar: Beyond Narcos demolishes the standard good versus evil telling of his story. The authorities were not hunting Pablo down to stop his cocaine business. They were taking it over.

**American Made: Who Killed Barry Seal?
Pablo Escobar or George HW Bush**

War on Drugs Series Book 2

Set in a world where crime and government coexist, *American Made* is the jaw-dropping true story of CIA pilot Barry Seal that the Hollywood movie starring Tom Cruise is afraid to tell.

Barry Seal flew cocaine and weapons worth billions of dollars into and out of America in the 1980s. After he became a government informant, Pablo Escobar's Medellin Cartel offered a million for him alive and half a million dead. But his real trouble began after he threatened to expose the dirty dealings of George HW Bush.

American Made rips the roof off Bush and Clinton's complicity in cocaine trafficking in Mena, Arkansas.

"A conspiracy of the grandest magnitude." Congressman Bill Alexander on the Mena affair.

The Cali Cartel: Beyond Narcos

War on Drugs Series Book 3

An electrifying account of the Cali Cartel, beyond its portrayal on Netflix.

From the ashes of Pablo Escobar's empire rose an even bigger and more malevolent cartel. A new breed of sophisticated mobsters became the kings of cocaine. Their leader was Gilberto Rodríguez Orejuela – known as the Chess Player, due to his foresight and calculated cunning.

Gilberto and his terrifying brother, Miguel, ran a multi-billion-dollar drug empire like a corporation. They employed a politically astute brand of thuggery and spent $10 million to put a president in power. Although the godfathers from Cali preferred bribery over violence, their many loyal torturers and hitmen were never idle.

Clinton, Bush and CIA Conspiracies: From the Boys on the Tracks to Jeffrey Epstein

War on Drugs Series Book 4

In the 1980s, George HW Bush imported cocaine to finance an illegal war in Nicaragua. Governor Bill Clinton's Arkansas state police provided security for the drug drops. For assisting the CIA, the Clinton Crime Family was awarded the White House. The #clintonbodycount continues to this day, with the deceased including Jeffrey Epstein.

This book features harrowing true stories that reveal the insanity of the drug war. A mother receives the worst news about her son. A journalist gets a tip that endangers his life. An unemployed man becomes California's biggest crack dealer. A DEA agent in Mexico is sacrificed for going after the big players.

The lives of Linda Ives, Gary Webb, Freeway Rick Ross and Kiki Camarena are shattered by brutal experiences. Not all of them will survive.

Pablo Escobar's Story (4-book series)

"Finally, the definitive book about Escobar, original and up-to-date." – UNILAD

"The most comprehensive account ever written." – True Geordie

Pablo Escobar was a mama's boy, who cherished his family and sang in the shower, yet he bombed a passenger plane and formed a death squad that used genital electrocution.

Most Escobar biographies only provide a few pieces of the puzzle, but this action-packed 1000-page book reveals everything about the king of cocaine.

Mostly translated from Spanish, Part 1 contains stories untold in the English-speaking world, including:

The tragic death of his youngest brother, Fernando.

The fate of his pregnant mistress.

The shocking details of his affair with a TV celebrity.

The presidential candidate who encouraged him to eliminate their rivals.

The Mafia Philosopher

"A fast-paced true-crime memoir with all of the action of Goodfellas." – UNILAD

"Sopranos v Sons of Anarchy with an Alaskan-snow backdrop." – True Geordie Podcast

Breaking bones, burying bodies and planting bombs became second nature to Two Tonys, while working for the Bonanno Crime Family, whose exploits inspired The Godfather.

After a dispute with an outlaw motorcycle club, Two Tonys left a trail of corpses from Arizona to Alaska. On the run, he was pursued by bikers and a neo-Nazi gang, blood-thirsty for revenge, while a homicide detective launched a nationwide manhunt.

As the mist from his smoking gun fades, readers are left with an unexpected portrait of a stoic philosopher with a wealth of charm, a glorious turn of phrase and a fanatical devotion to his daughter.

Party Time

An action-packed roller-coaster account of a life spiralling out of control, featuring wild women, gangsters and a mountain of drugs.

Shaun Attwood arrived in Phoenix, Arizona, a penniless business graduate from a small industrial town in England. Within a decade, he became a stock-market millionaire. But he was leading a double life.

After taking his first ecstasy pill at a rave in Manchester as a shy student, Shaun became intoxicated by the party lifestyle that would change his fortune. Years later, in the Arizona desert, he became submerged in a criminal underworld, throwing parties for thousands of ravers and running an ecstasy ring in competition with the Mafia mass murderer, Sammy 'The Bull' Gravano.

As greed and excess tore through his life, Shaun had eye-watering encounters with Mafia hitmen and crystal-meth addicts, enjoyed extravagant debauchery with superstar DJs and glitter girls, and ingested enough drugs to kill a herd of elephants. This is his story.

Hard Time

"Makes the Shawshank Redemption look like a holiday camp."
– NOTW

After a SWAT team smashed down stock-market millionaire Shaun Attwood's door, he found himself inside Arizona's deadliest jail and locked into a brutal struggle for survival.

Shaun's hope of living the American Dream turned into a nightmare of violence and chaos, when he had a run-in with Sammy "the Bull" Gravano, an Italian Mafia mass murderer.

In jail, Shaun was forced to endure cockroaches crawling in his ears at night, dead rats in the food and the sound of skulls getting cracked against toilets. He meticulously documented the conditions and smuggled out his message.

Join Shaun on a harrowing voyage into the darkest recesses of human existence.

Hard Time provides a revealing glimpse into the tragedy, brutality, dark comedy and eccentricity of prison life.

Featured worldwide on Nat Geo Channel's Locked-Up/Banged-Up Abroad Raving Arizona.

Prison Time

Sentenced to 9½ years in Arizona's state prison for distributing ecstasy, Shaun finds himself living among gang members, sexual predators and drug-crazed psychopaths. After being attacked by a Californian biker, in for stabbing a girlfriend, Shaun writes about the prisoners who befriend, protect and inspire him. They include T-Bone, a massive African American ex-Marine, who risks his life saving vulnerable inmates from rape, and Two Tonys, an old-school Mafia murderer, who left the corpses of his rivals from Arizona to Alaska. They teach Shaun how to turn incarceration to his advantage, and to learn from his mistakes.

Shaun is no stranger to love and lust in the heterosexual world, but the tables are turned on him inside. Sexual advances come at him from all directions, some cleverly disguised, others more sinister.

Resigned to living alongside violent, mentally ill and drug-addicted inmates, Shaun immerses himself in psychology and philosophy, to try to make sense of his past behaviour, and begins applying what he learns, as he adapts to prison life. Encouraged by Two Tonys to explore fiction as well, Shaun reads over 1000 books which, with support from a brilliant psychotherapist, Dr Owen, speed along his personal development. As his ability to deflect daily threats improves, Shaun begins to look forward to his release with optimism and a new love waiting for him. Yet the words of Aristotle from one of Shaun's books will prove prophetic: "We cannot learn without pain."

Un-Making a Murderer: The Framing of Steven Avery and Brendan Dassey

Innocent people do go to jail. Sometimes mistakes are made. But even more terrifying is when the authorities conspire to frame them. That's what happened to Steven Avery and Brendan Dassey, who were convicted of murder and are serving life sentences.

Un-Making a Murderer is an explosive book, which uncovers the illegal, devious and covert tactics used by Wisconsin officials, including:

– Concealing Other Suspects

– Paying Expert Witnesses to Lie

– Planting Evidence

– Jury Tampering

The art of framing innocent people has been in practice for centuries and will continue until the perpetrators are held accountable. Turning conventional assumptions and beliefs in the justice system upside down, *Un-Making a Murderer* takes you on that journey.

HARD TIME BY SHAUN ATTWOOD

CHAPTER 1

Sleep deprived and scanning for danger, I enter a dark cell on the second floor of the maximum-security Madison Street jail in Phoenix, Arizona, where guards and gang members are murdering prisoners. Behind me, the metal door slams heavily. Light slants into the cell through oblong gaps in the door, illuminating a prisoner cocooned in a white sheet, snoring lightly on the top bunk about two thirds of the way up the back wall. Relieved there is no immediate threat, I place my mattress on the grimy floor. Desperate to rest, I notice movement on the cement-block walls. *Am I hallucinating?* I blink several times. The walls appear to ripple. Stepping closer, I see the walls are alive with insects. I flinch. So many are swarming, I wonder if they're a colony of ants on the move. To get a better look, I put my eyes right up to them. They are mostly the size of almonds and have antennae. American cockroaches. I've seen them in the holding cells downstairs in smaller numbers, but nothing like this. A chill spread over my body. I back away.

Something alive falls from the ceiling and bounces off the base of my neck. I jump. With my night vision improving, I spot cockroaches weaving in and out of the base of the fluorescent strip light. Every so often one drops onto the concrete and resumes crawling. Examining the bottom bunk, I realise why my cellmate is sleeping at a higher elevation: cockroaches are pouring from gaps in the decrepit wall at the level of my bunk. The area is thick with them. Placing my mattress on the bottom bunk scatters them. I walk towards the toilet, crunching a few under my shower sandals. I urinate and grab the toilet roll. A cockroach darts from the centre of the roll onto my hand, tickling my fingers. My arm jerks as if it has a mind of its own, losing the cockroach and the toilet roll. Using a towel, I wipe the bulk of them off the bottom bunk, stopping only to shake the odd one off my hand. I unroll my mattress. They begin to regroup and inhabit my mattress. My adrenaline is pumping so much, I lose my fatigue.

Nauseated, I sit on a tiny metal stool bolted to the wall. *How will I sleep? How's my cellmate sleeping through the infestation and my arrival?* Copying his technique, I cocoon myself in a sheet and lie down, crushing more cockroaches. The only way they can access me now is through the breathing hole I've left in the sheet by the lower half of my face. Inhaling their strange musty odour, I close my eyes. I can't sleep. I feel them crawling on the sheet around my feet. *Am I imagining things?* Frightened of them infiltrating my breathing hole, I keep opening my eyes. Cramps cause me to rotate onto my other side. Facing the wall, I'm repulsed by so many of them just inches away. I return to my original side.

The sheet traps the heat of the Sonoran Desert to my body, soaking me in sweat. Sweat tickles my body, tricking my mind into thinking the cockroaches are infiltrating and crawling on me. The trapped heat aggravates my bleeding skin infections and bedsores. I want to scratch myself, but I know better. The outer layers of my skin have turned soggy from sweating constantly in this concrete oven. Squirming on the bunk fails to stop the relentless itchiness of my skin. Eventually, I scratch myself. Clumps of moist skin detach under my nails. Every now and then I become so uncomfortable, I must open my cocoon to waft the heat out, which allows the cockroaches in. It takes hours to drift to sleep. I only manage a few hours. I awake stuck to the soaked sheet, disgusted by the cockroach carcasses compressed against the mattress.

The cockroaches plague my new home until dawn appears at the dots in the metal grid over a begrimed strip of four-inch-thick bullet-proof glass at the top of the back wall – the cell's only source of outdoor light. They disappear into the cracks in the walls, like vampire mist retreating from sunlight. But not all of them. There were so many on the night shift that even their vastly reduced number is too many to dispose of. And they act like they know it. They roam around my feet with attitude, as if to make it clear that I'm trespassing on their turf.

My next set of challenges will arise not from the insect world, but from my neighbours. I'm the new arrival, subject to scrutiny about my charges just like when I'd run into the Aryan Brotherhood prison gang on my first day at the medium-security Towers jail a year ago. I wish my cellmate would wake up, brief me on the mood of the locals and introduce me to the head of the white gang. No such luck. Chow is announced over a speaker system in a crackly robotic voice, but he doesn't stir.

I emerge into the day room for breakfast. Prisoners in black-and-white bee-striped uniforms gather under the metal-grid stairs and tip dead cockroaches into a trash bin from plastic peanut-butter containers they'd set as traps during the night. All eyes are on me in the chow line. Watching who sits where, I hold my head up, put on a solid stare and pretend to be as at home in this environment as the cockroaches. It's all an act. I'm lonely and afraid. I loathe having to explain myself to the head of the white race, who I assume is the toughest murderer. I've been in jail long enough to know that taking my breakfast to my cell will imply that I have something to hide.

The gang punishes criminals with certain charges. The most serious are sex offenders, who are KOS: Kill On Sight. Other charges are punishable by SOS – Smash On Sight – such as drive-by shootings because women and kids sometimes get killed. It's called convict justice. Gang members are constantly looking for people to beat up because that's how they earn their reputations and tattoos. The most serious acts of violence earn the highest-ranking tattoos. To be a full gang member requires murder. I've observed the body language and techniques inmates trying to integrate employ. An inmate with a spring in his step and an air of confidence is likely to be accepted. A person who avoids eye contact and fails to introduce himself to the gang is likely to be preyed on. Some of the failed attempts I saw ended up with heads getting cracked against toilets, a sound I've grown familiar with. I've seen prisoners being extracted on stretchers who looked dead – one had yellow fluid leaking from his head. The constant violence gives me nightmares, but the reality is that I put myself in here, so I force myself to accept it as a part of my punishment.

It's time to apply my knowledge. With a self-assured stride, I take my breakfast bag to the table of white inmates covered in neo-Nazi tattoos, allowing them to question me.

"Mind if I sit with you guys?" I ask, glad exhaustion has deepened my voice.

"These seats are taken. But you can stand at the corner of the table."

The man who answered is probably the head of the gang. I size him up. Cropped brown hair. A dangerous glint in Nordic-blue eyes. Tiny pupils that suggest he's on heroin. Weightlifter-type veins bulging from a sturdy neck. Political ink on arms crisscrossed with scars. About the same age as me, thirty-three.

"Thanks. I'm Shaun from England." I volunteer my origin to show I'm different from them but not in a way that might get me smashed.

"I'm Bullet, the head of the whites." He offers me his fist to bump. "Where you roll in from, wood?"

Addressing me as wood is a good sign. It's what white gang members on a friendly basis call each other.

"Towers jail. They increased my bond and re-classified me to maximum security."

"What's your bond at?"

"I've got two $750,000 bonds," I say in a monotone. This is no place to brag about bonds.

"How many people you kill, brother?" His eyes drill into mine, checking whether my body language supports my story. My body language so far is spot on.

"None. I threw rave parties. They got us talking about drugs on wiretaps." Discussing drugs on the phone does not warrant a $1.5 million bond. I know and beat him to his next question. "Here's my charges." I show him my charge sheet, which includes conspiracy and leading a crime syndicate – both from running an Ecstasy ring.

Bullet snatches the paper and scrutinises it. Attempting to pre-empt his verdict, the other whites study his face. On edge, I wait for him to respond. Whatever he says next will determine whether I'll be accepted or victimised.

"Are you some kind of jailhouse attorney?" Bullet asks. "I want someone to read through my case paperwork." During our few minutes of conversation, Bullet has seen through my act and concluded that I'm educated – a possible resource to him.

I appreciate that he'll accept me if I take the time to read his case. "I'm no jailhouse attorney, but I'll look through it and help you however I can."

"Good. I'll stop by your cell later on, wood."

After breakfast, I seal as many of the cracks in the walls as I can with toothpaste. The cell smells minty, but the cockroaches still find their way in. Their day shift appears to be collecting information on the brown paper bags under my bunk, containing a few items of food that I purchased from the commissary; bags that I tied off with rubber bands in the hope of keeping the cockroaches out. Relentlessly, the cockroaches explore the bags for entry points, pausing over and probing the most worn and vulnerable regions. *Will the nightly swarm eat right through the paper?* I read all morning, wondering whether my cellmate has died in his cocoon, his occasional breathing sounds reassuring me.

Bullet stops by late afternoon and drops his case paperwork off. He's been charged with Class 3 felonies and less, not serious crimes, but is facing a double-digit sentence because of his prior convictions and Security Threat Group status in the prison system. The proposed sentencing range seems disproportionate. I'll advise him to reject the plea bargain – on the assumption he already knows to do so, but is just seeking the comfort of a second opinion, like many un-sentenced inmates. When he returns for his paperwork, our conversation disturbs my cellmate – the cocoon shuffles – so we go upstairs to his cell. I tell Bullet what I think. He is excitable, a different man from earlier, his pupils almost non-existent.

"This case ain't shit. But my prosecutor knows I done other shit, all kinds of heavy shit, but can't prove it. I'd do anything to get that sorry bitch off my fucking ass. She's asking for something bad to happen to her. Man, if I ever get bonded out, I'm gonna chop that bitch into pieces. Kill her slowly though. Like to work her over with a blowtorch."

Such talk can get us both charged with conspiring to murder a prosecutor, so I try to steer him elsewhere. "It's crazy how they can catch you doing one thing, yet try to sentence you for all of the things they think you've ever done."

"Done plenty. Shot some dude in the stomach once. Rolled him up in a blanket and threw him in a dumpster."

Discussing past murders is as unsettling as future ones. "So, what's all your tattoos mean, Bullet? Like that eagle on your chest?"

"Why you wanna know?" Bullet's eyes probe mine.

My eyes hold their ground. "Just curious."

"It's a war bird. The AB patch."

"AB patch?"

"What the Aryan Brotherhood gives you when you've put enough work in."

"How long does it take to earn a patch?"

"Depends how quickly you put your work in. You have to earn your lightning bolts first."

"Why you got red and black lightning bolts?"

"You get SS bolts for beating someone down or for being an enforcer for the family. Red lightning bolts for killing someone. I was sent down as a youngster. They gave me steel and told me who to handle and I handled it. You don't ask questions. You just get blood on your steel. Dudes who get these tats without putting work in are told to cover them up or leave the yard."

"What if they refuse?"

"They're held down and we carve the ink off them."

Imagining them carving a chunk of flesh to remove a tattoo, I cringe. He's really enjoying telling me this now. His volatile nature is clear and frightening. *He's accepted me too much. He's trying to impress me before making demands.*

At night, I'm unable to sleep. Cocooned in heat, surrounded by cockroaches, I hear the swamp-cooler vent – a metal grid at the top of a wall – hissing out tepid air. Giving up on sleep, I put my earphones on and tune into National Public Radio. Listening to a Vivaldi violin concerto, I close my eyes and press my tailbone down to straighten my back as if I'm doing a yogic relaxation. The playful allegro thrills me, lifting my spirits, but the wistful adagio provokes sad emotions and tears. I open my eyes and gaze into the gloom. Due to lack of sleep, I start hallucinating and hearing voices over the music whispering threats. I'm at breaking point. Although I have accepted that I committed crimes and deserve to be punished, no one should have to live like this. I'm furious at myself for making the series of reckless decisions that put me in here and for losing absolutely everything. As violins crescendo in my ears, I remember what my life used to be like.